Fundamentals of Machine Learning

Fundamentals of Machine Learning

Thomas P. Trappenberg

Dalhousie University

OXFORD
UNIVERSITY PRESS

Great Clarendon Street, Oxford, OX2 6DP,
United Kingdom

Oxford University Press is a department of the University of Oxford.
It furthers the University's objective of excellence in research, scholarship,
and education by publishing worldwide. Oxford is a registered trade mark of
Oxford University Press in the UK and in certain other countries

© Oxford University Press 2020

The moral rights of the author have been asserted

First Edition published in 2020

Impression: 1

Published in the United States of America by Oxford University Press
198 Madison Avenue, New York, NY 10016, United States of America

British Library Cataloguing in Publication Data

Data available

Library of Congress Control Number: 2019945424

ISBN 978–0–19–882804–4

DOI: 10.1093/oso/9780198828044.001.0001

Printed and bound by
CPI Group (UK) Ltd, Croydon, CR0 4YY

Acknowledgements

The material in this book has been inspired by several great resources. I would specifically like to acknowledge the influence of Andrew Ng's lecture notes for several parts in this book, especially some basic Bayesian formulations and examples. The excellent book of Francois Cholett on deep learning with Python is very much recommended for both the wonderful explanation of deep learning techniques and the implementation in Keras. We follow much of the presentation of automatic differentiation by the review of Baydin, Pearlmutter, Radul, and Siskind (JMLR 2018) which we recommend for further insights.

Many colleagues have contributed considerably to this book. In particular, I would thank Paul Hollensen, Patrick Connor, and Hossein Parvar for a lot of help with some very rough initial drafts of the manuscript. Thanks to Aditi Nair for her careful reading and good questions, and to Justin Tam for pointing out some rough sections. I would like to thank Will Stone for good ideas and producing Figure 1.7B, and Evangelos Milios for further suggestions. A very special thanks to Farzaneh Sheikhnezhad Fard. Her clear implementation of basic concepts and discussions of deep reinforcement learning have shaped much of the corresponding chapter. Finally, a very special thanks to all my students who took my classes over the last several years and have challenged me to think deeper about machine learning, and to investigate the roots of assumptions that we make.

Preface

Machine learning is exploding, both in research and industrial applications. Although much of the machine learning ideas have been around for many years, the latest break-throughs are based on several advances. One is the availability of large datasets with labeled data. Another is the availability of fast specialized processors such as graphics processing units (GPUs). In addition, progress is fueled by a deeper understanding of building models and learning from data, as well as some new techniques that brought everything together.

There are now a variety of wonderful books and online resources available on machine learning. So why another book? There are several reasons why I felt compelled to offer my contribution here. Many recent books focus on specific aspects of machine learning, in particular deep learning on the one hand and Bayesian methods on the other. In this book I try to develop a bridge or mutual understanding of what often seems to be viewed as two opposite ends of machine learning. I would like to argue that both approaches are important, have specific strengths in specific application areas, and that a combined view of machine learning and scientific modeling is useful. While this book places some focus on general machine learning methods, I believe that the insight and rigor of probabilistic modeling approaches aid to the general understanding, which in turn offers help in applying machine learning techniques more efficiently.

Another reason that I hope this book is appreciated is that I like to keep explanations brief while still providing some ideas about the deeper reasoning about the methods. It is important to keep this style of the book in mind as treatments and examples are deliberately minimal by design. Also, most explanations are deliberately brief in contrast to more traditional teaching books. My hope is to motivate and guide the reader sufficiently enough to consult further resources for advanced studies. I find this particularly important in an age where there are wonderful resources available on the Internet. I do not claim to cover all details of machine learning, but my hope is to provide the fundamentals for a good understanding that can help to guide further studies.

This book tries to strive a balance between the rigor of mathematical arguments and general outlining principle ideas. In this book, I use mathematical notation mainly as descriptors to keep presentations brief and to show the general form of some equations. For the most part, this book does not include rigorous mathematical proofs or derivations, but I hope to give enough details to see how results can be derived. I know that some readers might tend to avoid mathematical notations, but I would like to encourage these individuals to see them as providing a short form of a story. by contrast, other readers might find my simplifications debatable in a strict mathematical context. However, I think mathematical tools are useful at the level intended here to communicate ideas.

This book includes a brief overview of some older machine learning techniques such as support vector machines and decision trees. While these approaches might be considered shallow or old-fashioned with respect to deep learning, they have still important practical applications as they might provide solutions to applications that do not require the increased complexity of deep models. We will not dwell for very long into the theory of these traditional methods even though some of the stated formulas seem complex. However, I hope that mentioning some of these ideas, such as kernel methods or Lagrange methods for optimizations with constraints, will add to the foundation of studying more theoretical aspects that are often assumed in modern research papers. This is particularly the case for support vector machines for which there is a rich theory.

Since I have a personal interest in how the brain works, I did include some comments on the relations of machine learning and the brain. The brain is often quoted as inspiration for machine learning methods like neural networks. On the other hand, machine learning is also inspirational for neuroscience by giving us some ideas of possible information processing principles that could be at work in the brain, or at highlighting differences.

In the first chapter we will tour the main ideas of machine learning in order to see where this journey will take us. The next three chapters are designed to apply some machine learning methods. I decided to begin with applications before going through the more rigorous background since applying machine learning methods is not difficult with high-level programming to implement and use a variety of models. These chapters are intended to get you started to run some experiments on your own, and to gain some experience of what we want to achieve with machine learning. Chapter 2 is a brief outline of programming with Python of the kind we need in this book, and Chapters 3 and 4 show how to use sklearn and Keras to implement some of the methods.

The second part of the book comprising the following four chapters is intended to take a deeper look into the foundations of machine learning and scientific modeling in general. This includes a formalization of regression and gradient descent optimization, and discussions of the probabilistic aspects in modeling. The final section of the book comprises the last three chapters which are dedicated to three important and hopefully interesting advanced aspects of machine learning. The first is recurrent neural networks, which capture temporal aspects in modeling; the second is reinforcement learning, which captures learning of agents and is hence a much more general setting of learning machines; and the last chapter consists of some brief thoughts on the impact of machine learning on our society.

Contents

II FOUNDATIONS
REGRESSION AND PROBABILISTIC MODELING

1 Introduction

This chapter provides a high-level overview of machine learning, in particular of how it is related to building models from data. We start with a basic idea in the historical context and phrase the learning problem in a simple mathematical term as function approximation as well as in a probabilistic context. In contrast to more traditional models we can characterize machine learning as nonlinear regression in high-dimensional spaces. This chapter seeks to point out how diverse sub-areas such as deep learning and Bayesian networks fit into the scheme of things and aims to motivate the further study with some examples of recent progress.

1.1 The basic idea and history of machine learning

Machine learning is literally about building machines, often in software, that can learn to perform specific tasks. Examples of common tasks for machine learning is recognizing objects from digital pictures or predicting the location of a robot or a self-driving car from a variety of sensor measurements. These techniques have contributed largely to a new wave of technologies that are commonly associated with artificial intelligence (AI). This books is dedicated to introducing the fundamentals of this discipline.

The recent importance of machine learning and its rapid development with new industrial applications has been breath taking, and it is beyond the scope of this book to anticipate the multitude of developments that will occur. However, the knowledge of basic ideas behind machine learning, many of which have been around for some time, and their formalization for building probabilistic models to describe data are now important basic skills. Machine learning is about modeling data. Describing data and uncertainty has been the traditional domain of Bayesian statistics and probability theory. In contrast, it seems that many exciting recent techniques come from an area now called deep learning. The specific contribution of this book is its attempt to highlight the relationship between these areas.

We often simply say that we learn from data, but it is useful to realize that data can mean several things. In its most fundamental form, data usual consist of measurements such as intensity of light in a digital camera, the measurement of electric potentials in Electroencephalography (EEG), or the recording of stock-market data. However, what we need for learning is a teacher who provides us with information about what these data should predict. Such information can take many different forms. For example, we might have a form of data that we call labels, such as the identity of objects in a digital photograph. This is exactly the kind of information we need to learn optical object recognition. The teacher provides examples of the desired answers that the student (learner) should learn to predict for novel inputs.

Fundamentals of Machine Learning, Thomas P. Trappenberg, Oxford University Press (2020).
© Oxford University Press. DOI: 10.1093/oso/9780198828044.001.0001

Learning will always involve optimizing an objective function, and we will see that the objective function can easily be formulated with specific examples of the desired answers for a learner. This kind of guidance in a learning algorithms is traditionally called "supervised learning." At the other extreme, we might not have any labels, which has traditionally been called unsupervised learning. However, a teacher still needs to provide some guidance in form of an objective, such as ordering data with certain rules. An example of this is clustering, such as when a teacher specifies a distance measure like the Euclidean distance between feature vectors. We will see that such methods are important for representational learning. Finally, a much more general form of learning is a setting where the teacher provides some guidance but the learner, in addition, has to explore possible actions to find novel solutions. Such learning is formalized in reinforcement learning where the objective functions is a slightly more general form compared to the simpler supervised learning. While we will encounter all these different types of learning in this book, most of the fundamentals of learning theory and building models can be demonstrated in the simplest setting of supervised learning.

In machine learning, we are trying to solve problems with computers without explicitly programming them for a specific tasks. We will still need to program the learning machine, and we often have to make some adjustments of such programs for a specific task. However, such an approach is somewhat more general than coding a specific logic for a specific problem. Programming general learning machines instead of specific solutions to a problem is desirable specifically for tasks that would be difficult to program in an explicit rule-based system. A classic example that we will discuss in some length is that of character recognition, as illustrated in Fig. 1.1; writing a program that can translate a visual representation of a character, say the letter A to the computer-interpretable meaning of this character such as representing this letter as the ASCII string 01000001 which is not easy when considering all the shapes and styles that this character can take.

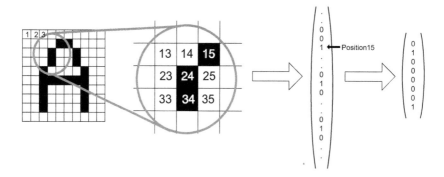

Fig. 1.1 Illustration of a letter-recognition tasks which takes a digital iamge, translates the pixel values into a large vector, and then transform it into a vector that represents the meaning of the letter.

Machine learning might sound like a niche area of science and you might wonder why there is now so much interest in this discipline, both academically and in industry.

The reason is that machine learning is really about modeling data. Modeling is the basis for advanced object recognition, data mining, and, ultimately, intelligent systems. Machine learning is the analytic engine in areas such as data science, big data, data analytics, and, to some extend, to science in general in the sense of building quantitative models.

Machine learning has a long history with traces far back in time (see Fig. 1.2). The first genuine public recognition and accompanying widespread excitement among scientists about learning machines came in the late 1950s and early 1960s with work like Arthur Samuel's self-learning checkers program. Samuel devised a program with reinforcement learning that ultimately learned to outperform its creator. Around this time, Richard Bellman established much of the mathematical foundation of reinforcement learning. One of the first general learning machines that are now considered to be neural networks was invented by Karl Steinbuch in Germany. Frank Rosenblatt invented much of the systematic foundation of neural networks and started to build neural network computers together with Charles Wightman, such as the Mark I Perceptron. Neural networks were popularized again in the 1980s, influenced by David Rumelhart and Geoffrey Hinton, and Terry Sejnowski studied their connection to the brain. Of course, there are many many more inspiring researchers such as Yoshua Bengio, Yann LeCun, and Jürgen Schmidthuber, to name but a few.

We are now in an era of "deep learning", with important recent developments that are responsible for the popularity of machine learning today. This has a great deal to do with the availability of appropriate data and the availability of faster computers, but also to smart techniques that make it possible to scale models to much larger domains. A great example of the recent progress in deep reinforcement learning is the ability of a computer to learn to play video games. Video games from the old Atari platform have become a useful paradigm for a new class of benchmarks that go beyond the classical data sets for machine learning from the University of California Irvine UCI machine learning repository that have dominated the benchmarks in the past. Atari games are somewhat simplified worlds while still presenting more learning in environments that humans have to figure out. In these benchmarks only visual input is given, made up of the computer frames of the video game, and feedback is only provided with how well the player performed in the game.

While these above examples have been widely popularized as the new forefront in AI, much of the scientific progress in machine learning is related to its embedding with probabilistic methods and statistical learning theories. Some pioneers in this domain are Vladislaw Vapnik and Judea Pearl. The development of statistical machine learning and Bayesian networks has influenced the field strongly in the last twenty years, and the domain of Bayesian reasoning is essential for the deeper understanding of machine learning. Some scientists are now working on more general probabilistic programming methods that to some extent go beyond the recent standard in machine learning applications. The aim of this book is to introduce machine learning at a more practical level so that it can be applied immediately by practitioners, at least in its basic form, and then to discuss the foundations in more general terms to help practitioners to learn more about the general theoretical underpinning of machine learning.

In the next three chapters we learn how to apply machine learning with the help of Python-based programming frameworks based on Python libraries such as Sklearn

Fig. 1.2 Some pioneers of machine learning. From top-left to bottom-right: Arthur Samuel playing checkers; Richard Bellman, who formalized reinforcement learning; Karl Steinbuch, who invented the 'learn matrix'; Frank Rosenblatt and Charles Wightman; who implemented a neural computer; Terry Sejnowski and Geoffrey Hinton discussing the Boltzmann machine circa 1983 (Courtesy of Geoffrey Hinton); and David Rummelhardt.

and keras. The next several chapters explore the principle behind supervised learning in the form of regression and classifications. We thereby switch frequently between a functional and a probabilistic framework. A refresher on the basic probability formalism is included in this discussion. In the last few chapters we will discuss some more advanced machine learning issues and methods, including recurrent networks and reinforcement learning.

1.2   Mathematical formulation of the basic learning problem

Much of what is currently most associated with the success of machine learning is supervised learning, sometimes also called predictive learning. The basic task of supervised learning is that of taking a collection of input data **x**, such as the pixel values of an image, measured medical data, or robotic sensor data, and predicting an output value **y** such as the name of an object in an image, the state of a patient's health, or the location of obstacles. It is common that each input has many components, such as many millions of pixel values in an image, and it is useful to collect these values in a mathematical structure such as a vectors (1-dimensional), a matrix (2-dimensional), or a tensor that is the generalization of such structures to higher dimensions. We often refer to machine learning problems as high-dimensional which refers, in this context, to the large number of components in the input structure and not to the dimension of the input tensor.

We use the mathematical terms vector, matrix, and tensor mainly to signify a data structure. In a programming context these are more commonly described as 1-dimensional, 2-dimensional, or higher-dimensional arrays. The difference between arrays and tensors (a vector and matrix are special forms of a tensor) is, however, that the mathematical definitions also include rules on how to calculate with these data structures. This book is not a course on mathematics; we are only users of mathematical notations and methods, and mathematical notation help us to keep the text short while being precise. We follow here a common notation of denoting a vector, matrix, or tensor with **bold-faced** letters, whereas we use regular fonts for scalars. We usually call the input vector a **feature vector** as the components of this are typically a set feature values of an object. The output could also be a multi-dimensional object such as a vector or tensor itself. Mathematically, we can denote the relations between the input and the output as a function

$$y = f(\mathbf{x}). \tag{1.1}$$

We consider the function above as a description of the **true underlying world**, and our task in science or engineering is to find this relation. In the above formula we considered a single output value and several input values for illustration purposes, although we see later that we can extend this readily to multiple output values.

Before proceeding, it is useful to clarify our use of the term "feature." Features represent components that describe the inputs to our learning systems. Feature values are often measured data in machine learning. Sometime the word "attributes" is used instead. In the most part, we use these terms interchangeably. However, sometimes researchers make a small distinction betwen the terms, using attributes to denote unique content while using feature as a derived value, such as the square of an attribute. This strict distinction is usually not crucial for the understanding of the context so our use of the term feature includes attributes.

Returning to the world model in equation 1.1, the challenge for machine learning is to find this function, or at least to approximate it sufficiently. Machine learning offers several approaches to deal with this. One approach that we will predominantly follow is to define a general parameterized function

$$\hat{y} = \hat{f}(\mathbf{x}; \mathbf{w}). \tag{1.2}$$

This formula describes how we make a parameterized hypothesis in which we specify a function $\hat{f}$ that depends on parameters $\mathbf{w}$ to approximate the desired input-output relation. This function is called a **model**:

> *A model is an approximation of a system to study specific aspects of the system and to predict behavior*

This often means that not all of the underlying world has to be captured in depth. For example, a building engineer might make a model of a bridge to tests its static without including the aesthetic aspects that an architect might emphasize in a model. In our context the word model is synonymous with approximation. We have indicated in the formula that this model is an approximation of the desired relation by using a hat symbol above the y and the f. However, we frequently drop the hat symbol when the relation is clear from the context. Also, in the context of machine learning, a model typically includes parameters so that their presence in the notation is synonymous with a model.

Coming up with the right parameterized approximation function is the **hard problem in machine learning**, and we will later discuss several choices. There are methods to develop the approximation function from the data systematically, generally called non-parametric methods. At this point we assume that we have a parameterized approximation function.

We often specify the set of parameters as a vector $\mathbf{w}$ behind a semi-colon in the function arguments. A more appropriate mathematical statement would be that equation 1.2 defines a set of functions in the parameter space. **Learning** is the challenge of finding the values for these parameters that best describe the data, and even better, predicting future outputs y from inputs x. So, the parameters are estimated from data $w = w(x, y)$. Searching for these parameters is done with a learning algorithm. A common way of realizing such a learning algorithm is to define a function that describes the goal of learning, such as minimizing the number of wrong classifications. We call this function the **loss function** $\mathcal{L}$, although other terms are sometimes used in the literature such as objective function, error function, or risk. A common algorithm to minimize such a loss function for a set of given data is to use an algorithm called **gradient descent**, which is an iterative method over the training data that changes the parameters along the negative gradient $\nabla_w \mathcal{L}$ of the loss function,

$$w_i \leftarrow w_i - \alpha \nabla_w \mathcal{L} \tag{1.3}$$

where α is called the learning rate and

$$\nabla_w = \begin{pmatrix} \frac{\partial}{\partial w_1} \\ \cdot \\ \cdot \\ \cdot \\ \frac{\partial}{\partial w_n} \end{pmatrix}. \tag{1.4}$$

is the Nabla operator which signifies the gradient. This is a typical learning algorithm to find the parameters of a model based on example data. We elaborate on this algorithm later.

While the gradient descent can find parameters to minimize the loss of the training data, our real goal is to find the values of $\mathbf{w}$ that best predicts data that have not been seen before. Just describing the training data acts somewhat more like a memory, but being able to **generalize** is the main goal of machine learning. A good solution of the machine (model) learning problem is represented by a point in the parameter space that approximates best the true underlying world. However, since we usually don't know the true underlying world, we estimate how good this model is by evaluating how good new predictions are.

In some applications of supervised learning we want to predict a continuous output variable. For example, we might want to predict the price of a house from the size information. This is called **regression**. In contrast, sometimes we want to predict discrete values such as the categories of object in a picture. This is called **classification**. The output variable y in classification is called a **label**. It is now common to refer generally refer to the output of the supervised learner as label, even in the case of regression where we have a continuous "label." We will see later that regression and classification are closely related; for example, binary classification can be seen as a regression problems with a discrete function $f(x)$ such as a sign function which would give us two labels, positive and negative.

An important part of our treatment of machine learning is to consider cases with uncertainty. For example, we might not be able to predict an exact label or output value, and we would be best-served if we consider the probability that a certain value will occur. This is very important for several reasons. For example, it is quite common that the process under investigation includes random (stochastic) factors or hidden (latent) factors that create variations in results even for the same sensory states. Thus, we pose that the true underlying world model we seek to describe is better described by a probability density function

$$p(Y = y|\mathbf{x}). \tag{1.5}$$

This function gives the probability density, or probability mass in the case of categorical data, of the label Y having a value y given that we have an input vector $\mathbf{x}$. The arguments of density functions are provided after the vertical bar, and we write random variables as upper-case letters and we specify specific values with lower-case letters.

Formulating machine learning in a probabilistic (stochastic) context has been most useful and provides us with the formalization that created many insights. In the probabilistic framework we are then modeling a density function

$$\hat{p}(Y = y|\mathbf{x}; \mathbf{w}). \tag{1.6}$$

Density function approximation is in some sense a special case of function approximation as the density function is still a function, albeit with some constraints such as a normalization $\int p(y)\mathrm{d}y = 1$. However, modeling density functions is also the more general case for modeling functions in the sense that they proivide the probabilistic information of how likely label values are given a certain input.

A probabilistic framework can be used for a more general formulation of learning. Given a parameterized model as written in equation 1.6, we want to know for all possible parameters how likely they are to describe the data well. This is not necessarily a single solution, and ideally we would like to know the probability density function of the parameters given by the data,

$$p(\mathbf{w}|y, \mathbf{x}). \tag{1.7}$$

This general approach of using probabilistic models and data to estimate model parameters, and in turn make predictions, is the essence of Bayesian modeling. We will introduce this more general learning paradigm. However, many of the current machine learning algorithms use a learning principle where learning only uses the most likely parameters given the data,

$$\mathbf{w}^* = \text{argmax}_w p(\mathbf{w}|y, \mathbf{x}).\tag{1.8}$$

Such a maximum *a posteriori* choice, or some point estimates derived from related principles such as the maximum likelihood estimate, are currently the dominant forms of machine learning. While limited in a Bayesian sense, these approximations have been very useful to build practical applications of machine learning. Of course, at this point we still need to find the specific form of the probability function $p(\mathbf{w}|y, \mathbf{x})$, which in itself is a subject of a hypothesis in the Bayesian framework. The point here is to suggest how useful a probabilistic formalism is in machine learning. We will discuss these thoughts more later in this book.

Formulating specific probabilistic models for problems with many stochastic factors is demanding. An important and useful way to formulate multivariate probabilistic models is the area of **causal models**. Such models provide specific probabilistic models of the components that provide the necessary foundations of the inference engine. Inference here means that the system can be used to "argue" about a solution in a probabilistic sense or to derive predictions. Such systems are the domain of Bayesian networks, and we will include an introduction to this important domain in this book as it provides an important aspect of machine learning. To some extent we will argue that probabilistic models and deep neural networks represent somewhat a diverse spectrum of machine learning models, but we will also argue that they can be viewed in a unified way. Fig. 1.3 shows a famous example form Judea Pearl, one of the inventors of this important modeling framework.

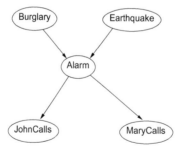

Fig. 1.3 An example of a graphical representation of a causal model.

In Bayesian networks we model entities that build the causal structure of the problem. It hence has a much stronger theoretical predictive strength and explanatory ability than many other machine learning models. However, in practice we rarely know about the generative elements, and machine learning models that are more general such as neural networks represent an often more practical method. Nature might have combined such strategies in the brain, where sensory input is transformed into a semantic space in which some approximation of Bayesian reasoning can be implemented. Learning about those different aspects of modeling and machine learning is hence a useful approach in this dynamic area.

1.3 Non-linear regression in high-dimensions

The simplest example of supervised machine learning is linear regression. In linear regression we assume a linear model such as the function,

$$y = w_0 + w_1 x. \tag{1.9}$$

This is a low-dimensional example with only a single feature, value x, and a scalar label, value y. Most of us learned in high school to use mean square regression. In this method we choose as values for the offset parameter w_0 and the slope parameter w_1 the values that minimize the summed squared difference between the regressed and the data points. This is illustrated in Fig. 1.4A. We will later explain this procedure in more detail. This is an example where data are used to determine the parameters of a parameterized model, and this model with the fitted parameters can then be used to predict y values for new x values. This is in essence supervised learning.

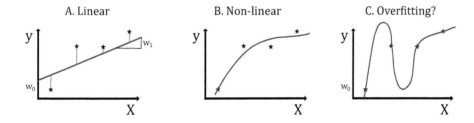

Fig. 1.4 Data points and possible models to fit these data. (A) Linear regression, (B) a non-linear function, and (C) another non-linear function that might overfit the data.

What makes modern machine learning go beyond this type of modeling is that we are now usually describing data in high dimensions (many features) and to use non-linear functions. This seems straight forward, but there are several problems in practice going down this route. For example, Fig. 1.4B shows a non-linear function that seems somewhat to describe the pattern of the data much better than the linear model in Fig. 1.4A. However, the non-linear model shown in Fig. 1.4C is also a solution. It even goes through all the training points. This is a particularly difficult problem. If we are allowed to increase the model complexity arbitrarily, then we can always find a model which goes through all the data points. However, the data points might have a simple relation, such as the linear one of Fig. 1.4A, and the variation only represents noise. Fitting the data point with this noise as in Fig. 1.4C does therefore mean that we are **overfitting** the data.

So a major problem when fitting data with fairly general non-linear functions is the complexity of the function in terms of the number of parameters, such as the order of the polynomial or the number of nodes in neural networks, as discussed further later in this chapter. We will later discuss methods to prevent overfitting in more detail, but at this point it is already useful to consider some systematics. For example, in the linear model we have some systematic **bias** of the data in that all but the first data point lay above the model curve, and this trend we would also expect to show in new data points if the correct model is the one shown in Fig. 1.4B. In contrast new data points when evaluating with the model on the right would have large variations as the line clearly overshoots in order to hit the training points. This increase of **variance** in the test data is one indication of overfitting. It is hence instructive to study the difference between the error of the training set and the test set as shown in Fig.1.5.

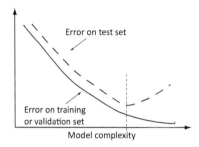

Fig. 1.5 Illustration of bias-variance trade-off. Overfitting shows when the error of the test set is increasing, relative to the training error.

The need to find the right balance between these two effects is called the **bias-variance trade-off**. When the models are too low-dimensional we expect that both errors are high but that both curves stay close to each other. In contrast, when we have plenty of parameters it is possible to make the training error small, while this leads to overfitting and hence an increase in the test error. This bias-variance trade-off is quite important in practical applications of machine learning to guide the developer to the appropriate model choice. There are important techniques under the umbrella term **regularization** with the aim of helping to make the data more regular with respect to the model and hence preventing overfitting.

Building nonlinear models is a challenge in itself as the choices are infinite. We could consider a polynomial of order n, that can be written as

$$y = w_0 + w_1 x + w_2 x^2 + ... + w_n x^n. \tag{1.10}$$

The above function is a function in one dimension. If we have more feature values we could end up with functions that depend on a combination of the feature values such as

$$y = w_0 + w_1 x_1 + w_2 x_2 + w_3 x_1 x_2 + w_4 x_1^2 x_2, ... \tag{1.11}$$

Also, using a polynomial as a non-linear function is only one possible choice of many. We could add trigonometric functions, or some functions which we just make up. We will later consider mainly functions that have been termed artificial neural networks. These functions can be represented graphically, as shown in Fig.1.6. Each node in such a graph is also called a neuron as it resembles somewhat the conjectured basic functionality of a biological neuron in the brain. Such an artificial neuron weights

A: Node (neuron)   B: Network

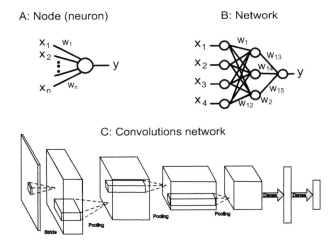

C: Convolutions network

Fig. 1.6 Basic elements of an artificial neural network (ANN). Each node represents an operation of summing weighted inputs and applying an non-linear transfer functions to this net input. The output of each node can become the input of another node or represent the output of the networks.

each individual input with an adjustable parameter, sums this weighted input, and then applies a non-linear function such as a $\tanh$ function on this summed input. The output of each node is hence,

$$y_j = \tanh(\sum_i w_{ji} x_i). \qquad (1.12)$$

This output can be the input to another node, and we can in such a way build elaborate functions with graphs of such nodes as shown in Fig.1.6B. We will later elaborate on specific network architectures that represent specific classes of non-linear functions that will be useful for specific applications. We will specifically explore how networks with many layers of neurons have advanced the capabilities of learning machines considerably, which is now known as **deep learning**.

An example of a network type called a convolutional neural network is illustrated in Fig.1.6C. It is now common that such networks have tens and even hundreds of layers. Deep neural networks are hence a form of high-dimensional non-linear fitting function, and preventing overfitting is therefore a very important component in deep learning. Deep networks have many free parameters, and large data sets (big data) have therefore been important for the recent progress in this area, in combination with other techniques to prevent overfitting such as a technique called dropout that we will discuss later. In general, one can think about techniques to prevent overfitting by restricting the possible range of the parameters. While relying on big data is one simple solution, making complex systems work with a limited amount of training data is the much more interesting challenge.

In the next section we will see that basic implementation of machine learning methods is not difficult when using application programs that implement these techniques. This is good news. However, a deeper understanding of the methods is necessary to make these applications and their conclusion appropriate. The machine learning algorithms will come up with some predictions, and evaluating whether these predictions are sensible is an important part of machine learning. Machine learning education needs therefore to go beyond learning how to run an application program. This book aims to find a balance between practical applications and their theoretical foundation.

1.4 Recent advances

Many advances have been made in recent years based on machine learning, in particular with deep learning methods for image processing, natural language processing, and more general data analytics. Many companies are now enthusiastic about data analytics, using data in a wider sense to gain insights into customer profiles or other data mining tasks. Machine learning is an important part of a data analytics engine. Data analytics often require additional care such as data security to ensure privacy, the ability to acquire and maintain large data collections, and also to make results available in a form useful for humans. We will not delve into many of these aspects but concentrate instead on the data modeling aspects.

One of the most visible impacts of deep learning has been made in computer vision through convolutional neural networks. The basic applications in this area are mostly based on recognition networks and methods for semantic segmentation. However, such methods have now also advanced object localization, object tracking, and scene understanding, to name but a few. Some examples from my own projects are shown in Fig. 1.7. The left-hand image shows semantic segmentation to identify and localize crop and weed for a robotic farming application. The right-hand image shows an application of fish tracking for aquaculture applications.

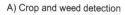

A) Crop and weed detection   B) Fish detection and tracking

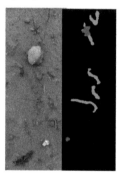
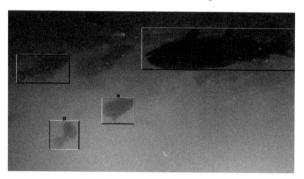

Fig. 1.7 Some examples in computer vision using deep networks. A) Detection of crop (green) and weed (red) to enable automated weeding for farm robotics. The crop is onion in an early growing stage (Courtesy of Nexus Robotics Inc.). B) Recognition, localization, and tracking of fish for fish health monitoring in aquaculture (Courtesy of ReelData Inc.).

Another area that has seen a huge improvement is the area of natural language processing (NLP). It has long been an important tasks to build programs that understand natural languages for applications such as translation, sentiment analysis, or to enable some form of formal analysis of technical reports. Various methods for sequence modeling have contributed greatly to this area, in particular recurrent neural networks, discussed later in this book.

A developing area in machine learning are generative models. Generative models are models that can make examples of instances of a class. For example, a generative models can learn about cars from examples and then generate images of new cars by itself. Such networks could then be used in some creative way. Examples of systems that can learn generative models are variational autoencoders (VAEs) and generative adversarial networks (GANs). These methods demonstrate an important advance: the ability to capture the probabilistic structure of objects which in turn can be exploited in various ways.

Machine learning methods have shown that it can produce solutions to problems that have previously been intractable. For example, computer programs to play the Chinese board game "Go" have been mostly available only at an advance novice level until a few years ago. However, in 2016, a machine learning program called "Alpha-Go" that combined cleverly supervised and reinforcement learning was able to beat a player, Mr. Lee Sedol, who is considered one of the best players of the last decade and had previously won sixteen world titles. Go was considered to be a real challenge for AI systems as it was considered to rely a lot on "gut feelings" rather than quantifiable strategies. It was therefore a huge success when computers, which had only reached levels of an advanced beginner a few years prior, could win against such an accomplished player.

Finally, AI has always been strongly associated with the understanding of the human mind. While the subject of this book is far from explaining human intelligence, the advances in machine learning have shed light on some aspects of human cognitive and brain processes. For example, generative models with sparseness constraints are able to reproduce the form of representations that brain scientists have measured in the early visual cortex, and there is a lot of evidence, by comparing brain imaging data to deep learning vision systems, that there are some aspects covered by such networks. Bayesian reasoning and reinforcement learning are areas that are now inspiring new approaches in psychiatry. The brain has many aspects that are not captured by current machine learning models, but these models capture some aspects of application domains that have long been difficult to program with traditional computers.

1.5   No free lunch, but worth the bite

Neural networks and other models, such as support vector machines and decision trees, are fairly general models in contrast to Bayesian models that are usually much better at specifying a causal structure of interpretable entities. More specific models should outperform more general model as long as they faithfully represent the underlying structure of the world model. This fact is captured by David Wolpert's "No free lunch" theorem, which states that there is not a single algorithms that covers all applications better than some other algorithms. The best model is, of course, the real world model, as discussed earlier, which we generally do not know. Applying machine learning algorithms is therefore somewhat of an art and requires experience and knowledge of the constraints of the algorithms. Discussions of what is an appropriate model are sometimes cumbersome and can distract us from making good use of them. We take a more practical approach, letting a user define what an appropriate contribution is for a machine learning model. For example, the best accuracy of a prediction might not always be the goal, and other considerations such as the speed of processing, the number of required training data, or the ability to interpret data can be important factors. We will therefore include brief discussions of some classic machine learning algorithms even if they do not represent the latest research in this area.

An interesting remark that often cops up in discussions of some machine learning algorithms and, in particular, neural networks is that these methods are commonly described, and somewhat criticized, as being **black box** methods. By "back box" we usually mean that the internal structure is not known. However, the machine learning models usually live in a computer where we can inspect all the components; these methods are hence known as white box methods. A better way to describe the difficulties with the ability human have in interpreting machine learning models is due to the fact that trained deep learning models are commonly complex models that implement complex decision rules. While some application might have as a goal the learning of human interpretable decision rules, other might rather be interested in achieving better prediction performance, which often requires more fine-grained rules.

We will see in Chapter 3 that writing a program to apply machine learning algorithms to data is often not very difficult. New algorithms will often find their way to graphical data mining tools, which makes them available to an even larger application community. However, applying such algorithms correctly in different application domains can be challenging and it is well known that some experience is required. We therefore concentrate in the following on explaining what is behind these algorithms and how different theoretical concepts are explored by them. Some understanding of the algorithms is absolutely necessary to avoid pitfalls in their application.

The basic first step for the application of ML methods is how to represent the data. We mentioned already some different data structures of inputs such as vectors or tensors. However, there are usually many different possible ways to represent a problem numerically. In the past it has been crucial to work out an appropriate high-level data representation such as summary statistics to keep the dimensionality of the model low. However, the recent progress in deep learning made it possible to treat this representation itself as part of the learning problem. Representational learning has thus become an important part of machine learning.

Once the problem has been defined by representing the data and possible goals in an appropriate way, and once the appropriate ML algorithm has been chosen, it is then the main challenge to choose good parameters of the algorithms, such as the number of neurons or layers of neurons in neural networks, which kernel to use in support vector machines, how many training steps to take in gradient descent learning, or how many data to use for learning versus validation. We call these parameters of the algorithms the **hyperparameters**. Choosing the right hyperparameters is commonly a major question, and to make it clear from the start, there is no simple answer. Thinking about how to approach this question with appropriate experiments and to understand the options and possible approaches is thus a major part of machine learning applications. The point I want to raise here is that learning about the algorithms rather than simply applying them is a direction worth taking.

Part I

A practical guide to machine learning

2 Scientific programming with Python

This chapter is a brief introduction to scientific programming with Python with an emphasis on some mathematical operations that will form the basis of many algorithms. This will specifically include working with matrices and convolutions. Python is a high-level programming language similar to Matlab and R that has gained increasing popularity in the machine learning community. The main reason we use Python in this book is that it is freely available and now provides considerable support for machine learning, with packages such as sklearn and keras that we will discuss and utilize in this book. We assume some familiarity with programming concepts and concentrate on a quick introduction to the specific environment and supporting libraries used in this book as well as some basic operations such as convolutions that will be important in later algorithms. The programs in this book are based on Python 3, and we assume that all relevant packages are installed. At this point we need the NumPy and the Matplotlib libraries as well as the `Jupyter` programming environments. Comprehensive documentation and tutorials for Python and related tools are available at <https://www.python.org>.

2.1 Programming environment

We will be using a programming environment called Jupyter. Specifically, we will be using the Jupyter notebook that allows us to write code with a simple editor and display comments and outputs in the same file. Jupyter is accessed through the browser and contains form fields in which code and comments can be added. These fields can then be executed and the feedback from print commands or figure plots are displayed after each block within the same document. This makes it very useful in documenting brief code and small exercises. An example program is shown in Fig. 2.1. All example programs in this book are available as Jupyter files on the web.

The Jupyter notebook has an interface to launch the Python interpreter and to run individual sections or all the code. The header with comments is produced by executing a text cell. This is useful to produce some documentations. Also, the notebook can be distributed with the output that can facilitate communications about code. The numbers on the left shows a consecutive number of calls to the interpreter. In the shown example, the first program cell was run first to load the libraries, and then the second cell was run twice; this is why a [3] is displayed in front of this cell. When the program is running, an [*] is displayed. The second cell produces the output 4, which is displayed after the cell.

A more advanced environment for bigger programs with more traditional programming support is Spyder. This tool includes an editor, a command window, and further programming support such as displays of variables and debugging support. This pro-

Fundamentals of Machine Learning, Thomas P. Trappenberg, Oxford University Press (2020).
© Oxford University Press. DOI: 10.1093/oso/9780198828044.001.0001

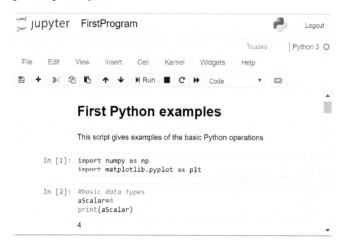

Fig. 2.1 An example of a Python program within the Jupyter notebook. The example code is discussed further later in the chapter.

gram mimics more traditional programming environment such as the ones found in Matlab and R. An example view of Spyder is shown in Fig. 2.2. On the left is the editor window that contains a syntax-sensitive display to write the programs, and on the right is the console to launch line commands such as executing and interpreting the code. As Python is an interpreted language, it is possible to work with the programs in an interactive way, such as running a simulation and than plotting results in various ways. The Spyder development environment is recommended for bigger projects.

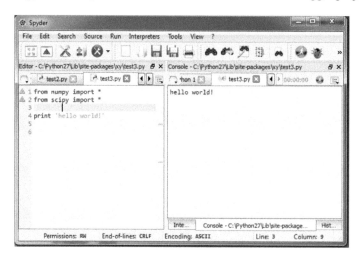

Fig. 2.2 The Spyder programming environment for Python.

2.2 Basic language elements

2.2.1 Basic data types and arrays

As a general purpose programming language, Python contains basic programing concepts such as basic data types, loops, conditional statements, and subroutines. We will briefly review the associated syntax with examples that are provided in file `FirstProgram.ipynb`. In addition to such basic programming constructs, all major programming languages such as Python are supported by a large number of libraries that enable a wide array of programming styles and specialized functions. We are here mainly interested in basic scientific computing, in contrast to system programming, and for this we need multidimensional arrays. We therefore base almost all programs in this book on the NumPy library. NumPy provides basic support of common scientific constructs and functions such as trigonometric functions and random number generators. Most importantly, it provides support for N-dimensional arrays. NumPy has become the standard in scientific computing with Python. We will use this well-established constructs to implement vectors, matrices and higher dimensional arrays. While there is a separate matrix class, this construct is limited to a two dimensional structure and has not gained widespread acceptance.

An established way to import the NumPy library in our programs is to map them to the name space "np" with the command `import numpy as np`. In this way, the specific methods or functions of NumPy are accessed with the prefix `np.`. In addition to importing NumPy, we always import a plotting library as plotting results will be very useful and a common way to communicate results. We specifically use the popular PyPlot package of the Matploitlib library. Hence, we nearly always start our program with the two lines

Listing 2.1 FirstProgram.ipynb (part 1)

```
import numpy as np
import matplotlib.pyplot as plt
```

In the following, we walk through a program in the Jupyter environment called `FirstProgram`. These lines of code are intended to show the syntax of the basic programming constructs that we need in this book. We start by demonstrating the basic data types that we will be using frequently. We are mainly concerned with numerical data, of which a scalar is the simplest example,

Listing 2.2 FirstProgram.ipynb (part 2) with output

```
#basic data types
aScalar=4
print(aScalar)

4
```

We here show the code as well as the response of running the program with the `print()` function. Comment lines can be included with the hash-tag symbol #. The type of the variables are dynamically assigned in Python. That is, a variable name and corresponding memory space is allocated the first time a variable with this name is used on the left hand side of an assignment operator "=". In this case it is an interger value, but we could also assign a real-valued variable with textttaScalar=4.0.

Most of the time we will be working on a large collection of data so that we need a concept to access the data collection. In Python, there are several forms of lists. For example, a basic 1-dimensional list is given in the basic Python stack by enclosing a semi-colon-separated list in square brackets such as

Listing 2.3 FirstProgram.ipynb (part 3) with output

```
aList = [1,2,3]
print(aList)

[1, 2, 3]
```

Such lists are useful for collecting data. However, since we need to perform well-defined mathematical operations on lists of data, it is useful to introduce a more versatile construct of such data collections in forms of a NumPy array.

Before proceeding, it might be good to review some of the naming conventions. A basic data structure for a collection of data is called an "array" in computer science. In contrast to these simple data structure concepts, the mathematical concepts of a vector or matrix are different in that they include well defined mathematical operations on these data structures. Thus, the mathematical concept of a vector is a 1-dimensional array on which some operations are defined, such as adding two vectors with the same dimension by adding their components, or multiplying a vector with a scalar by multiplying each component of the vector with a scalar. Similar, a matrix is a 2-dimensional construct with correspondingly defined operation. We can even generalize this to higher dimensions, and such mathematical constructs are called tensors. It is convenient to view a vector or matrix operation just as a special case of the general tensor operations.

To create a NumPy array we use the NumPy function `array()`. For example, a 1-dimensional Python list can be turned into a NumPy vector like,

Listing 2.4 FirstProgram.ipynb (part 4) with output

```
aVector=np.array([1,2,3])
print(aVector)
print(aVector[0], aVector[-1])
print(aVector[1:3])

[1 2 3]
1 3
[2 3]
```

As shown in the second print statement, we can access an element of the array with indices in square brackets. The first element in an array has the index 0. Hence, the print command returns the value 1. It is useful to think about this index as the offset from the first element. The index -1 accesses the last element in the vector. The third print command shows how to access a range of indices. Unfortunately, there is no distinction between a row vector and a column vector in NumPy, so this needs some more careful considerations when a distinction is necessary. We return to this point in a moment.

Similar to defining a vector with NumPy, a 2-dimensional array with the appropriate definition of mathematical operations is called a matrix and can be defined and accessed with NumPy like,

Listing 2.5 FirstProgram.ipynb (part 5) with output

```
aMatrix=np.array([[1,2,3],[4,5,6]])
print(aMatrix)
print(aMatrix[1,2])

[[1 2 3]
 [4 5 6]]
6
```

The notation indicates that a 2-dimensional array is considered in the Python syntax as a 1-dimensional list of a 1-dimensional list. Note how individual array elements are accessed; the first index specifies the position in the column, and the second index specifies the position in the row. This is equivalent to the common mathematical notation for matrices. With this we can revise the notation for the vectors above by defining a row vector as

Listing 2.6 FirstProgram.ipynb (part 6)

```
aVector=np.array([[1,2,3]])
```

This can then be converted into a column vector with the help of the transpose operation

Listing 2.7 FirstProgram.ipynb (part 7) with output

```
print(aVector.T)

[[1]
 [2]
 [3]]
```

After defining such NumPy arrays we can apply mathematical function on these NumPy arrays. For example, some element-wise operations on matrices are

Listing 2.8 FirstProgram.ipynb (part 8) with output

```
matrix2=np.array([[5,5,6],[7,8,9]])
result1=aMatrix * matrix2  #element-wise
result2 = aMatrix ** 3  #element-wise exponentiation:
result3 = aMatrix > 3  #find the indices where (matrix > 3)
print(result1,result2,result3)

[[ 5 10 18]
 [28 40 54]]
[[  1   8  27]
 [ 64 125 216]]
[[False False False]
 [ True  True  True]]
```

A basic matrix multiplication, also called a dot product or inner product, is implemented as function np.dot(a,b) and in Python 3 also as operator @,

Listing 2.9 FirstProgram.ipynb (part 9) with output

```
result=aMatrix @ matrix2.T
print(result)

[[ 33  50]
 [ 81 122]]
```

We have thereby included the transpose operation through the operator specification
".T". Such operator specification are common in object-oriented programming constructs.

We are often in need of accessing subsets of data in arrays and also merging arrays.
To access a subset of an array we can first generate an index vector called idx below,
which specifies the indices we want to process such as the first and second element in
the second row of the matrix, called aMatrix, defined earlier

Listing 2.10 FirstProgram.ipynb (part 10) with output
```
idx =[[1],[0,2]]
print(aMatrix[idx])

[4  6]
```

Another useful example is to make a vector with a list,

Listing 2.11 FirstProgram.ipynb (part 11)
```
x=np.arange(10)
```

which is the same as array(range(10)), and to extract every second element of a
vector,

Listing 2.12 FirstProgram.ipynb (part 12) with output
```
print(x[::2])

[0  2  4  6  8]
```

The array indexing is the same as x[0:-1:2] because the default boundaries for the
first and second limits is the first and last element. Merging two arrays is done with
the NumPy concatenate() method,

Listing 2.13 FirstProgram.ipynb (part 13) with output
```
result=np.concatenate((aMatrix,matrix2),axis=0)
print(result)

[[1  2  3]
 [4  5  6]
 [5  5  6]
 [7  8  9]]
```

A useful command to check the size and orientation of a matrix is

Listing 2.14 FirstProgram.ipynb (part 14) with output
```
result.shape

(4,  3)
```

As already mentioned, the first index specifies the row going downwards and the
second index specifies the column going to the right. We sometimes want to reorder
the elements of an array which can be done with a reshape function,

Listing 2.15 FirstProgram.ipynb (part 15) with output

```
print(result.reshape(2,6))

[[1 2 3 4 5 6]
 [5 5 6 7 8 9]]
```

So far, we have discussed the basic numerical data types that we need. Besides these numerical data types, there are of course, others such as characters. Text data a simply enclosed in parenthesis like.

Listing 2.16 FirstProgram.ipynb (part 16) with output

```
text='Hello_World!'
print(text)

Hello World!
```

2.2.2 Control flow

In the following, we show three fundamental programming constructs, that of loops, conditional statements, and functions. To loop through some code, one can use the following construct,

Listing 2.17 FirstProgram.ipynb (part 17) with output

```
for i in range(4):
    print(i)

0
1
2
3
```

which starts at i=0 and goes in steps of one until i=3. Note that Python is sensitive to the code position; the indented code represents the block of statements executed inside the loop. A conditional statement takes the form

Listing 2.18 FirstProgram.ipynb (part 18)

```
if scalar<1:
    print("true")
else:
    print("false")

false
```

Again note the indentation to specify the block of code for each condition.

2.2.3 Functions

This book tries to use minimal examples that do not require advanced code structuring techniques such as object oriented-programming, although those techniques are available in Python. The basic code reuse technique is of course the definition of a function. In Python this can be done with the following template. To structure code better, specifically to define some code that can be reused, we have the option to define functions like

Listing 2.19 FirstProgram.ipynb (part 19)
```
def func(arg1, arg2=10):
    arg=arg1+arg2
    return arg;

a=1
print(func(2), func(a,2))

12  3
```

Simple variables are passed by value in Python, but more complex objects might be referred by reference. It is therefore wise to be careful when changing the content of calling variables in the functions. The function can be called with an argument, and we showed in the example how to provide a default argument.

It is also useful to define an inline version of a function, such as defining logistic sigmoid function

Listing 2.20 FirstProgram.ipynb (part 20)
```
lsig = lambda x: 1 / (1 + exp(-x))
```

We will use this inline function below to plot it.

2.2.4 Plotting

Plotting graphs for data is a useful scientific tool, and we will be using the the popular scientific plotting library Matplotlib <http://matplotlib.org/>, specifically the pyplot package that provides a slightly simpler interface within the matplotlib package. We imported this library already at the beginning of the code. Using this library, an example of a basic line plot is given in the following code.

Listing 2.21 FirstProgram.ipynb (part 21)
```
#plotting
x=arange(100)    #same as array(range(100))
y=np.sin(0.1*x)
plt.plot(x,y)
```

When you summit plots in an assignment or paper, you always need axis labels to know what is plotted. This can be done with

Listing 2.22 FirstProgram.ipynb (part 22)
```
plt.xlabel("x")
plt.ylabel("y")
```

If we want to plot the above inline function, we need to generate an array of arguments x. Below we provide three possible versions for this.

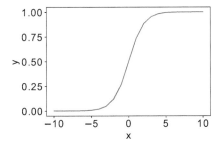

Fig. 2.3 Examples of a plot for the sigmoid function $f(x) = \frac{1}{1+e^{-x}}$ with the Matplotlib library.

Listing 2.23 FirstProgram.ipynb (part 23)
```
x=np.array([])
for i in range(21):
    x=np.append(x,(i-10))

x = np.array([i-10 for i in range(21)])
x = np.linspace(-10,10,21)
```

Plotting this function is simply achieved with the following commands

Listing 2.24 FirstProgram.ipynb (part 24)
```
plt.plot(x,lsig(x))
plt.rcParams.update({'font.size': 20})
plt.xlabel('x'); plt.ylabel('y')
plt.savefig('tmp.pdf', format='pdf')
```

The `plot(x,y)` is enough to plot the basic graph in the Jupyter environment, though iPython might need a `plt.show()` to trigger the display. The resulting plot is shown in Fig. 2.3. The example code shows how to change the font size of the axis labels, is often useful when including graphs in documents. The final command shows how to save the figure into a pdf file.

2.2.5 Timing the program

Some of the programs might need some time to run, and it might be necessary to estimate the time of running with some smaller examples and measuring the time. This can be done in the following way.

Listing 2.25 FirstProgram.ipynb (part 25) with output
```
import time
tic = time.clock()
toc = time.clock()
print(toc - tic)

2.2214871933101676e-05
```

2.3 Code efficiency and vectorization

Machine learning is about working with large collections of data. Such data are kept in data bases, spreadsheets, or simply in text files, but to work with them we load them into arrays. Since we define operations on such arrays, it is better to treat these arrays as vectors, matrices, or generally as tensors. Traditional programming languages such as C and Fortran require us to write code that loops over all the indices in order to specify operations that are defined on all the data. For example, as provided in the program `MatrixMultiplication.ipynb`, let us define two random $n \times n$ matrices with the NumPy random number generator for uniformly distributed numbers,

Listing 2.26 MatrixMultiplication.ipynb (fragment)
```
a=np.random.rand(n,n)
b=np.random.rand(n,n)
```

and a matrix of zeros with the same size,

Listing 2.27 MatrixMultiplication.ipynb (fragment)
```
c=np.zeros((n,n))
```

We can than write the code of adding two numbers with an explicit loop over all indices as

Listing 2.28 MatrixMultiplication.ipynb (fragment)
```
for i in range(n):
    for j in range(n):
        c[i][j]=a[i][j]+b[i][j]
```

In high-level programming languages like Python, Matlab, and R, it is common to write such operations in a compact form like

Listing 2.29 MatrixMultiplication.ipynb (fragment)
```
c=a+b
```

It is now common to call this style of programming a vectorized code. Such a vectorized code is not only much easier to read, but it is also essential to write efficient code. The reason for this is that the system programmers can implement such routines very efficiently, and this is difficult to match with the more general but inefficient explicit index operation.

To demonstrate the efficiency issue, let us measure the time of operations for a matrix multiplication. We start as usual by importing the standard NumPy and Matplotlib libraries, and we also import a timer routine with

Listing 2.30 MatrixMultiplication.ipynb (fragment)
```
import time
```

We then define a method called `matmulslow` that implements a matrix multiplication with an explicit iteration over the indices,

Listing 2.31 MatrixMultiplication.ipynb (fragment)

```
def matmulslow(a,b):
    m = a.shape[1]
    c=np.zeros((m,m))
    for i in range(m):
        for j in range(m):
            for k in range(m):
                c[i,j]=c[i,j]+a[i,k]*b[k,j]
    return c;
```

and a fast version of this operation in the method `matmulfast` which call the NumPy method `dot`,

Listing 2.32 MatrixMultiplication.ipynb (fragment)

```
def matmulfast(a,b):
    return np.dot(a,b);
```

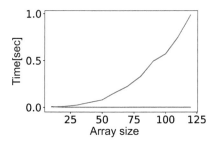

Fig. 2.4 Execution time of a matrix multiplication for different sizes of the matrices. The red line show the execution times for a element-wise implementation, whereas the blue line shows the execution times of the vectorized version with the build-in function. Using build-in functions is much more efficient than component-wise programming of this matrix multiplication.

We then evaluate the time these routines take with the following test code,

Listing 2.33 MatrixMultiplication.ipynb (fragment)

```
size=np.array([])
time1=np.array([])
time2=np.array([])
for n in range(10,130,10):

    size=np.append(size,n)
    a=np.random.rand(n,n)
    b=np.random.rand(n,n)
    c=np.zeros((n,n))

    timestart = time.clock()
    c = matmulslow(a,b)
    time1 = np.append(time1,time.clock()-timestart)

    timestart = time.clock()
    c = matmulfast(a,b)
    time2 = np.append(time2,time.clock()-timestart)
```

The resulting time graph is shown in Fig. 2.4. This not only shows that the time difference can be substantial for larger arrays, but that the scaling is very different. Some concern that interpreted computer languages are slow comes from the inefficient implementations of programmers not used to this style of programming. It is often the most challenging part for experienced programmers of C-like languages to adopt to this vectorized code, but such a programming style is essential to produce efficient code.

2.4 Data handling

In this section we will be using some famous data sets to practice handling of data. We start with the iris dataset that has been a benchmark for many traditional statistics and machine learning methods. We than briefly explore the MNIST data of handwritten digits and some basic image-handling routines.

2.4.1 Basic plots of iris data

Since machine learning requires data, we are commonly faced with importing data from files. There are a variety of tools to handle specific file formats. The most basic one is to reading data from text files. We can then manipulate the data and plot them in a form which can help us to gain insights into the information we want to get from the data. We will discuss some classical machine learning examples. These data are now often included in the libraries so that it will save us some time. However, preparing data to be used in machine learning is a large part of applying machine learning in practice. The following examples are provided in the program HouseMNIST.ipynb.

We start here with the example of the well-known classification problem of iris flowers. The iris dataset was collected from a field on the same day at the Gaspé region of eastern Quebec in Canada. These data were first used by the famous British statistician Ronald Fisher in a 1936 paper. The data consist of 150 samples, 50 samples of each of 3 species of the iris flower called iris Setosa (0), iris Versicolour (1), and iris Virginica (2). For our purpose, we usually simply give each class a label such as a number, as shown in the bracket after the flower names in this example.

The dataset is given on the book's web page with three text files, named iris.data, feature_names.txt, and target_names.txt, to start practising data handling. These are basic text files and their contents can be inspected by loading them into an editor. We are now exploring these data with with the program iris.ipynb. The data file contains both the feature values and the class label, and we can load these data into a NumPy array with the NumPy functions loadtxt. Printing out the shape of the array reveals that there are 150 lines of data, 1 for each sample, and 5 columns. The first four values are the measured length and width of septals and pedals of the flowers. The last number is the class label. The following code separates this data array into feature matrix and a target vector for all the samples. We also show how text can be handled with the NumPy function genfromtxt.

Listing 2.34 ExampleIris1.ipynb (part 1)

```
import numpy as np
import matplotlib.pyplot as plt

iris_data = np.loadtxt('iris.data', delimiter=',')
print(iris_data.shape)

features = iris_data[:,0:4]
target = iris_data[:,4]

feature_names = np.genfromtxt('feature_names.txt', delimiter=',',
    dtype='str')
feature_names = np.delete(feature_names,-1)
target_names = np.genfromtxt('target_names.txt', delimiter=',', dtype
    ='str')
```

With the data in the form of NumPy arrays, it is then easy to apply functions on these arrays to calculate properties of interest. For example, we can calculate the sum of all the septal width and the pedal width, the second and fourth column respectively, with the command

Listing 2.35 ExampleIris1.ipynb (part 2)

```
print(features[:,[1,3]].sum(axis=0))
```

It is also useful to make plots, such as plotting the average of the feature values across the samples in a bar graph where we also indicated the standard deviation with error bars.

Listing 2.36 ExampleIris1.ipynb (part 3)

```
plt.bar(np.arange(1,5),features.mean(axis=0))
plt.errorbar(np.arange(1,5),features.mean(axis=0), features.std(axis
    =0),linestyle='None', marker='o',c='r')
plt.show()
```

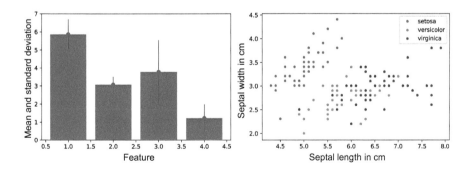

Fig. 2.5 Summary statistics (left) and scatter plot (right) of Fisher's iris data.

While using such summary statistics is a common way of characterizing data, in the age of advanced computer graphics it is often useful to try and plot the data. For example, a scatter plot of the data points where we would characterize the flowers only by the pedal length and width can be generated according to the following code. Both of these plots are shown in Fig. 2.7

Listing 2.37 ExampleIris1.ipynb (part 4)

```
plt.scatter(features[:50,0],features[:50,1], s=10, c='r', label =
    target_names[0])
plt.scatter(features[50:100,0],features[50:100,1], s=10, c='g', label
    = target_names[1])
plt.scatter(features[100:,0],features[100:,1], s=10, c='b', label =
    target_names[2])
plt.legend(loc='upper_right')
plt.xlabel(feature_names[0])
plt.ylabel(feature_names[1])
plt.show()
```

2.4.2 House data, NMIST, and Panda

Fig. 2.6 Examples of web sites with many data that can be used to develop machine learning solutions.

There are now many collections of data that contain common benchmark data. A classic collection maintained by the University of California at Irvine, called the UCI machine learning repository, has been instrumental in the development of machine learning methods. Today there are several more rich collections such as Kaggle or OpenML (see Fig. 2.6). A Kaggle collection is provided at <https://www.kaggle.com>. This site does not only provide data but is also well known for facilitating competitions on data science. Often, data are provided in spreadsheets such as the .csv file format or can be written into this format form a data base. And example is the file house.csv which originates in Kaggle and is also provided on this book's webpage that contains over 200,000 entries of basic information regarding house sales in King County. A very convenient way to read and explore these data is with the Panda library. Panda is a data analysis library that contains tools for reading plotting and doing some basic data analysis. Using the following lines, we can read the house data and provide a summary statistics:

Listing 2.38 HouseMNIST.ipynb (part 1)

```
import numpy as np
import matplotlib.pyplot as plt
import pandas as pd

df = pd.read_csv('houses.csv')
df.describe(include='all')
```

The variable df is a data frame which is a construct in Panda that contains the values and further information. We will be using mainly NumPy arrays that allow us simpler vector and matrix operations. We can take some data from the Panda data frame and read them into an array. The following program does this and also plots the first ten data points for the house price against the living area in square feet.

Listing 2.39 HouseMNIST.ipynb (part 2)

```
Y = df['price_(grands)'].values
X = df['sqft_living'].values
plt.plot(X[:10],Y[:10],'x')
```

	price	bedrooms	bathrooms	sqft_living
count	21613	21613	21613	21613
mean	540000	3.37	2.11	2080
std	367000	0.93	0.77	918
min	75000	0	0	290
25%	321000	3	1.75	1427
50%	450000	3	2.25	1910
75%	645000	4	2.5	2550
max	7700000	33	8	13540

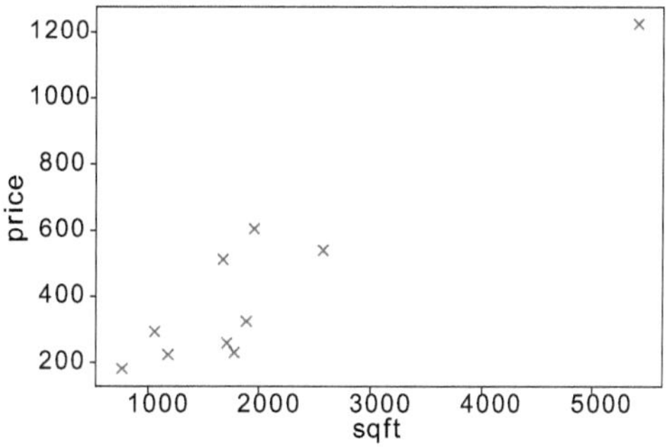

Fig. 2.7 House price versus size of living area for houses sold in King County.

Another famous data set that we will use later is the MNIST dataset originally given from the website <http://yann.lecun.com/exdb/mnist> in a compressed form. These data are often included in machine learning packages, though here we should point out another great collection of data which is provided by <https://www.openml.org>. The MNIST data set contains hand-written numbers first collected by the National Institute for Standrads (NIST) and modified (hence the M) be centered in 28×28 images. The specific data set is called mnist_784 as it has 784 attributes (28×28 pixels) and is available at <https://www.openml.org/d/554>.

The Openml web site provides a variety of formats to download their data. Since we can download these data also in the csv format, we can use a similar code as in the house example. This version shows how to read several columns into a data matrix. Since each image is written into a line, we have to reshape each input vector into a matrix before plotting it. An example is shown in Fig. 2.8A.

Listing 2.40 HouseMNIST.ipynb (part 3)

```
df = pd.read_csv('mnist_784.csv')
x = df.iloc[:,0:784].values
y = df.iloc[:,784].values

img=x.reshape(70000,28,28)
plt.imshow(img[5], cmap='binary')
```

A) MNIST example

B) jpg image

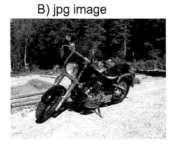

Fig. 2.8 (A) Example of an MNIST image. (B) Photograph of the author's motorbike.

2.5 Image processing and convolutional filters

This section dives into some image processing concepts and reviews convolution operations that become important later in this book. It is therefore important to review this section well. Also, the discussion gives us the opportunity to practice Python programing a bit more.

We have already displayed gray-scale images that were given by 2-dimensional matrices where each component stands for a gray level of one pixel. In order to represent color images we just need now three channels that each stands for one primary colors, red (R), green (G), and blue (B). Such RGB images are represented in a tensor of $M \times N \times 3$, where M and N are the size of horizontal and vertical resolutions in pixels. Reading and displaying an image file is incorporated in the Matplotlib library, though there are also a variety of other packages that can be used. For example, given a test image such as motorbike.jpg from the book's web page as shown in Fig. 2.8B, a program to read this image into an array and to plot it is

Listing 2.41 CV1.ipynb (part 1)

```
import numpy as np
import matplotlib.pyplot as plt

img=plt.imread('motorbike.jpg');
plt.imshow(img)
img.shape
```

The shape function reveals that this image has a resolution of 600×800 pixels with three color channels.

A main application of machine learning is object recognition, and we will now give an example of how we could accomplish this with a filter that highlights specific features in an image. Let's assume we are looking for a red spot of a certain size in a photograph. Lets say we are given a picture as an RGB image like that is shown in Fig.2.9A. The corresponding program to read this image into an array and to plot it is

Listing 2.42 CV1.ipynb (part 2)
```
img=plt.imread('red_dot_small.png'); img=img[:,:,:3]
plt.imshow(img)
img.shape
```

This is a very small image of size (8,8,3). We had to strip off the fourth channel of the loaded png array as this picture format includes a channel in which a transparency color can be specified. We can modify this image by changing pixels. For example, the code

Listing 2.43 CV1.ipynb (part 3)
```
img[6,5,1]=0; img[6,5,2]=0
plt.imshow(img)
```

creates a new red pixel resulting in the image shown in Fig. 2.9B. We use this image for the following discussion.

The red spot that we want to detect with the following program is the structure in the upper left and not the red pixel with coordinate (6,5) that we just added by hand above. We added this red pixel to discuss how we can distinguish between the main red object we are looking for and other red objects in the picture. It is interesting to look at the red, green, and blue channels separately, as shown in Fig. 2.9C. Each of these plots can be produced with a code as in the following example for the red channel.

Listing 2.44 CV1.ipynb (part 4)
```
img_r=np.zeros((8,8,3))
img_r[:,:,0]=img[:,:,0]
plt.imshow(img_r)
```

Interestingly, when looking at the color channels, one can see that there is a lot of red in the figure, as well as green and blue. The reason that we perceive the red blobs in the original figure is that there is less green and less blue in these areas.

We can use this fact to handcraft a filter that looks for red pixels. In particular, since a red pixel is characterized by a large value in the red channel and small values in the other channels, we can define a red index by

Listing 2.45 CV1.ipynb (part 5)
```
red_idx=2*img[:,:,0]-img[:,:,1]-img[:,:,2]
```

The value of the variable `red_idx` is only large if the red channel has a large value and if the green and blue channels have small values. This red index is shown in Fig. 2.9D. By taking the maximum of this resulting map we find the index (6,5) which is the pixel with the highest red index.

Listing 2.46 CV1.ipynb (part 6)
```
plt.imshow(red_idx, cmap='gray')
max_idx=np.argmax(red_idx)
max_position=np.unravel_index(max_idx, (8,8))
print(max_position)
```

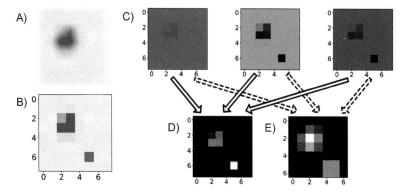

Fig. 2.9 (A) An original image of a red dot and (B) the modified image that is used for the discussion. (C) Display of the content of the three color channels. (D) Illustration of a color index for a single pixel from the three color channels and (D) result of a convolution.

In order to look for the larger 2×2 red patch in the image, we can define a 2×2 matrix which we call a filter. This filter swept over the image in the following way: we place the 2×2 matrix in the upper-left corner of the image and multiply the filter element with the corresponding image elements and then sum all the products. For the red patch recognition we define three filters, one for each color channel, which we then add together.

Listing 2.47 CV1.ipynb (part 7)

```
# 2x2 convolution
f1=np.array([[2,2],[2,2]])
f2=np.array([[-1,-1],[-1,-1]])
f3=np.array([[-1,-1],[-1,-1]])
y=np.zeros((7,7))
for i in range(7):
    for j in range(7):
        y[j,i]=np.sum(f1*img[j:j+2,i:i+2,0]+f2*img[j:j+2,i:i+2,1]+f3*
            img[j:j+2,i:i+2,1])
plt.imshow(y, cmap='gray')
max_idx=np.argmax(y)
max_position=np.unravel_index(max_idx, (7,7))
print(max_position)
```

The maximum of the resulting map is now at the location of the larger red patch as shown in Fig. 2.9E.

The operation that we have just implemented–that of element-wise multiplication of two matrices, adding up the resulting values and repeating this for all positions of the filter–is an operation called convolution. Thus the operation above represents a 2-dimensional convolution over each channel with possibly different filters, and then an addition of all the channels. We will now discuss in more detail a single convolution, but it is good to keep in mind that the real operations we need in deep neural networks are convolutions over channels and adding channels.

For a 1-dimensional discrete signal, a convolution is defined mathematically as

$$(f * x)(t) = \sum_{t'=0}^{T} f(t')x(t + t').$$

(2.1)

We used here the notation of t for the running variable as this is often applied to time series. Of course, this is only a notation and we could chose any symbol we like. A convolution for a continuous signals that spans an infinite time in the form of its mathematically formula is

$$(f * x)(t) = \int_{-\infty}^{\infty} f(t')x(t - t')dt'.$$

(2.2)

In this notation, which has been historically more common in engineering, the filter is reversed (flipped) compared to the discrete definition above. In machine learning circles, the plus sign seems now to be the dominant way of formulating the convolution, and because we will learn this value of the filter, this part of the definition does not influence the results. A function like the filter appearing in an integral as above is mathematically called a kernel function.

It is straight forward to generalize a convolution to n-dimensional data. Mathematically, a complete n-dimensional convolution can be written as

$$(f * g)(x_1, ..., x_n) = \int_{-\infty}^{\infty} \cdots \int_{-\infty}^{\infty} f(x_1', ..., x_n')g(x_1 - x_1', ..., x_n - x_n')dx_1'...dx_n',$$

(2.3)

where we used the letter g for the signal. g is here an n-dimensional array. Such an n-dimensional structure with the corresponding rules of operations is mathematically called a tensor. For example, a 3-dimensional tensor would be a cube, and convoluting them with another 3-dimensional tensor (cube) would result in another 3-dimensional tensor (cube). The discrete 2-dimensional case can be written as

$$(f * g)(u, v) = \sum_{u'=0}^{U} \sum_{v'=0}^{V} f(u', v')g(u + u', v + v').$$

(2.4)

We used here the nomenclature u and v for the coordinates of the signal. These letters are often used for the pixel space in digital cameras.

It is now common that software packages have already function implementations for convolution operations. However, it might be useful to note that most implementations are based on the convolution theorem which states the convolution of two tensors becomes a point-wise multiplication in Fourier space. Hence, one first applies an FFT (Fast Fourier Transform) to the tensors, multiplies the results pointwise, and then uses an inverse FFT to get the corresponding convolution.

The 2-dimensional convolution brings us back to our red spot example. In this case, we did a 2-dimensional convolution in each color channel and then added (or subtracted) the color channels with corresponding coefficients:

$$(f * g)(u, v) = \sum_{u'=0}^{U} \sum_{v'=0}^{V} \sum_{c} f(u', v', c)g(u + u', v + v', c).$$

(2.5)

Hence, this operation to find the red spot is really a convolution over space and addition over channel (convadd). This operation is illustrated in Fig. 2.10. This operation has

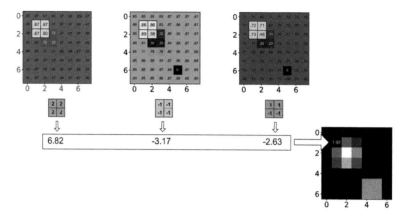

Fig. 2.10 Illustration of 2 dimensional convolutions with adding of channels. In this example different 2×2 filters are placed over the color channel and the corresponding elements are multiplied and then added up. The filter is then moved by an amount of pixels specified by the stride parameter until all the image was covered.

become the workhorse in computer vision with convolutional neural networks that we explore later in this book.

It is useful to mention that applications of convolutions are sometimes modified slightly to accommodate the preservation of the signal size. We have seen that the output of a convolution has a reduced size that depends on the size of the filter. Sometimes we want the output image to be the same size. We can achieve this by simply adding appropriate columns and rows to the input image. This is called padding, and padding with zeros is a common choice. Of course, this method can introduce some artifacts that might not be desirable.

Finally, it is interesting to note that edge detectors are an important part of computer vision systems. For example, we can apply to an image a 2×2 filter with 1s on the left column and -1s on the right column,

$$\begin{pmatrix} -1 & 1 \\ -1 & 1 \end{pmatrix}$$

For example, if we have an image with two color like

$$\begin{pmatrix} 0 & 0 & 0 & 1 & 1 & 1 \\ 0 & 0 & 0 & 1 & 1 & 1 \\ 0 & 0 & 0 & 1 & 1 & 1 \\ 0 & 0 & 0 & 1 & 1 & 1 \end{pmatrix}$$

then the filtered image would be

$$\begin{pmatrix} 0 & 0 & 2 & 0 & 0 \\ 0 & 0 & 2 & 0 & 0 \\ 0 & 0 & 2 & 0 & 0 \end{pmatrix}$$

which highlights an horizontal edge. An example of applying this filter to the image on the left-hand image of Fig. 2.11 results in the right-hand image in the same figure.

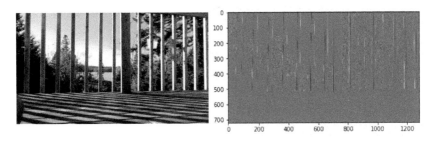

Fig. 2.11 An example of simple edge detector on the first component of a JPG image.

Of course, our filter is very small and only shows edges with significant changes between two consecutive edges. There are therefore better designs of edge detectors, such as the Canny edge detector. These techniques combine such gradient filters with Gaussian smoothing and removal of some spurious cases. Also, a continuous version of edge filters is, for example, described by Gabor functions such as the ones shown in Fig. 2.12a and b. A Gabor function is described by a sinusoidally-modulated Gaussian,

$$f(u,v) = e^{-\frac{u^2+\gamma v^2}{2*\sigma^2}} \cos(\frac{2\pi}{\lambda}u + \varphi). \tag{2.6}$$

The example of a 64^2 pixel filter with parameters $\gamma = 0.5$, $\sigma = 10$, $\lambda = 32$, and $\varphi = \pi/2$ is shown in Fig. 2.12a. This filter can be rotated with a rotation matrix

$$\begin{pmatrix} x \\ y \end{pmatrix} \leftarrow \begin{pmatrix} \cos(\varphi) & \sin(\varphi) \\ -\sin(\varphi) & \cos(\varphi) \end{pmatrix} \begin{pmatrix} x \\ y \end{pmatrix} \tag{2.7}$$

as shown in Fig. 2.12b for $\varphi = \pi$. Interestingly, such functions describe some of the neurons in the primary visual cortex of primates. Detecting edges seems therefore a good first step to process images, a fact that we will encounter again in later discussion.

A. Gabor function with \phi = \pi/2   B. Rotated version of A

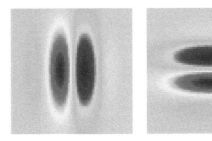

Fig. 2.12 Example of Gabor functions for (a) vertical and (b) horizontal edge detection.

3   Machine learning with sklearn

The open-source series of libraries called scikit build on the NumPy and SciPy libraries
for more domain-specific support. In this chapter we briefly introducing the scikit-learn
library, or sklearn for short. This library started as a Google Summer of Code project
by David Cournapeau and developed into an open source library which now provides
a variety of well-established machine learning algorithms. These algorithms together
with excellent documentation are available at <http://scikit-learn.org>.

The goal of this chapter is to show how to apply machine learning algorithms
in a general setting using some classic methods. In particular, we will show how to
apply three important machine learning algorithms, a support vector classifier (SVC),
a random forest classifier (RFC), and a multilayer perceptron (MLP). While many
of the methods studied later in this book go beyond these now classic methods, this
does not mean that these methods are obsolete. Quite the contrary; many applications
have limited amounts of data where some more data-hungry techniques such as deep
learning might not work. Also, the algorithms discussed here are providing some form
of baseline to discuss advanced methods like probabilistic reasoning and deep learning.
Our aim here is to demonstrate that applying machine learning methods based on such
machine learning libraries is not very difficult. It also provides us with an opportunity
to discuss evaluation techniques that are very important in practice.

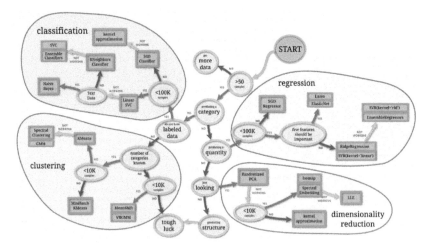

Fig. 3.1 Illustration of sklearn components and a typical workflow for different data and machine
learning goals.

Fundamentals of Machine Learning, Thomas P. Trappenberg, Oxford University Press (2020).
© Oxford University Press. DOI: 10.1093/oso/9780198828044.001.0001

An outline of the algorithms and a typical work flow provided by scikit-learn, or sklearn for short, is shown in Fig. 3.1. The machine learning methods are thereby divided into classification, regression, clustering, and dimensionality reduction. We will later discuss the ideas behind the corresponding algorithms, specifically in the second half of this chapter, though we start by treating the methods first as a black-box. We specifically outline in this chapter a typical machine learning setting for classification. In some applications it is possible to achieve sufficient performance without much need of knowing exactly what these algorithms do, although we will later show that applying machine learning to more challenging cases and avoiding pitfalls requires some deeper understanding of the algorithms. Our aim for the later part of this book is therefore to look much deeper into the principles behind machine learning including probabilistic and deep learning methods.

3.1 Classification with support vector machines, random forests, and multilayer perceptrons

We will show here how to apply three different types of machine learning classifiers using sklearn implementations, that of a support vector classifier (SVC), a random forest classifier (RFC), and a multilayer perceptron (MLP). We therefore concentrate on the mechanisms and will discuss what is behind these classifiers using the classical example of the iris flowers dataset that we discussed in the previous chapter to demonstrate how to read data into NumPy arrays. We will start with the SVC, which is support vector machine (SVM)[1]. The sklearn implementation is actually a wrapper for the SVMLIB implementation by Chih-Chung Chang and Chih-Jen Lin that has been very popular for classification applications. Later in this chapter describe more of the math and tricks behind this method, but for now we use it to demonstrate the mechanics of applying this method.

To apply this machine learning technique of a classifier to the iris data-set in the program `IrisClassificationSklearn.ipynb`. The program starts as usual by importing the necessary libraries. We then import the data similar to the program discussed in the previous chapter. We choose here to split the data into a training set and a test set by using every second data point as training point and every other as a test point. This is accomplished with the index specifications `0:-1:2` which is a list that starts at index "0", iterates until the end specified by index "−1" and uses a step of "2." Since the data are ordered and well balanced in the original data file, this will leave us also with a balanced dataset. Balance here means here that we have the same, or nearly the same, number data in the training set for each class. It turns out that this is often important for the good performance of the models. Also, instead of using the names features and target, we decided to shorten the notation by denoting the input features as x and the targets as y values.

---

[1]SVM was the original common name for this technique as it originated for classification problems. Later, the techniques were generalized to support vector regression, and we follow here the abbreviation used in sklearn.

Listing 3.1 IrisClassificationSklearn.ipynb (part 1) with output

```
import numpy as np
import matplotlib.pyplot as plt

iris_data = np.loadtxt('iris.data',delimiter=',')
x_train = iris_data[0:-1:2,0:4]
y_train = np.int32(iris_data[0:-1:2,4])
x_test = iris_data[1:-1:2,0:4]
y_test = np.int32(iris_data[1:-1:2,4])
print(x_train.shape)

(74, 4)
```

The next section of code encapsulates a basic machine learning session. In the first step we specify the model, which is here a support vector classifier (SVC) from the SVM methods of sklearn. We then apply a training algorithm provided in the fit function that requires the training data, both feature values and labels, as this is supervised learning. After the model is trained, we can use the trained model to predict new data. We use the prediction method on the feature values of the test data to predict the corresponding labels. Finally, we evaluate how good the predictions are by comparing the predicted labels with the test labels. In this case we simply count the percentage of correct labels, which is called the accuracy. The accuracy for this evaluation is around 0.97 percent, which corresponds to only two incorrect classifications.

Listing 3.2 IrisClassificationSklearn.ipynb (part 2) with output

```
from sklearn import svm
# model
model = svm.SVC(kernel='linear')
# train
model.fit(x_train,y_train)
# prediction
y_predicted=model.predict(x_test)
#evaluation
print('Percentage correct (accuracy) of SVM : ', np.mean(y_test ==
    y_predicted))

Percentage correct (accuracy) of SVM :   0.972972972972973
```

Before we move on to discuss evaluations in some more detail, let us apply another model, that of the popular random forest classifier. The corresponding code is:

Listing 3.3 IrisClassificationSklearn.ipynb (part 3) with output

```
from sklearn.ensemble import RandomForestClassifier
# model
model = RandomForestClassifier(n_estimators=10)
# train
model.fit(x_train,y_train)
# prediction
y_predicted=model.predict(x_test)
#evaluation
print('Percentage correct (accuracy) of RFC : ', np.mean(y_test ==
    y_predicted))

Percentage correct (accuracy) of RFC :   0.9459459459459459
```

The result of this classifier is round 95 percent, equating to four misclassifications. This accuracy is slightly less than the previous results with the SVM classifier, which seems to indicate that the SVM method is superior to RFs. However, this conclusion should not be made as argued further later in this chapter. Here, we simply want to show that the framework of applying different models and to show that the results here are similar.

Finally, we show an example implementation of a basic neural network called an MLP in sklearn. In the next chapter, we will elaborate on this technique as neural networks have been a major contributor to deep learning that have been behind much of the recent machine learning success and which will be an important part of our later discussions. The main point here is to show that neural networks can also be framed using the basic model definition, trained by fitting the mode parameters to the training data and making predictions on test data.

Listing 3.4 IrisClassificationSklearn.ipynb (part 4) with output

```
from sklearn.neural_network import MLPClassifier
#model
model= MLPClassifier(hidden_layer_sizes=(10, 20, 10))
# train
model.fit(x_train, y_train)
# prediction
y_predicted=model.predict(x_test)
#evaluation
print('Percentage correct (accuracy) of MLP: ', np.mean(y_test ==
    y_predicted))

Percentage correct (accuracy) of MLP :   0.96
```

Running this code repeatedly will give different performances values in every run. Most often, these values will be smaller than the ones achieved with SVM and RF, but some are even larger. This demonstrates that more careful consideration of such methods is important.

3.2 Performance measures and evaluations

We used the percentage of misclassification as an objective function to evaluate the performance of the model. This is a common choice and often a good start in our examples, but there are other commonly used evaluation measures that we should understand. Let us consider first a binary classification case where it is common to call one class "positive" and the other the "negative" class. This nomenclature comes from diagnostics such as trying to decide if a person has a disease based on some clinical tests. We can then define the following four performance indicators,

- True Positive (TP): Number of correctly predicted positive samples
- True Negative (TN): Number of correctly predicted negative samples
- False Positive (FP): Number of incorrectly predicted positive samples
- False Negative (FN): Number of incorrectly predicted negative samples

These numbers are often summarized in a confusion matrix, and such a matrix layout is shown in Fig. 3.2A.

If we have more than two classes we could generalize this to measures of True Class 1, True Class 2, True Class 3, False Class 1, etc. It is convenient to summarize these numbers in a matrix which lists the true class down the columns and the predicted label along the rows. An example of a confusion matrix for the iris dataset that has three classes is shown in Fig. 3.2B. The plot is produced with the following code.

Listing 3.5 IrisClassificationSklearn.ipynb (part 5)
```
from sklearn import metrics, model_selection
# Confusion Matrix
cm = metrics.confusion_matrix(y_test, y_predicted)
plt.matshow(cm)
plt.colorbar()
plt.ylabel('True_label')
plt.xlabel('Predicted_label')
plt.show()
```

We used a sklearn function to calculate the confusion matrix, although it is easy and recommended as an exercise to reproduce the sklearn function in your own implementation by simply using the `model.predict()` function and comparing the predictions directly with the test labels.

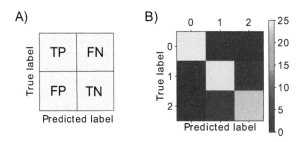

Fig. 3.2 (A) Outline of confusion matrix with two classes. (B) Example of a confusion matrix for the iris dataset when classified using an SVM.

Many different measures have been proposed in the literature which can be related to this basic measurements. For example, if we want to know the ratio (percentage) of correct classification regardless of the class, then we can look at the accuracy, as previously used. This can be written as

$$\text{Accuracy} = \frac{TP + TN}{TP+TN+FP+FN}. \tag{3.1}$$

The denominator is therefore of course the set of all data. The true positive rate (TPR) is defined as the number of TP relative to all positive predictions, some of which might be false,

$$\text{True Positive Rate (TPR)} = \frac{TP}{TP+FN}. \tag{3.2}$$

This measure is also called recall, in the computer science arena of information retrieval, or sensitivity, as this tells how discriminatory our classifier is. Of course, this becomes 100% when simply recalling all samples as positive. It is thus important to balance this with the false positive rate (FPR),

$$\text{False Positive Rate} = \frac{FP}{FP+TN}, \tag{3.3}$$

which we want to make small. This measure is also called fall out and is the complement to specificity: 1-specificity. In many cases we have the option of trading off TPR and FPR by changing some parameters in the algorithm. The resulting trade-off is commonly visualized as an ROC curve. ROC stands for receiver operating characteristics, which comes from their historical use in evaluating communication equipment. Some examples of ROC curves are shown in Fig. 3.3. Ideally, we want the TPR to be one and the FPR to be zero, which corresponds to a point in the upper-left corner. While this is not typically the case in practice, we want this curve at least to come as close as possible to this point. Or in other words, we want the area under the curve to be close to 1. In contrast, a random binary classification corresponds to the diagonal curve in this plot, which has a value of 0.5, as the area under this curve. Hence, when comparing two algorithm, we generally prefer an algorithm that has a larger area under the ROC curve, or an area that is close to 1. For many applications we have curves that are somewhere in between the two.

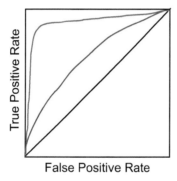

Fig. 3.3 Example of an ROC curve. The ideal classifier is in the upper-left corner.

While we have already mentioned several measures, there are many more definitions floating around in the literature. For example, the precision is defined as

$$\text{Precision} = \frac{TP}{TP+FP}, \tag{3.4}$$

and the recall is defined as

$$\text{Recall} = \frac{TP}{TP+FN}. \tag{3.5}$$

A popular way to summarize the precision and recall is to take their harmonic mean

$$F_1 = 2 \cdot \frac{\text{precision} \cdot \text{recall}}{\text{precision} + \text{recall}}. \tag{3.6}$$

This measure has the index 1 because it is the balanced choice of the more general definition that weights the two terms differently:

$$F_\beta = (1 + \beta^2) \cdot \frac{\text{precision} \cdot \text{recall}}{\beta^2 \cdot \text{precision} + \text{recall}}. \tag{3.7}$$

These measures can also be generalized to more than two classes by treating the positive class as the one under investigation and lumping the others into the negative class. There are many routines in sklearn to calculate these values from the test set. For example, the values mentioned above can be calculated for the iris example, as shown in the following code.

Listing 3.6 IrisClassificationSklearn.ipynb (part 6) with output

```
# Model Evaluation
print('\n_The_main_classification_metrics_for_iris_data:\n\n',metrics
    .classification_report(y_test, y_predicted))

The main classification metrics for iris data:

precision    recall  f1-score    support

0        1.00      1.00      1.00         25
1        0.80      0.96      0.87         25
2        0.95      0.75      0.84         24

avg / total      0.92      0.91      0.90        74
```

There are many more definitions and even different terms for the same measures. While this can be confusing it is easy to look up the specific definition. What is more important to realize is that the appropriateness of these measures are not give *a priori* but depend on what the user is seeking. That is, a good measure should encapsulate the importance that a user places onto specific characteristics. This is similar to discussing which of a range of cars is better. Some might find that greater horsepower is good, while others want a car to consume as little petrol as possible. Hence, there is no simple, best measure.

3.3 Data handling

3.3.1 Cross-validation

The performance of a model on the training data can always be improved and even made perfect on the training data when making the model more complex. This is the essence of overfitting. Basically, we can always write a model that can memorize a finite dataset. However, machine learning is about generalization that can only be measured with data points that have not been used during training. This is why in the examples earlier we split our data into a training set and into a test set.

Just splitting the data into these two sets is sufficient if we have enough. In practice, having enough labeled data for supervised training is often a problem. We therefore now introduce a method that is much better in using the data to their full potential. The method is called k-fold cross-validation for evaluating a model's performance. This method is based on the premise that all the data are used at some time for training and testing (validation) at some point throughout the evaluation procedure. For this, we partition our data into k partitions as shown in Fig. 3.4 for $k = 4$. In this example we assumed to have a dataset with twenty samples, so that each partition would have five samples. In every step of the cross-validation procedure we are leaving one partition out for validating (testing) the trained model and use the other $k - 1$ partitions for training. Hence, we get k values for our evaluation measure, such as accuracy. We could then simply use the average as a final measure for the accuracy of the model's fit. However, since we have several measures, we now have the opportunity to look at the distribution itself for more insights. For example, we could also report the variance if we assume a Gaussian distribution of the performance of the different models that result from training with different training sets.

Of course, the next question is then what should the value of k be? As always in machine learning, the answer is not as simple as merely stating a number. If we have only a small number of data, then it would be wise to use as many data as possible for training. Hence, an N-fold cross-validation, where N is the number of samples, would likely be useful. This is also called leave-one-out cross-validation (LOOCV). However, this procedure also requires N training sessions and evaluations which might be computationally too expensive with larger datasets. The choice of k is hence important to balance computational realities. We of course assume here that all samples are 'nicely' distributed in the sense that their order in the dataset is not biased. For example, cross-validation would be biased if we have data points from one class in the first part of the dataset and the other in the second part. A random resampling of the dataset is a quick way of avoiding most of these errors. Sklearn has of course a good way of implementing this. A corresponding code is given below.

Listing 3.7 IrisClassificationSklearn.ipynb (part 7)

```
# cross-validation
x = iris_data[:,0:4]
y = iris_data[:,4]
CV=10
scores = model_selection.cross_val_score(svm.SVC(kernel='linear'), x,
    y, cv=CV)

print("Accuracy on iris data: %0.4f (+/- %0.4f)", (scores.mean(),
    scores.std()))
```

In all these procedures it is of utmost importance to ensure that predictions are made on data that have never been seen in the training set before. Using test cases that have been contaminated by training data is called information or data leakage. Data leakage is a common problem as errors can easily creep into our code, for example by providing false indices to our data arrays. Testing on data that have not even been entered on the computer during training is a good way to ensure this data integrity.

We have here discussed the cross-validation procedure for testing a model, so a better name would probably be cross-testing. We will later see that this technique is often used in validation to tune hyperparameters as discussed further later in this chapter, but it is good to realize that cross-validation is foremost and iterative evaluation procedure that can be used beyond hyperparameter learning.

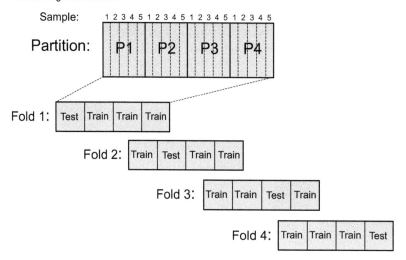

Fig. 3.4 Illustration of four-fold cross-validation on a dataset with twenty samples. In each fold, another partition of the data is taken out for testing the results of training the model on the rest of the data.

As stressed earlier, cross-validation is really an evaluation procedure for a model with a given labeled dataset. In the end, which model should we choose? In practice, it is common to use cross-validation mainly for hyperparameter tuning and to report performances in scientific papers. However, it is also common to retrain the model with all given data as training points for application purposes because it is assumed that a model with most training data will perform best in generalization.

3.3.2 Bagging and data augmentation

Having enough training data is often a struggle for machine learning practitioners. The problems of not having enough training data are endless. For one, this might reinforce the problem with overfitting or even prevent using a model of sufficient complexity at the start. Support vector machines are fairly simple (shallow) models that have the advantage of needing less data than deep learning methods. Nevertheless, even for these methods we might only have a limited amount of data to train the model.

A popular workaround has been a method called bagging, which stands for "bootstrap aggregating." The idea is therefore to use the original dataset to create several more training datasets by sampling from the original dataset with replacement. Sampling with replacement, which is also called boostrapping, means that we could have several copies of the same training data in the dataset. The question then is what good they can do. The answer is that if we are training several models on these different datasets we can propose a final model as the model with the averaged parameters. Such a regularized model can help with overfitting or challenges of shallow minima in the learning algorithm. We will discuss this point further when discussing the learning algorithms in more detail later.

While bagging is an interesting method with some practical benefits, the field of data augmentation now often uses more general ideas. For example, we could just add some noise in the duplicate data of the bootstrapped training sets which will give the training algorithms some more information on possible variations of the data. We will later see that other transformation of data, such as rotations or some other form of systematic distortions for image data is now a common way to train deep neural networks for computer vision. Even using some form of other models to transfom the data can be helpful, such as generating training data synthetically from physics-based simulations. There are a lot of possibilities that we can not all discuss in this book, but we want to make sure that such techniques are kept in mind for practical applications.

3.3.3 Balancing data

We have already mentioned balancing data, but it is worthwhile pausing again to look at this briefly. A common problem for many machine learning algorithms is a situation in which we have much more data for one class than another. For example, say we have data from 100 people with a decease and data from 100,000 healthy controls. Such ratios of positive and negative class are not uncommon in many applications. A trivial classifier that always predicts the majority class would then get 99.9 per cent correct. In mathematical terms, this is just the prior probability of finding the class, which sets the baseline somewhat for better classifications. The problem is that many learning methods that are guided by simple loss measures such as this accuracy will mostly find this trivial solution. There have been many methods proposed to prevent such trivial solutions of which we will only mention a few here.

One of the simplest methods to counter imbalance of data is simply to use as many data from the positive class as the negative class in the training set. This systematic under-sampling of the majority class is a valid procedure as long as the sub-sampled data still represent sufficiently the important features of this class. However, it also means that we lose some information that is available to us and the machine. In the example above this means that we would only utilize 100 of the healthy controls in the training data. Another way is then to somehow enlarge the minority class by repeating some examples. This seems to be a bad idea as repeating examples does not seem to add any information. Indeed, it has been shown that this technique does not usually improve the performance of the classifier or prevent the majority overfitting problem. The only reason that this might sometimes work is that it can at least make sure the learning algorithms is incremented the same number of times for the majority and the minority class.

Another method is to apply different weights or learning rates to learn examples with different sizes to the training set. One problem with this is to find the right scaling of increase or decrease in the training weight, but this technique has been applied successfully in many case, including deep learning.

In practice it has been shown that a combination of both strategies under-sampling the majority class and over-sampling the minority class can be most beneficial, in particular when augmenting the over-sampling with some form of augmentation of the data. This is formalized in a method called SMOTE: synthetic minority over-sampling technique. The idea is therefore to change some characteristics of the over-sampled data such as adding noise. In this way there is at least a benefit of showing the learner variations that can guide the learning process. This is very similar to the bagging and data augmentation idea discussed earlier.

3.3.4 Validation for hyperparameter learning

Thus far we have mainly assumed that we have one training set, which we use to learn the parameters of the parameterized hypothesis function (model), and a test set, to evaluate the performance of the resulting model. In practice, there is an important step in applying machine learning methods which have to do with tuning hyperparameters. Hyperparameters are algorithmic parameters beyond the parameters of the hypothesis functions. Such parameters include, for example, the number of neurons in a neural network, or which split criteria to use in decision trees, discussed later. SVMs also have several parameters such as one to tune the softness of the classifier, usually called C, or the width of the Gaussian kernel γ. We can even specify the number of iterations of some training algorithms. We will later shed more light on these parameters, but for now it is important only to know that there are many parameters of the algorithms itself beyond the parameters of the parameterized hypothesis function (model), which can be tunes. To some extent we could think of all these parameters as those of the final model, but it is common to make the distinction between the main model parameters and the hyperparaemeters of the algorithms.

The question is then how we tune the hyperparameters. This in itself is a learning problem for which we need a special learning set that we will call a validation set. The name indicates that it is used for some form of validation, although it is most often used to test a specific hyperparameters setting that can be used to compare different settings and to choose the better one. Choosing the hyperparameters itself is therefore a type of learning problem, and some form of learning algorithms have been proposed. A simple learning algorithm for hyperparameters would be a grid search where we vary the parameters in constant increments over some ranges of values. Other algorithms, like simulated annealing or genetic algorithms, have also been used. A dominant mode that is itself often effective when used by experienced machine learners is the hand-tuning of parameters. Whatever method we choose, we need a way to evaluate our choice with some of our data.

Therefore, we have to split our training data again into a set for training the main model parameters and a set for training the hyperparameters. The former we still call the training set, but the second is commonly called the validation set. Thus, the question arises again how to split the original training data into a training set for model parameters and the validation set for the hyperparameter tuning. Now, we can of course use the cross-validation procedure as explained earlier for this. Indeed, it is very common to use cross-validation for hyperparameter tuning, and somehow the name of the cross-validation coincides with the name of the validation step. But notice that the cross-validation procedure is a method to split data and that this can be used for both hyperparameter tuning and evaluating the predicted performance of our final model.

Once more, it is important to stress that the validation error should not be reported as our estimate of the final performance of our model. Using the validation data is a type of learning itself, and the model is thus tuned to these specific values. Such an error can be made arbitrarily small with some form of overfitting. Thus, we need a test set which has not been used in any way during the training and model selection, so neither in the training of the primary model parameters nor in the selection of hyper-partameters to estimate a generalization error. Using any of the test data in training, or even any derived information of test data in training, can lead to a drastic underestimation of the generalization error. We called this above already data or information leakage, and such information contamination can completely invalidate the prediction of the model performance on unseen data. Therefore, we must set aside another part of the data that has never been used in training or hyperparameter tuning. We call this set the test set. We could again then use a cross-validation scheme itself for the combined training/validation and test set. This nested use of cross-validation does add some complexity but is highly recommended when the dataset is small.

3.4   Dimensionality reduction, feature selection, and t-SNE

Before we dive deeper into the theory of machine learning, it is good to realize that we have only scratched the surface of machine learning tools in the sklearn toolbox. Besides classification, there is of course regression, where the label is a continuous variable instead of a categorical. We will later see that we can formulate most supervised machine learning techniques as regression and that classification is only a special case of regression. Sklearn also includes several techniques for clustering which are often unsupervised learning techniques to discover relations in data. Popular examples are k-means and Gaussian mixture models (GMM). We will discuss such techniques and unsupervised learning more generally in later chapters. Here we will end this section by discussing some dimensionality reduction methods.

As stressed earlier, machine learning is inherently aimed at high-dimensional feature spaces and corresponding large sets of model parameters, and interpreting machine learning results is often not easy. Several machine learning methods such as neural networks or SVMs are frequently called a blackbox method. However, there is nothing hidden from the user; we could inspect all portions of machine learning models such as the weights in support vector machines. However, since the models are complex, the human interpretability of results is challenging. An important aspect of machine learning is therefore the use of complementary techniques such as visualization and dimensionality reduction. We have seen in the examples with the iris data that even plotting the data in a subspace of the 4-dimensional feature space is useful, and we could ask which subspace is best to visualize. Also, a common technique to keep the model complexity low in order to help with the overfitting problem and with computational demands was to select input features carefully. Such feature selection is hence closely related to dimensionality reduction.

Today we have more powerful computers, typically more training data, as well as better regularization techniques so that input variable selection and standalone dimensionality reduction techniques seems less important. With the advent of deep learning we now often speak about end-to-end solutions that starts with basic features without the need for pre-processing to find solutions. Indeed, it can be viewed as problematic to potential information. However, there are still many practical reasons why dimensionality reduction can be useful, such as the limited availability of training data and computational constraints. Also, displaying results in human readable formats such as 2-dimensional maps can be very useful for human-computer interaction (HCI).

A traditional method that is still used frequently for dimensionality reduction is principle component analysis (PCA). PCA attempts to find a new coordinate system of the feature representation which orders the dimensions according to how spread the data are along these dimensions. The reasoning behind this is that dimensions with a large spread of data would offer the most sensitivity for distinguishing data. This is illustrated in Fig. 3.5. The direction of the largest variance of the data in this figure is called the first principal component. The variance in the perpendicular direction, which is called the second principal component, is less. In higher dimensions, the next principal components are in further perpendicular directions with decreasing variance along the directions. If one were allowed to use only one quantity to describe the data, then one can choose values along the first principal component, since this would capture an important distinction between the individual data points. Of course, we lose some information about the data, and a better description of the data can be given by including values along the directions of higher-order principal components. Describing the data with all principal components is equivalent to a transformation of the coordinate system and thus equivalent to the original description of the data.

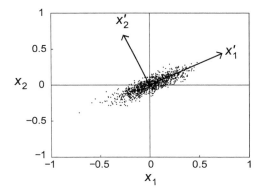

Fig. 3.5 Example of feature pairs (x_1, x_2) values drawn from a 2-dimensional probability distribution with mean zero. It also shows a new coordinate system with the first principle component x_1' and the perpendicular direction along the second pronciple component x_2'.

There are several extensions to PCA that are worth considering in the machine learning context. In particular, independent component analysis (ICA) seeks to find new coordinates that minimize the statistical dependence between the new features. Let **s** be independent source signals, and consider that the features that we usually measure for a system are linear combinations of these source signals,

$$\mathbf{x} = \mathbf{W}\mathbf{s} \qquad (3.8)$$

where **W** is a mixing matrix. A typical application is that of the so-called cocktail party problem where say n speakers are talking (which would be the source signal) and we have n microphones in the room (which would be the measured signal). If we want to derive the source signal from the measured signal, we have to find the inverse of this mixing matrix. In this situation we don't even know the mixing matrix, so the question is how we find the inverse of a matrix that we do not know. A solution is that we make certain assumptions, such as the fact that the speaker should speak independently and hence that the signals are statistically independent. In this way we can formulate the demixing problem as a minimization problem, that of finding the demiximg matrix that would minimize a measure of dependency such as the Kullback–Leibler divergence. We will talk about such statistical measures in more detail later. While this type of ICA does not directly reduce the dimension of the problem, having an feature space spanned by independent features helps to investigate some meaningful independent subspaces. A generalization of these ideas is captured in non-negative matrix factorization.

Finally, another popular method for dimensionality reduction and a common technique to visualize high-dimensional data in 2-dimensional spaces is a technique called t-distributed stochastic neighbor embedding (t-SNE). This technique tries to minimize distance between the similarities of data points in the high-dimensional feature space with the distance of their low-dimensional representation. Such techniques are implemented in sklearn. The code following shows the application of PCA and t-SNE for the iris dataset. The resulting scatter plot in Fig. 3.6 demonstrate that the iris Setosa flowers are easily distinquishable from the other two classes, but that there are a few examples of overlap between iris Versicolour and iris Virginica. Such techniques are important when considering machine learning as the analytics engine for data mining and data science.

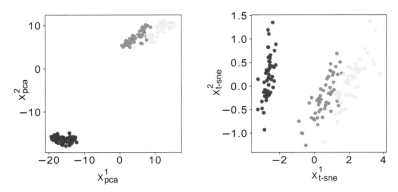

Fig. 3.6 Example of first two principle components of the iris data (left) and the corresponding t-SNE representation (right).

Listing 3.8 IrisTSNE.ipynb

```
# adapted from Alexander Fabisch
import numpy as np
import matplotlib.pyplot as plt
from sklearn.datasets import load_iris
from sklearn.decomposition import PCA
from sklearn.manifold import TSNE

iris = load_iris()
X_tsne = TSNE(learning_rate=100).fit_transform(iris.data)
X_pca = PCA().fit_transform(iris.data)

plt.figure(figsize=(10, 5))
plt.subplot(121)
plt.scatter(X_tsne[:, 0], X_tsne[:, 1], c=iris.target)
plt.subplot(122)
plt.scatter(X_pca[:, 0], X_pca[:, 1], c=iris.target)
plt.show()
```

3.5 Decision trees and random forests

As stressed at the beginning of this chapter, our main aim here was to show that applying machine learning methods is made fairly easy with application packages like sklearn, although one still needs to know how to use techniques like hyperparameter tuning and balancing data to make effective use of them. In the next two sections we want to explain some of the ideas behind the specific models implemented by the random forrest classifier (RPF) and the support vector machine (SVM). This is followed in the next chapter by discussions of neural networks. The next two section are optional in the scnsc that following the theory behind them really require knowledge of additional mathematical concepts that are beyond our brief introductory treatment in this book. Instead, the main focus here is to give a glimpse of the deep thoughts behind those algorithms and to encourage the interested reader to engage with further studies. The asterisk in section headings indicates that these sections are not necessary reading to follow the rest of this book.

We have already used a random forrest classifier (RFC), and this method is a popular choice where deep learning has not yet made an impact. It is worthwhile to outline the concepts behind it briefly since it is also an example of a non-parametric machine learning method. The reason is that the structure of the model is defined by the training data and not conjectured at the beginning by the investigator. This fact alone helps the ease of use of this method and might explain some of its popularity, although there are additional factors that make it competitive such as the ability to build in feature selection. We will briefly outline what is behind this method. A random forest is actually an ensemble method of decision trees, so we will start by explaining what a decision tree is.

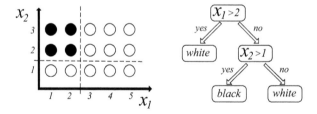

Fig. 3.7 Example data of two classes with black and white discs and a corresponding decision tree for classification on the right.

Let us consider the training data

$$\mathcal{D}_{\text{train}} = \{(\mathbf{x}^{(i)}, y)\}, \tag{3.9}$$

where the attribute vector has N_f components. For example, the data on the left in Fig. 3.7 have two attributes called x_1 and x_2. The algorithm calculates how to split the data iteratively by considering which attribute could classify the training data best at this level of a decision function. If we first split the data along the vertical dashed line, then we can already classify a large number of data correctly. We can split the remaining data further using the second attribute.

The question in practice then is which attribute and corresponding attribute value we use to split the data. A popular choices to make this decision is a measure called "information gain" or a related measure called "Gini impurity." For the information gain we calculate the entropy of the data before and after the split. The entropy H describes how uniform the data are, with larger values of the entropy indicating more homogeneous data. Thus, for our classification purpose, we look for splits that separate the data well and hence lead to a lower entropy in each partition. The Shannon entropy is formally calculated as

$$H = -\sum_y p(y)log_2 p(y), \tag{3.10}$$

where $p(y)$ is the probability of a label. Thus in our example Fig. 3.7 the entropy before the split is $H = -4/15\log_2(4/15) - 11/15\log_2(11/15) \approx 0.84$. The weighted average entropy of the indicated vertical split is $H = 6/15(-4/6\log_2(4/6) - 2/6\log_2(2/6)) - 9/15 * 0 \approx 0.37$. This is an information gain of around 0.47. When we split the data as proposed with the dashed horizontal line, then the weighted entropy is $H = 10/15 * (-4/10 * log_2(4/10) - 6/10 * log_2(6/10)) \approx 0.45$ which leads only to a information gain of 0.39. All the other possible splits have lower information gain than the first choice. As mentioned earlier, some decision trees use the Gini impurity instead of the entropy to measure how diverse the data are in a set, which is defined as

$$G = 1 - \sum_y p^2(y). \tag{3.11}$$

The results are very similar, but the Gini impurity is numerically less demanding. A nice features of decision trees is that the algorithm does a form of feature (attribute) selection based on some information theoretic measures. A downside is that it does not usually consider combinatorial features.

The decision tree for the iris data can be calculated with sklearn as demonstrated with the code in Listing 3.9. In this code we add in the data as previously shown at the beginning of this chapter and define and train a tree model provided in sklearn. This model gets about 95 per cent correct. Sklearn also provides an interface to a graphing software called graphviz that can plot a graph of the decision trees. The resulting graph for the iris dataset is shown in Fig. 3.8. This tree nicely represents rules on individual features. For example, the first node says to look at the third feature, the petal length, and if this feature is less or equal to 0.7 then this is an example of the first class, the iris Setosa. The graph also shows the Gini impurity value for each subset of the data under the selection condition. The Gini impurity is zero if all examples are from one class.

A common problem with decision trees is that they tend to overfit decisions along the way that are made from individual features. This is where the random forest idea comes into play. A random forest is a ensemble method which makes decisions based on an ensemble of decision trees. The different decision trees are created by creating different training sets for each of them by randomly sampling. This has already been discussed as bagging. Since a decision tree is a non-parametric method, this can be particularly effective way to create a variety of trees where a vote of all the trees in the end can make better decisions as it prevents some form of overfitting. This is why it is common in practice to use random forests instead of a single decision tree.

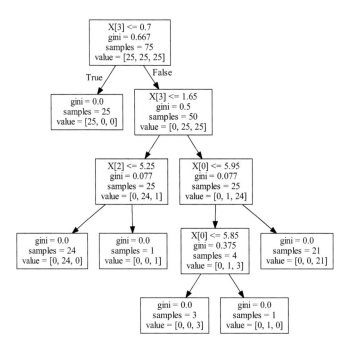

Fig. 3.8 Example of a decision tree trained on the iris dataset.

Listing 3.9 IrisDecisionTree.ipynb

```python
import numpy as np
from sklearn import tree

iris_data = np.loadtxt('iris.data',delimiter=',')

x_train = iris_data[0:-1:2,0:4]
y_train = np.int32(iris_data[0:-1:2,4])
x_test = iris_data[1:-1:2,0:4]
y_test = np.int32(iris_data[1:-1:2,4])

# model
model = tree.DecisionTreeClassifier()
# train
model.fit(x_train,y_train)
# prediction
y_predicted=model.predict(x_test)
#evaluation
print('Percentage correct (accuracy) of DTC: ', np.mean(y_test ==
    y_predicted))

import graphviz
dot_data = tree.export_graphviz(model, out_file=None)
graph = graphviz.Source(dot_data)
graph
```

3.6 Support vector machines (SVM)

3.6.1 Linear classifiers with large margins

In this section we outline the basic idea behind support vector machines (SVM) that have been instrumental in a first wave of industrial applications due to their robustness and ease of use. A warning: SVMs have some intense mathematical underpinning, although our goal here is to outline only some of the mathematical ideas behind this method. It is not strictly necessary to read this section in order to follow the rest of the book, but it does provide a summary of concepts that have been instrumental in previous progress and are likely to influence the development of further methods and research. This includes some examples of advanced optimization techniques and the idea of kernel methods. While we mention some formulae in what follows, we do not derive all the steps and will only use them to outline the form to understand why we can apply a kernel trick. Our purpose here is mainly to provide some intuitions.

SVMs, and the underlying statistical learning theory, was largely invented by Vladimir Vapnik in the early 1960s, but some further breakthroughs were made in the late 1990s with collaborators such as Corinna Cortes, Chris Burges, Alex Smola, and Bernhard Schölkopf, to name but a few. The basic SVMs are concerned with binary classification. Fig. 3.9 shows an example of two classes, depicted by different symbols, in a 2-dimensional attribute space. We distinguish here attributes from features as follows. Attributes are the raw measurements, whereas features can be made up by combining attributes. For example, the attributes x_1 and x_2 could be combined in a feature vector $(x_1, x_1 x_2, x_2, x_1^2, x_2^2)^T$. This will become important later. Our training set consists of m data with attribute values $\mathbf{x}^{(i)}$ and labels $y^{(i)}$. We put the superscript index i in brackets so it is not mistaken as a power. For this discussion we chose the binary labels of the two classes as represented with $y \in \{-1, 1\}$. This will simplify some equations.

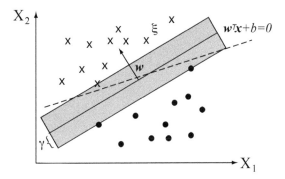

Fig. 3.9 Illustration of linear support vector classification.

The two classes in the Fig. 3.9 can be separated by a line, which can be parameterized as

$$w_1 x_1 + w_2 x_2 - b = 0 \qquad (3.12)$$

$$\mathbf{w}^T\mathbf{x} - b = 0. \tag{3.13}$$

While the first line shows the equation with its components in two dimensions, the next expression in a matrix notation is the same in any dimension. Of course, in three dimensions we would talk about a plane. In general, we will talk about a hyperplane in any dimensions. The particular hyperplane is the dividing or separating hyperplane between the two classes. We also introduce what the margin γ, which is the perpendicular distance between the dividing hyperplane and the closest point.

The main point to realize now is that the dividing hyperplane that maximizes the margin is most likely to be a good choice. Why is that? We should assume that the training data, shown in the figure, are some unbiased examples of the true underlying density function describing the distribution of points within each class and thus representative of the most likely data. It is then likely that new data points, which we want to classify, are close to the already existing data points. Thus, if we make the separating hyperplane as far as possible from each point, then we probably won't make mistaken classification on future data points. Or, in other words, a separating hyperplane like the one shown as dashed line in the figure, is likely to offer poorer generalization than the maximum margin hyperplane. Thus, the maximum margin hyperplane can be considered the best choice if we assume that both classes have the same expected variation from the training data. Such a maximum margin classifier can hence be expected to be a good choice.

Let us formalize the maximization of the margin a bit more mathematically. Learning a linear maximum margin classifier on labeled data means finding the parameters $\mathbf{w}$ and b that maximizes the margin. For this we could computer the distances of each point from the hyperplane, which is simply a geometric exercise,

$$\gamma^{(i)} = y^{(i)}\left(\left(\frac{\mathbf{w}}{||\mathbf{w}||}\right)^T\mathbf{x}^{(i)} + \frac{b}{||\mathbf{w}||}\right). \tag{3.14}$$

The vector $\mathbf{w}/||\mathbf{w}||$ is the normal vector of the hyperplane, a vector of unit length perpendicular to the hyperplane. The norm $||\mathbf{w}||$ is the Euclidean length of the vector $\mathbf{w}$. The margin we want to maximize is the distance to the closest point,

$$\gamma = \min_i \gamma^{(i)}. \tag{3.15}$$

We can formulate the maximum margin calculation by realizing from Egn 3.14 that maximizing γ is equivalent to minimizing $||\mathbf{w}||$, or, equivalently, of minimizing

$$\min_{\mathbf{w},b} \frac{1}{2}||\mathbf{w}||^2. \tag{3.16}$$

Of course, we want to maximize this margin under the constraint that no training data should lay within the margin. Since we have the freedom to chose a scale, we can defines this distance as 1, so that the decision boundaries become

$$\mathbf{w}^T\mathbf{x}^{(i)} + b \geq 1 \quad \text{for} \quad y^{(i)} = 1 \tag{3.17}$$

$$\mathbf{w}^T\mathbf{x}^{(i)} + b \leq -1 \quad \text{for} \quad y^{(i)} = -1. \tag{3.18}$$

These equations can be combined into one equation when we use labels for the set $y = \{-1, 1\}$, namely

$$-(y^{(i)}(\mathbf{w}^T\mathbf{x}+b)-1) \geq 0. \tag{3.19}$$

So, to summarize, we have a quadratic minimization problem (Eq. 3.16) with the linear inequalities Eeg.3.19) as constraint. Optimization with constraints can be formalized with the Lagrange formalism. For this, we simply add the constraints to the main objective or loss function with some parameters α_i that are generally called Lagrange multipliers,

$$\mathcal{L}^P(\mathbf{w},b,\alpha_i) = \frac{1}{2}||\mathbf{w}||^2 - \sum_{i=1}^{m}\alpha_i[y^{(i)}(\mathbf{w}^T\mathbf{x}+b)-1]. \tag{3.20}$$

Lagrange multipliers determine how well the constraints are observed. In the case of $\alpha_i = 0$, the constraints do not matter. In order to conserve the constraints, we should thus make these values as large as we can. Finding the maximum margin classifier is hence given by the so-called primal problem

$$p^* = \min_{\mathbf{w},b}\max_{\alpha_i}\mathcal{L}^P(\mathbf{w},b,\alpha_i) \tag{3.21}$$

However, Vapnik went a step further by realizing that the margin can also be maximized by maximizing the so-called dual Lagrangian

$$d^* \max_{\alpha_i}\min_{\mathbf{w},b}\mathcal{L}^D(\mathbf{w},b,\alpha_i), \tag{3.22}$$

since one can show that

$$p^* \leq d^*. \tag{3.23}$$

Note that in these formulae we interchange the minimum and maximum operations. While we will not derive this dual problem, the reason for this step is the following. While it is straightforward to solve the primal optimization problem, solving the dual problem leads to a formulation in which we can use a kernel trick, discussed later to generalize the method to non-linear cases. Moreover, the equality holds when the optimization function and the constraints are convex.[2] So, if we minimize $\mathcal{L}$ by looking for solutions of the derivatives $\frac{\partial\mathcal{L}}{\partial\mathbf{w}}$ and $\frac{\partial\mathcal{L}}{\partial b}$, we get

$$\mathbf{w} = \sum_{i=1}^{m}\alpha_i y^{(i)}\mathbf{x}^{(i)} \tag{3.24}$$

$$0 = \sum_{i=1}^{m}\alpha_i y^{(i)} \tag{3.25}$$

Substituting this into the optimization problem, we get the final form of our optimization problem,

$$\max_{\alpha_i}\sum_i\alpha_i - \frac{1}{2}\sum_{i,j}y^{(i)}y^{(j)}\alpha_i\alpha_j\mathbf{x}^{(i)T}\mathbf{x}^{(j)}, \tag{3.26}$$

subject to the constraints

$$\alpha_i \geq 0 \tag{3.27}$$

---

[2]Under these assumptions, there are other conditions that hold, called the Karush–Kuhn–Tucker conditions, that are useful in providing proof of the convergence of the methods outlined here.

$$\sum_{i=1}^{m} \alpha_i y^{(i)} = 0. \tag{3.28}$$

From this optimization problem it turns out that the α_is of only a few examples, those ones that are lying on the margin, are the only ones which have $\alpha_i \neq 0$. The corresponding training examples are called support vectors. The actual optimization can be done with several algorithms. John Platt developed the sequential minimal optimization (SMO) algorithm that is very efficient for this optimization problem. Please note that the optimization problem is convex and can thus be solved very efficiently without the danger of getting stuck in local minima.

Once we find the support vectors with corresponding α_is, we can calculate $\mathbf{w}$ from Egn 3.24 and b from a similar equation. Then, if we are given a new input vector to be classified, this can then be calculated with the hyperplane Egn 3.13 as

$$y = \begin{cases} 1 & \text{if } \sum_{i=1}^{m} \alpha_i y^{(i)} \mathbf{x}^{(i)T} \mathbf{x} > 0 \\ -1 & \text{otherwise} \end{cases}, \tag{3.29}$$

Since this is only a sum over the support vectors, which should be only a few data points from the training set, classification becomes very efficient after training.

3.6.2 Soft margin classifier

Thus far we have only discussed the linear separable case, but how about the case when there are overlapping classes? It is possible to extend the optimization problem by allowing some data points to be in the margin while penalizing these points somewhat. We therefore include some slag variables ξ_i that reduce the effective margin for each data point, but we add a penalty term to the optimization that penalizes if the sum of these slag variables are large,

$$\min_{\mathbf{w},b} \frac{1}{2} ||\mathbf{w}||^2 + C \sum_i \xi_i, \tag{3.30}$$

subject to the constraints

$$y^{(i)} (\mathbf{w}^T \mathbf{x} + b) \geq 1 - \xi_i \tag{3.31}$$

$$\xi_i \geq 0 \tag{3.32}$$

. The constant C is a free parameter in this algorithm. Making this constant large means allowing fewer points to be in the margin. This parameter must be tuned and it is advisable at least to try to vary this parameter in order to verify that the results do not dramatically depend on an initial choice.

3.6.3 Non-linear support vector machines

We have treated the case of overlapping classes while assuming that the best we can do is a linear separation. However, what if the underlying problem is separable with a function that might be more complex? An example is shown in Fig. 3.10. Non-linear separation and regression models are of course much more common in machine learning, and we will now look into the non-linear generalization of the SVM.

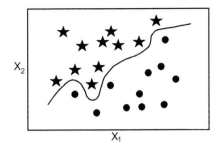

Fig. 3.10 Example of a non-linear separation between two classes.

Let us illustrate the basic idea with an example in two-dimensions. A linear function with two attributes that span the 2-dimensional feature space is given by

$$y = w_0 + w_1 x_1 + w_2 x_2 = \mathbf{w}^T \mathbf{x}, \qquad (3.33)$$

with

$$\mathbf{x} = \begin{pmatrix} 1 \\ x_1 \\ x_2 \end{pmatrix} \qquad (3.34)$$

and weight vector

$$\mathbf{w}^T = (w_0, w_1, w_2). \qquad (3.35)$$

Let us say that we cannot separate the data with this linear function but that we could separate it with a polynomial that include second-order terms like

$$y = \tilde{w}_0 + \tilde{w}_1 x_1 + \tilde{w}_2 x_2 + \tilde{w}_3 x_1 x_2 + \tilde{w}_4 x_1^2 + \tilde{w}_5 x_2^2 = \tilde{\mathbf{w}} \phi(\mathbf{x}). \qquad (3.36)$$

We can view the second equation as a linear separation on a feature vector

$$\mathbf{x} \rightarrow \phi(\mathbf{x}) = \begin{pmatrix} 1 \\ x_1 \\ x_2 \\ x_1 x_2 \\ x_1^2 \\ x_2^2 \end{pmatrix}. \qquad (3.37)$$

This can be seen as mapping the attribute space $(1, x_1, x_2)$ to a higher-dimensional space with the mapping function $\phi(\mathbf{x})$. We call this mapping a feature map. The separating hyperplane is then linear in this higher-dimensional space. Thus, we can use the above linear maximum margin classification method in non-linear cases if we replace all occurrences of the attribute vector $\mathbf{x}$ with the mapped feature vector $\phi(\mathbf{x})$.

There are only three problems remaining. One is that we don't know what the mapping function should be. The somewhat ad-hoc solution to this problem will be that we try out some functions and see which one works best. We will discuss this further later in this chapter. The second problem is that we have the problem of overfitting as we might use too many feature dimensions and corresponding free parameters w_i. In the next section, we provide a glimpse of an argument why SVMs might address this problem. The third problem is that with an increased number of dimensions the evaluation of the equations becomes more computational intensive. However, there is a useful trick to alleviate the last problem in the case when the calculations always contain only dot products between feature vectors. An example of this is the solution of the minimization problem of the dual problem in the earlier discussions of the linear SVM. The function to be minimized in this formulation, Eqn 3.26 with the feature maps, only depends on the dot products between a vector $\mathbf{x}^{(i)}$ of one example and another example $\mathbf{x}^{(j)}$. Also, when predicting the class for a new input vector $\mathbf{x}$ from Eqn 3.24 when adding the feature maps, we only need the resulting values for the dot products $\phi(\mathbf{x}^{(i)})^T \phi(\mathbf{x})$. We now discuss that such dot products can sometimes be represented with functions called kernel functions,

$$K(\mathbf{x}, \mathbf{z}) = \phi(\mathbf{x})^T \phi(\mathbf{z}). \tag{3.38}$$

Instead of actually specifying a feature map, which is often a guess to start with, we could actually specify a kernel function. For example, let us consider a quadratic kernel function between two vectors $\mathbf{x}$ and $\mathbf{z}$,

$$K(\mathbf{x}, \mathbf{z}) = (\mathbf{x}^T \mathbf{z} + 1)^2. \tag{3.39}$$

We can then try to write this in the form of Eqn 3.38 to find the corresponding feature map. That is,

$$
\begin{align}
K(\mathbf{x}, \mathbf{z}) &= (\mathbf{x}^T \mathbf{z})^2 + 2\mathbf{x}^T \mathbf{z} + 1 \tag{3.40} \\
&= (x_1 z_1 + x_2 z_2)^2 + 2(x_1 z_1 + x_2 z_2) + 1 \tag{3.41} \\
&= x_1^2 z_1^2 + x_2^2 z_2^2 + 2x_1 z_1 x_2 z_2 + 2x_1 z_1 + 2x_2 z_2 + 1 \tag{3.42} \\
&= \phi(\mathbf{x})^T \phi(\mathbf{z}), \tag{3.43}
\end{align}
$$

with

$$
\phi(\mathbf{x}) = \begin{pmatrix} 1 \\ \sqrt{2}x_1 \\ \sqrt{2}x_2 \\ \sqrt{2}x_1 x_2 \\ x_1^2 \\ x_2^2 \end{pmatrix}. \tag{3.44}
$$

Except for the factors of $\sqrt{2}$ that do not matter as these can be absorbed into the definition of the weight parameters, this is the same as the mapping function we assumed earlier. Thus, instead of calculating a dot product in the 6-dimensional mapped space, we can calculate a dot product in the original 3-dimensional space and simply square the result. Also, savings of computational complexity become even more pronounced with higher-order polynomials where we can replace calculation of $O(n^2)$ with a fixed calculation in the original attribute space. There is an impressive saving of computations with this kernel trick.

While we have derived the corresponding feature map for a specific kernel function, this task is not always easy and not all functions are valid kernel functions. We must also be careful that the kernel functions still lead to convex optimization problems. In practice, only a small number of kernel functions are used. Besides the polynomial kernel mention so far, one of the most popular is the Gaussian kernel, also called radial basis function (RPF) kernel,

$$K(\mathbf{x}, \mathbf{z}) = \exp -\frac{||\mathbf{x} - \mathbf{z}||^2}{2\gamma^2}. \tag{3.45}$$

It is common to represent the width of this Gaussian with the parameter γ, which is a prominent hyperparameter of the SVM with an RBF kernel. It is interesting to note that this kernal function corresponds to a feature map that is formally infinitely large.

As mentioned earlier, a large feature space corresponds to a complex model with many parameters and hence has the potential to overfit easily. We must therefore finally look into this problem. The key insight here is that we are already minimizing the sum of the components of the parameters, or more precisely the square of the norm $||\mathbf{w}||^2$. This term can be viewed as regularization which favours a smooth decision hyperplane. Moreover, we have discussed two extremes in classifying complicated data: one was to use kernel functions to create high-dimensional non-linear mappings and hence have a high-dimensional separating hyperplane; the other method was to consider a low-dimensional separating hyperplane and interpret the data as overlapping. The last method includes a parameter C that can be used to tune the number of data points that we allow to sit within the margin. Thus, we can combine these two approaches to classify non-linear data with overlaps where the soft margins will in addition allow us to favour more smooth dividing hyperplanes.

In practice, we have to consider several free parameters when applying support vector machines and one of the first that must be chosen is which kernel function to use. Most packages have a number of choices implemented. In the following example we used the Gaussian kernel function with width parameter γ. Setting a small value for γ and allowing for a large number of support vectors (small C), corresponds to a complex model. In contrast, larger width values and regularization of constant C will increase the stiffness of the model and lower the complexity. In practice, we have to tune these parameters to get good results. To do this we need to use some form of validation set, and k-times cross-validation is often implemented in the related software packages.

An example of the SVM performance (accuracy) on some examples (iris dataset from the UCI repository; from Broadman and Trappenberg, 2006) is shown in Fig. 3.11 for several values of γ and C. It is often typical that there is a large area where the SVM works well and has only little variations in terms of performance. This robustness has helped to make SVMs practical methods that often outperform other methods. However, there is often also an abrupt onset of the region where the SVM fails, and some parameter tuning is hence required. While just trying a few settings might be sufficient, some more systematic methods such as grid search or simulated annealing are recommended.

3.6.4 Statistical learning theory and VC dimension

SVMs are good and practical classification algorithms for several reasons. In particular, they are formulated as a convex optimization problem that has many good theoretical properties and that can be solved with quadratic programming. They are formulated to

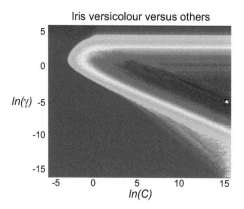

Fig. 3.11 Illustration of SVM accuracy for different values of parameters C abd γ.

take advantage of the kernel trick, they have a compact representation of the decision hyperplane with support vectors, and turn out to be fairly robust with respect to the hyper parameters. However, in order to act as a good learner, they need to moderate the overfitting problem discussed earlier. A great theoretical contributions of Vapnik and colleagues was the embedding of supervised learning into statistical learning theory and to derive some bounds that make statements on the average ability to learn form data. We briefly outline here the ideas and state some of the results without too much details, and we discuss this issue here entirely in the context of binary classification. However, similar observations can be made in the case of multiclass classification and regression. This section uses language from probability theory that we only introduce in more detail later. Therefore, this section might be best viewed at a later stage. Again, the main reason in placing this section is to outline the deeper reasoning for specific models.

As can't be stressed enough, our objective in supervised machine learning is to find a good model which minimizes the generalization error. To state this differently by using nomenclature common in these discussions, we call the error function here the risk function R; in particular, the expected risk. In the case of binary classification, this is the probability of missclassification,

$$R(h) = P(h(x) \neq y). \tag{3.46}$$

Of course, we generally do not know this density function. We assume here that the samples are iid (independent and identical distributed) data, and we can then estimate what is called the empirical risk with the help of the test data,

$$\hat{R}(h) = \frac{1}{m} \sum_{i=1}^{m} \mathbb{1}\left(h(\mathbf{x}^{(i)}; \theta) = y^{(i)}\right). \tag{3.47}$$

The function $\mathbb{1}$ is 1 if the argument is true and 0 otherwise. We use here m as the number of examples, but note that here this is the number of examples in the test (or validation) set, which is the number of all training data minus the ones used for training. Also, we will discuss this empirical risk further, but note that it is better to use the regularized version that incorporates a smoothness constraint such as

$$\hat{R}_{rmreg}(h) = \frac{1}{m} \sum_i \mathbb{1}(h(\mathbf{x}^{(i)}; \theta) = y^{(i)}) - \Lambda ||\mathbf{w}||^2 \tag{3.48}$$

in the case of SVM, where Λ is a regularization constant. Thus, wherever $\hat{R}(h)$ is used in the following, we can replace this with $\hat{R}_{\text{reg}}(h)$. Empirical risk minimization is the process of finding the hypothesis $\hat{h}$ that minimizes the empirical risk,

$$\hat{h} = arg \min_h \hat{R}(h). \tag{3.49}$$

As a side note, we will later talk about the maximum likelihood estimate (MLE), and the empirical risk is the MLE of the mean of a Bernoulli-distributed random variable with true mean $R(h)$. Thus, the empirical risk is itself a random variable for each possible hypothesis h. Let us first assume that we have k possible hypothesis h_i. We now draw on a theorem called the Hoeffding inequality that provides and upper bound for the sum of random numbers to its mean,

$$P(|R(h_i) - \hat{R}(h_i)| > \gamma) > 2 \exp(-2\gamma^2 m). \tag{3.50}$$

This formula states that there is a certain probability that we make an error larger than γ for each hypothesis of the empirical risk compared to the expected risk, although the good news is that this probability is bounded, and that the bound itself becomes exponentially smaller with the number of validation examples. This is already an interesting results, but we now want to know the probability that some, out of all possible hypotheses, are less than γ. Using the fact that the probability of the union of several events is always less or equal to the sum of the probabilities, one can show that with probability $1 - \delta$ the error of a hypothesis is bounded by

$$|R(h) - \hat{R}(h)| > \sqrt{\frac{1}{2m} \log \frac{2k}{\delta}}. \tag{3.51}$$

This is a great results since it shows how the error of using an estimate for the risk, the empirical risk that we can evaluate from the test (or validation) data, becomes smaller with training examples and with the number of possible hypotheses.

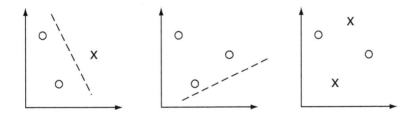

Fig. 3.12 Illustration of VC dimensions for the class of linear functions in two dimensions.

While the error scales only with the log of the number of possible hypotheses, the values still extend to infinite when the number of possible hypotheses extends to infinite, which more closely resembles the situation when we have parameterized hypotheses. However, Vapnik was able to show the following generalization in the infinite case. Given a hypotheses space with Vapnic–Chervonencis dimension VC(h), then, with probability $1 - \delta$, the error of the empirical risk compared to the expected risk (true generalization error) is

$$|R(h) - \hat{R}(h)| > O\left(\sqrt{\frac{VC}{m}\log\frac{m}{VC} + \frac{1}{m}\log\frac{1}{\delta}}\right). \qquad (3.52)$$

The VC dimensions is thereby a measure of how many points can be divided by a member of the hypothesis set for all possible label combinations of the point. For example, consider three arbitrary points in two dimensions as shown in Fig. 3.12, and let us consider the hypothesis class of all possible lines in two dimensions. We can always divide the three points under any class membership condition, of which two examples are also shown in the figure. By contrast, it is easy to find examples with four points that can not be divided by a line in two dimensions. The VC dimension of lines in two dimensions is thus $VC = 3.$[3]

3.6.5 Support vector regression

While we have mainly discussed classification in the last few sections, it is time to consider the more general case of regression and to connect these methods to the general principle of maximum likelihood estimation outlined in the previous chapter. It is again easy to illustrate the method for the linear case before generalizing it to the non-linear case similar to the strategy followed for SVMs.

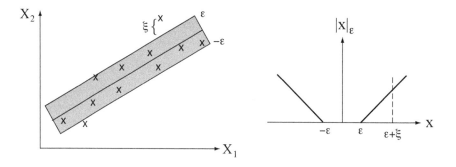

Fig. 3.13 Illustration of support vector regression and the ϵ-insensitive cost function.

The idea in support vector regression is that data points close to a regression line are expected to fluctuate but that we should not take outliers too much into account. This can be achieved with an error function which does not count deviations of data from the hypothesis that are less than ϵ form the hypothesis. Such an error function is often called an ϵ-insensitive error function and is illustrated in Fig. 3.13. The corresponding optimization problem is

---

[3]Three points of different classes can not be separated by a single line, but these are singular points that are not effective in the definition of VC dimension.

$$\min_{\mathbf{w},b} \frac{1}{2}||\mathbf{w}||^2 + C \sum_i (\xi_i + \xi^*), \qquad (3.53)$$

subject to the constraints

$$y^{(i)} - \mathbf{w}^T \mathbf{x} - b \geq \xi_i \qquad (3.54)$$
$$y^{(i)} - \mathbf{w}^T \mathbf{x} - b \geq \xi_i^* \qquad (3.55)$$
$$\xi_i, \xi_i^* \geq 0. \qquad (3.56)$$

The dual formulations again only depend on scalar products between the training examples, and the regression line can be also be expressed by a scalar product between the support vectors and the prediction vector,

$$h(\mathbf{x}; \alpha_i, \alpha_i^*) = \sum_{i=1}^{m} (\alpha_i - \alpha_i^*) \mathbf{x}_i^T \mathbf{x}. \qquad (3.57)$$

Thus, we can again use kernels to generalize the method to non-linear cases. In practice it has been more challenging to get SVR models to learn effectively and they are now mostly replaced by neural networks.

4   Neural networks and Keras

In this chapter we discuss the basic operation of an artificial neural network which is the major paradigm of deep learning. The name derives using an analogy to a biological brain. We start this introduction by outlining the basic operations of neurons in the brain and how these operations are abstracted by simple neuron models. We then build networks of artificial neurons that constitute much of the recent success of AI. We will concentrate in this chapter on using such techniques and will later come back to discussing their theoretical embedding.

4.1   Neurons and the threshold perceptron

The brain is composed of specialized cells. These cells include neurons, which are thought to be the main information-processing units, and glia, which have a variety of supporting roles. A schematic example of a neuron is shown in Fig. 4.1a. Neurons are specialized in electrical and chemical information processing. They have an extensions called an axon to send signals, and receiving extensions called dendrites. The contact zone between the neurons is called a synapse. A sending neuron is often referred to as the presynaptic neuron and the receiving cell is a postsynaptic neuron. When an neuron becomes active it sends a spike down the axon where it can release chemicals called neurotransmitters. The neurotransmitters can then bind to receiving receptors on the dendrite that trigger the opening of ion channels. Ion channels are specialized proteins that form gates in the cell membrane. In this way, electrically charged ions can enter or leave the neuron and accordingly change the voltage (membrane potential) of the neuron. The dendrite and cell body acts like a cable and a capacitor that integrates (sums) the potentials of all synapses. When the combined voltage at the axon reaches a certain threshold, a spike is generated. The spike can then travel down the axon and affect further neurons downstream.

This outline of the functionality of a neuron is, of course, a major simplification. For example, we ignored the description of the specific time course of opening and closing of ion channels and hence some of the more detailed dynamics of neural activity. Also, we ignored the description of the transmission of the electric signals within the neuron; this is why such a model is called a point-neuron. Despite these simplifications, this model captures some important aspects of a neuron functionality. Such a model suffices for us at this point to build simplified models that demonstrate some of the information-processing capabilities of such a simplified neuron or a network of simplified neurons. We will now describe this model in mathematical terms so that we can then simulate such model neurons with the help of a computer.

Warren McCulloch and Walter Pitts were among the first to propose such a simple model of a neuron in 1943 which they called the **threshold logical unit**. It is now often

Fundamentals of Machine Learning, Thomas P. Trappenberg, Oxford University Press (2020).
© Oxford University Press. DOI: 10.1093/oso/9780198828044.001.0001

A. Schematic neuron

B. Schematic synapse

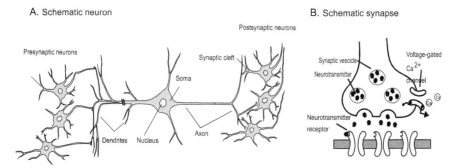

Fig. 4.1 A. Outline of the components of a neuron and its connectivity to other neurons in the brain that make up the neuronal network. B. Outline of a synaptic terminal where neurotransmitters are released that can trigger the opening of ion channels in the receiving neuron, which in turn triggers the change of the electric state of the neuron.

referred to as the McCulloch–Pitts neuron. Such a unit is shown in Fig. 4.2A with three input channels, although neurons have typically a much larger number of input channels. Input values are labeled by x with a subscript for each channel. Each channel has an associated **weight parameter**, w_i, representing the "strength" of a synapse.

The McCulloch–Pitts neuron operates in the following way. Each input value is multiplied with the corresponding weight value, and these weighted values are then summed together, mimicking the superposition of electric charges. Finally, if the weighted summed input is larger than a certain threshold value, w_0, then the output is set to 1, and 0 otherwise. Mathematically this can be written as

$$y(\mathbf{x}; \mathbf{w}) = \begin{cases} 1 & \text{if } \sum_i^n w_i x_i = \mathbf{w}^T \mathbf{x} > w_0 \\ 0 & \text{otherwise} \end{cases}. \tag{4.1}$$

This simple neuron model can be written in a more generic form that we will call the **perceptron**. In this more general model, we calculate the output of a neuron by applying an gain function g to the weighted summed input,

$$y(\mathbf{x}; \mathbf{w}) = g(\mathbf{w}^T \mathbf{x}), \tag{4.2}$$

where $\mathbf{w}$ are parameters that need to be set to specific values or, in other words, they are the parameters of our parameterized model for supervised learning. We will come back to this point later regarding how precisely to chose them. The original McCulloch–Pits neuron is in these terms a threshold perceptron with a threshold gain function,

$$g(x) = \begin{cases} 1 & \text{if } x > 0 \\ 0 & \text{otherwise} \end{cases}. \tag{4.3}$$

This threshold gain function is a first example of a non-linear function that transforms the sum of the weighted inputs. The gain function is sometimes called the activation function, the transfer function, or the output function in the neural network literature. Non-linear gain functions are an important part of artificial neural networks as further discussed in later chapters.

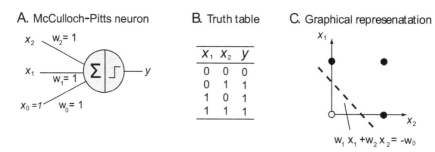

Fig. 4.2 Representation of the boolean OR function with a McCulloch–Pitts neuron, also called threshold linear unit.

The argument that McCulloch and Pitts brought forward with this model is that neurons can implement logic functions. This is illustrated in Fig. 4.2 for the Boolean OR function. This function output the true value (represented numerically as 1) if either of the inputs is on 1, and false (represented numerically as 0) otherwise. The truth table of this function is shown on the left in Fig. 4.2, and the threshold perceptron with two inputs is shown beside it. If either of the inputs x_1 and x_2 has a value of 1, then the output of the neuron should be $y = 1$, representing TRUE. Only if both inputs are 0 is the output value 0, representing FALSE. In terms of machine learning, the truth table represents all possible data points of the problem, and representing this function is thus akin memorizing all possible data points. We discussed earlier that the interesting part of machine learning is when only a limited amount of data is available at the learning phase and it has to generalize to unseen examples. However, the Boolean function is the smallest case of an interesting function representation problem that is worth discussing.

The decision line (or hyperplane in higher dimensions) of the threshold perceptron as a classifier is illustrated on the right side of Fig. 4.2 in the parameters space spanned by w_1 and w_2. This line is mathematically given by

$$w_1 x_1 + w_2 x_2 = \theta. \tag{4.4}$$

As can be seen from the graph, there are many solutions to this equation that can separate the data. In the last chapter, we discussed how the solution with the largest margin is expected to generalize well. The linear SVM can hence be thought of as a special case of a perceptron. While SVMs went on to find a way to generalize these methods to non-linear problems with the kernel trick, the following sections will take these perceptrons on a different path. Specifically, while SVMs tried to preserve a convex optimization problem with specific predefined transformations of the feature space, deep learning aims at learning appropriate transformations as discussed further below.

4.2 Multilayer perceptron (MLP) and Keras

To represent more complex functions with perceptron-like elements we are now building networks of artificial neurons. We will start with a multilayer perceptron (MLP) as shown in Fig.4.3. This network is called a two-layer network as it basically has two processing layers. The input layer simply represents the feature vector of a sensory input, while the next two layers are composed of the perceptron-like elements that sum up the input from previous layers with their associate weighs of the connection channels and apply a non-linear gain function $\sigma(x)$ to this sum,

$$y_i = \sigma(\sum_j w_{ij}x_j). \tag{4.5}$$

We used here the common notation with variables x representing input and y representing the output. The synaptic weights are written as w_{ij}. The above equation corresponds to a single-layer perceptron in the case of a single output node. Of course, with more layers, we need to distinguish the different neurons and weights, for example with superscipts for the weights as in Fig.4.3. The output of this network is calculated as

$$y_i = \sigma(w_{ij}^o \sigma(\sum_k w_{jk}^h x_k)). \tag{4.6}$$

where we used the superscript "o" for the output weights and the superscript "h" for the hidden weights. These formulae represent a parameterized function that is the model in the machine learning context.

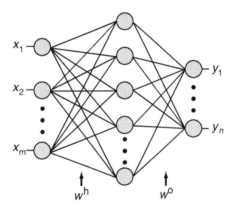

Fig. 4.3 A multilayer perceptron is a standard architecture of a neural network in which input is passed through hidden layers to the output layer. The weight values of the hidden layer is summarized in the weight matrix $\mathbf{w}^h$. The output values of the nodes in the hidden layer become the input to the output layer, which are scaled by the values of the connection strength as specified by the elements in the weight matrix $\mathbf{w}^o$.

The MLP model is included in the sklearn library. We have used this already in the last chapter, and we will implement them here again with Keras that is another library. The reason to switch to this library is that it is build on top of routines that can run the code on graphic processor units (GPUs). This is essential for deep learning as the size of the models will increase as we go along and the models have commonly be applied to large data sets. GPUs are processors that are optimized for array operations. Such operations are common in generating graphics. Most of our operations around neural networks can take advantage of these specilized processors as neural networks are based on matrix or tensor operations, including additions, multiplications, and convolution operations. Support for deep learning has specifically been developed by NVIDIA, so GPUs by this company are the main workhorses of deep learning.

There are several implementations that realize the basic array operations on GPUs. This includes Theano, a Python toolbox for multi-dimensional array operations, the Microsoft Cognitive Toolkit (CNTK) for deep-learning with support of Python, C#, C++, and Java, and Tensorflow, which is Google's support for deep learning. The implementation can be written directly with the help of these toolboxcs. Keras is a general layer on top of these applications that is ideal to outline the computational principles and support fast prototyping. We will use Keras in this book. A popular recent alternative is PyTorch that is recommended for further studies.

Let us discuss our first deep neural network with a new example, that of hand-written character cecognition, specifically the MNIST dataset. This dataset has dominated much of the early DNN developments and must be considered a classic by now. The data set consists of digitized examples of hand written numbers from 0 to 9. Each image consist of 28×28 pixels. An examples is shown as input in Fig. 4.4. We have already mentioned this data set in Chapter 2, but briefly, this benchmark dataset has 60,000 training examples and 10,000 test examples, and a developer is of course free to choose any portion of the 60,000 training images as the validation set.

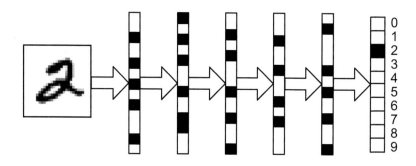

Fig. 4.4 A (relatively) deep neural network for the MNIST hand written character recognition benchmark.

A network with six layers is outlined in Fig. 4.4, and the corresponding program is included below. The first part of the program is concerned with the preparation of the data in the appropriate format such as gathering all the pixels in the image into a large vector of size 784 (=28×28) and rescaling it to a range of $[0, 1]$. Will later discuss why such a normalization is useful. Also, we change the labels into a 1-hot representation, which is a vector of length equal to the number of classes with 0s in all components except the position that indicates the label of this class. For example, with three classes we could have $1 \rightarrow [1, 0, 0], 2 \rightarrow [0, 1, 0], 3 \rightarrow [0, 0, 1]$. We can use the Keras function to_categorical() for this purpose.

Listing 4.1 MNIST_MLP.ipynb (part 1)

```
import numpy as np
import matplotlib.pyplot as plt
from keras import models, layers, optimizers, datasets, utils

(x_train, y_train), (x_test, y_test) = datasets.mnist.load_data()

x_train = x_train.reshape(60000, 784)/255
x_test = x_test.reshape(10000, 784)/255
y_train = utils.to_categorical(y_train, 10)
y_test = utils.to_categorical(y_test, 10)
```

We will later reuse this part of the program to test other models.

Similar to sklearn, we will now define a model, use a fit function to train the model, and evaluate it on the test data. The interesting part here is how the neural network can be specified in Keras. Keras provides two principle ways to specify models: one called sequential model which is limited to purely sequential models with single inputs and outputs, and the more general functional model which can be used to assemble more complex models. The functional model notation is not much more difficult and even slightly more sensible so that we will use this mode right away. A functional model in Keras is specified by specifying a general input, then specifying functions for layers and connecting them by specifying their individual inputs, and finally to collect a single model by calling a function `Model()` in which we specify the input and output of the entire model. Note that a function with two bracket pairs like the `Dense` function in this example means that the function returns a function, which is then called with the second argument list.

Listing 4.2 MNIST_MLP.ipynb (part 2)

```
inputs = layers.Input(shape=(784,))
x = layers.Dense(128, activation='relu')(inputs)
x = layers.Dense(128, activation='relu')(x)
x = layers.Dense(128, activation='relu')(x)
x = layers.Dense(128, activation='relu')(x)
x = layers.Dense(128, activation='relu')(x)
outputs= layers.Dense(10, activation='softmax')(x)

model = models.Model(inputs=inputs, outputs=outputs)
```

The MLP is characterized by a fully connected layer where each neuron of the previous layer is connected to every neuron in the receiving layer. Such layers are now commonly called dense layers. We have to specify the activation function for each layer if it is not linear, which is here the rectified linear function (relu)

$$g(x_i) = \begin{cases} x_i & \text{if } x_i > 0 \\ 0 & \text{otherwise,} \end{cases} \quad (4.7)$$

except the last layer for which the activation function is a softmax function

$$g(x_i) = \frac{e^{-x_i}}{\sum_j e^{-x_j}}. \quad (4.8)$$

The model has to be compiled. This is different from sklearn and the reason is that at this step the model is prepared for execution on GPUs if available. Most of the examples in this book are prepared to be small enough so that a GPU is not required. In the compilation step we specify which loss function to use, which optimizer we will use, and also which metric we use to evaluate the results. Of course, we have to discuss these choices in more detail, but for now we want to show that such networks with these popular choices can do remarkable well. It is common that this simple model results in a test accuracy of around 98 per cent on the MNIST dataset. In contrast, a comparable SVM achieves around 91 per cent on the MNIST dataset.

Listing 4.3 MNIST_MLP.ipynb (part 3) (with output)

```
model.compile(loss='categorical_crossentropy', optimizer='Nadam',
    metrics=['accuracy'])

history = model.fit(x_train, y_train, batch_size=128,
epochs=10, validation_data=(x_test, y_test))

score = model.evaluate(x_test, y_test)
print('Test_loss:', score[0],'Test_accuracy:', score[1])

Test loss: 0.09899666948468402 Test accuracy: 0.9759
```

The performance of the model after learning is of course of utmost importance for us. However, it is also very instructive and important for the development of the models to monitor the performance of the model during learning. We call such graphs **learning curves**. We can draw different type of curves, either evaluated on the training set or evaluated on the validation set. It is easy to plot such curves in Keras as the fit function already includes a history of evaluations as a callback function, and Keras provides the framework to code your own callback function. Other deep learning frameworks also commonly include a way to visualize the progress during learning. In the code above we assigned the returned pointer of the fit function to dictionary list variable `history`. The `key()` function lists the key names for the included values,

Listing 4.4 MNIST_MLP.ipynb (part 4)

```
print(history.history.keys())
```

which returns

Listing 4.5 MNIST_MLP.ipynb (part 5)

```
dict_keys(['val_loss', 'val_acc', 'loss', 'acc'])
```

Let us plot the accuracy learning curves

Listing 4.6 MNIST_MLP.ipynb (part 6)

```
# Plotting learning curves
plt.plot(history.history['acc'],'—')
plt.plot(history.history['val_acc'])
plt.ylabel('accuracy')
plt.xlabel('epoch')
plt.legend(['train', 'test'], loc='lower_right')
plt.show()
```

which results in the graph shown in Fig. 4.5. We can see that the validation accuracy, is fairly consistent around 0.975, while the training accuracy is increasing, which might be a sign of overfitting. The behaviour of such curves is quite useful observe when developing the model. It can provide some diagnostic values when the model is not learning properly.

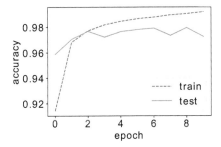

Fig. 4.5 Example of the learning curves. The blue dotted line corresponds to the accuracy over the training data, while the red solid line corresponds to the accuracy over the validation data.

4.3 Representational learning

Here, we are discussing feedforward neural networks which can be seen as implementing transformations or mapping functions from an input space to a latent space, and from there on to an output space. The latent space is spanned by the neurons in between the input nodes and the output nodes, which are sometime called the hidden neurons. We can of course always observe the activity of the nodes in our programs so that these are not really hidden. All the weights are learned from the data so that the transformations that are implemented by the neural network are learned from examples. However, we can guide these transformations with the architecture. The latent representations should be learned so that the final classification in the last layer is much easier than from the raw sensory space. Also, the network and hence the representation it represents should make generalizations to previously unseen examples easy and robust. It is useful to pause for a while here and discuss representations.

4.3.1 Signal decomposition and sparse features

To illustrate again the re-representation of a signal with filters, consider basic signal analysis. Let us consider time-varying signals that are represented with floating point values for each time step. Say we are sampling a EEG signal that is recorded from electric electrodes attached to the head with 500HZ. That is, we have one data point every 0.002 second. If we assume that a floating point is typically represented by computer word of 64 bits, then a 10-minute length would take over 2 MB of storage.

An example signal $x(t)$ is illustrate at the top in Fig. 4.6. While this is a relatively complicated signal, we have created this signal from two template signals that we call the **basis functions**. With these basis functions we can reconstruct the signal as

$$x(t) = a_1 y_1(t) + a_2 y_2(t) \tag{4.9}$$

Representing the original signal with these basis functions has a big advantage. For example, if we store a set of basis functions in several computers, then we can transmit the signal with only two numbers for the coefficients a_1 and a_2. Of course, we can not expect real signals to be made up of only these two basis functions. So in practice, we want to create a long list of "appropriate" basis functions. A common example for basis functions are sine waves which are usually good choices for periodic signals. A composition of a signal into such sine of cosine functions is called a Fourier transformation

$$x(t) = \int_0^{\infty} a(\lambda) \sin(2\pi\lambda t) + b(\lambda) \cos(2\pi\lambda t) \mathrm{d}\lambda \qquad (4.10)$$

Another common choice for more localized functions are functions somewhat similar to y_1 in the figure. Such functions are called wavelets and the corresponding decomposition is a wavelet transform. These functions are usually chosen by hand and have been designed specifically for certain applications. The filters in deep neural networks can be seen as representing a from of basis functions for a specific feature decomposition. The interesting part of neural networks is that these functions are learned from data so that we do not need to design basis functions by hand.

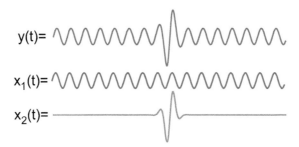

Fig. 4.6 Illustration of signal representation with templates.

Since we can take a large or even infinite number of basis functions into account, it is possible to represent any function with appropriate basis functions. However, having arbitrary basis function is also not the best choice. That is, if we have a long list of basis functions, then we might still need a large number of coefficients. Indeed, if we make the basis function a value at each time step, then we would just end up with the same representation as before for a signal for which we just store the value at each time point. An important insight to make efficient use of resources while extracting the "essence of signals" is to try and find sparse representations. A **sparse representation** is a representation where we might have a large number of basis functions in our dictionary (nodes in a deep network) but are only using a relatively small number of active nodes to represent each example. In our example this might correspond to

$$y(t) = a_1 x_1(t) + a_2 x_2(t) + a_3 x_3(t) + a_4 x_4(t) + a_5 x_5(t) + a_6 x_6(t) + ... \quad (4.11)$$

with a coefficient vector
$$\mathbf{a} = (1, 3, 0, 0, 0, 0, 0, ...). \qquad (4.12)$$

Sparse representations lead to considerable compressions such as being able to represent a continuous signal with only two numbers in our example. Sparse compression can be an important factor in machines to gain some "semantic knowledge" of the world. For example, there are many instantiations of objects such as cars, but my ability to characterize them with one word is equivalent to semantic knowledge and a form of sparse representation.

4.3.2 De-noising autoencoders and semantic compression

If compressed (or sparse) representations are so useful, can we force such representations in our neural networks? There are different techniques that will indeed force some compressed representations, including an architecture called an autoencoder outlined here as well some regularization methods discussed earlier.

A simple example of an autoencoder is shown in Fig. 4.7. In this network we start with an input layer that is connected to a smaller hidden layer and then to an output layer that is the same size as the input layer. The reason for choosing an output layer that has the same size as the input layer is that we want to build a mapping function that maps inputs to the same output. This is an example of unsupervised or self-supervised learning, as we do not require labels for this learning task, just raw data such as pictures.

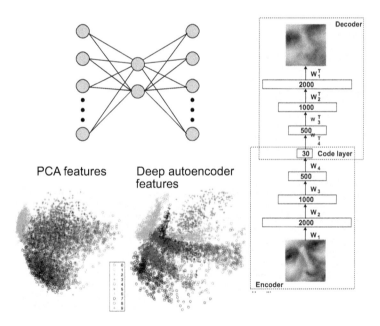

Fig. 4.7 Examples of autoencoders with the basic idea at the top, the deep autoencoder that kicked off deep learning and some comparisons of auto encoders to PCA. From Science, 313 (5786), G. E. Hinton, R. R. Salakhutdinov, Reducing the Dimensionality of Data with Neural Networks, pp. 504-507, DOI: 10.1126/science.1127647, Copyright © 2006, American Association for the Advancement of Science. Reprinted with permission from AAAS.

Why would we want to build such functions and isn't this simply the identity function? The main point is that the mapping function represented by this neural network is channeled through a small hidden layer that forces some compression. In this sense we try to extract useful filters. Sometimes this is described as semantic hashing as this compressed space might represent higher knowledge. Most of the actual implementation of such networks use a version where the inputs are somewhat corrupted by noise and the labels are the noiseless pattern. Such an architecture is called a de-noising autoencoder. Noise does actually help in this circumstance to force the solution away from a simple identity function and to generalize better to new unseen examples. The figure includes an example of t-SNE plots that show feature representation learned from the MNIST data set by an autoencoder compared to PCA (principal component analysis) that we mentioned earlier. The classes of the autoencoder are much better clustered which shows a useful organization of the latent space. We will come back to a more modern implementation of such strategies with variational autoencoders.

4.4 Convolutional neural Networks (CNNs)

4.4.1 Filters and convolutions

We mentioned earlier that an SVM is like an improved perceptron in that it takes regularization and some form of feature transformation into account. We should therefore ask ourselves why the MLP is then outperforming an SVM on the MNIST data which achieves only around 94 per cent with the sklearn implementation. The main difference is that here we used more layers with adjustable parameters compared to the SVM which we can view as a one-layer (smart) perceptron with an additional preprocessing step of transforming inputs into a high-dimensional representation of the feature space defined by the kernel. The use of additional layers with learned parameters allows for the learning of hierarchical features. We will illustrate this point in more detail later, but for now it is sufficient to say that deep learning enables the learning of hierarchical representations that are difficult to match with shallow (less sequential) operations. Increasing the number of layers has allowed successful applications of neural networks to more complex problems. Models with tens or even hundreds of layers are now not uncommon.

The question is then how we can make the neural networks scalable, as it not only takes more computer time to process the models, but also increases the demand on training examples to learn the increased number of parameters of more complex models. The answer is that we can build-in some assumptions into our network architecture. We will see this strategy several times. Here we discuss a particular important case, that of position invariance of features.

It is useful to realize that neurons represent detectors or filters for specific features, meaning that neurons become maximally activated for specific input patterns. This is easily understood in vision applications. We demonstrated this already in Chapter 2 when discussing convolutions. While we demonstrated convolutions there with predefined filters, we are now taking this a step further buy building networks based on convolutional operations in which the parameters of the filters are learned.

4.4.2 CNN and MNIST

The idea of designing position-invariant feature detectors in neural networks was first described by Fukushima in 1980. Back then, Fukushima worked for NHK, the Japanese public broadcaster, together with physiologists, as NHK was interested to understand the mechanisms of human vision. It was well known since the early 1960s from experiments by Hubel and Wiesel showing some neurons in the primary visual cortex, the first stage of visual processing in the cortex, are edge detectors, and that such features detectors must be combined in a way so that object recognition becomes invariant to the location in space.

Edge detectors are the workhorse of traditional computer vision, and we discussed in Chapter 2 how such filters are implemented with convolutions. The neural networks that we discussed then had to learn individual weights for each pixel location. Even if this network could learn to represent an edge detector, separate detectors have to be learned for each location in an image since edges can appear in all locations. Another way of thinking about convolution is that a neuron (specific filter) is applied to every possible location in the image. This leads us to the idea of weight sharing and convolutional neural networks (CNNs).

To discuss the implementation of this network type with Keras we go back to the MNIST benchmark example. The basic idea of a convolutional network is to replace the dense connections of regular networks, that are implemented with a matrix multiplication $\mathbf{h} = \mathbf{wx}$, with that of a convolution $\mathbf{h} = \mathbf{w} * \mathbf{x}$. Thus, the network looks a lot like the one shown in Fig. 4.4. While such a convolutional network has far fewer parameters than a dense network, implementing the convolution and running it efficiently on a computer is challenging. It is therefore that we need to use graphics processing units (GPUs). GPUs are special purpose processors that are designed for efficient matrix operations, and these processors have been very helpful in deep learning. In particular, NVIDIA has added specific support for deep learning operations, and it is such lower-level support on which we rely in the following. While there are specific frameworks that even support directly the programming with GPUs, such as Tensorflow or Theano, we chose here to apply Keras that is itself utilizing backends like Tensorflow and Theano, as well as other support on GPUs, to implement the operations we need in deep learning. Hence, as long as your programming environment is implemented to take advantage of GPUs, we can ignore the details and work on a higher level with system architectures. If you do not have a GPU than I recommend running the following MNIST examples on a smaller traning set.

The Keras program to apply a CNN to the MNIST data is shown in the following. The program starts by linking the required libraries and reading the data as we did earlier for the dense network (MLP). The only difference is that we now reshape the input data into a 2-dimensional array instead of the 1-dimensional feature vector for each example. Actually, the data is already in the form of 28×28 for each sample, but since Keras expects the number of channels we have still to reshape it into the form $28 \times 28 \times 1$.

Listing 4.7 MNIST_CNN.ipynb (part 1)

```
import keras
import numpy as np
import matplotlib.pyplot as plt
from keras import models, layers, optimizers, datasets, utils

(x_train, y_train), (x_test, y_test) = datasets.mnist.load_data()
x_train = x_train.reshape(60000, 28, 28, 1)/255
x_test = x_test.reshape(10000, 28, 28, 1)/255
y_train = utils.to_categorical(y_train, 10)
y_test = utils.to_categorical(y test, 10)
```

The model is then defined by the following code.

Listing 4.8 MNIST_CNN.ipynb (part 2)

```
inputs = layers.Input(shape=(28, 28, 1,))
x=layers.Conv2D(32, kernel_size=(3, 3),activation='relu')(inputs)
x=layers.Conv2D(64, (3, 3), activation='relu')(x)
x=layers.MaxPooling2D(pool_size=(2, 2))(x)
x=layers.Dropout(0.25)(x)
x=layers.Flatten()(x)
x=layers.Dense(128, activation='relu')(x)
x=layers.Dropout(0.5)(x)
outputs=layers.Dense(10, activation='softmax')(x)

model = models.Model(inputs=inputs, outputs=outputs)
```

The model starts with a convolutional layer that produces filtered images with thirty-two channels where each channel is the result of filtering with a separate filter. The size of the filter is specified with the `kernel_size` parameter. We used a rectified linear (RELU) activation functions that is common for deep networks. We then add another convolution layer. Since the output size is defined by the previous we don't have to include the input size. In this layer we expand the representation to sixty-four channels.

The next layer is a new type of layer that is produced by a fixed kernel type defining an operation that is called **max pooling**. Max pooling takes a consecutive patch of pixels, in this case a pooling size of (2,2), and replaces this with one pixel of the maximum of this patch. This will shrink the image size, in this example case by a half in each direction. Shrinking the image is important as we eventually want to get away from details of a picture to a higher-level (semantic) description of the input. Replacing some image patch with only the max value of its pixels seems to be a rather drastic way of doing this, and some other proposals have been offered. For example, we could take the average of the pixels. Such an average pooling is in practice not so much different than the max pooling operation. To reduce the signal size we could also shift the filter by more than one pixel every time it is applied. The number of pixels for which the filter is moved every time during a convolution operation is called a **stride**. More advanced techniques have been proposed, such as capsule networks, but these are beyond our discussion at this point.

The next layer we add is a dropout layer. This is actually not really a new layer but a post-processing of the current layer which turns off some of the nodes randomly. The probability of a neuron to be turned off is set to 25 per cent in our example. Dropout is a common technique to prevent overfitting. Overfitting in neural networks can happen when individual neurons become very sensitive to specific training examples, and turning neurons off randomly during training forces a more distributed representation. This can be seen as a type of data augmentation as the next layer has to learn noisy versions of the patterns and hence cannot specialize on single sharp features. Dropout is only turned on during training as we want all the neurons active during predictive recalls. Since dropout affects the training accuracy it is possible that the training accuracy is lower than the accuracy of the test set.

At the end, we feed this new representation of the image into a classification network which is an MLP in itself. The function `layers.Flatten()` does flatten the features into a 1-dimensional vector that is the input to the MLP. The rest of the code specifies how to train this network and how to evaluate it as with our previous examples.

Listing 4.9 MNIST_CNN.ipynb (part 3)

```
model.compile(loss=keras.losses.categorical_crossentropy,
optimizer=keras.optimizers.Adadelta(),
metrics=['accuracy'])

model.fit(x_train, y_train,
batch_size=128,
epochs=12,
verbose=1,
validation_data=(x_test, y_test))
score = model.evaluate(x_test, y_test, verbose=0)
print('Test_loss:', score[0])
print('Test_accuracy:', score[1])
```

CNNs improve the MNIST recognition even further and are now at the point where they can recognize most examples in the test set. Running this network in a reasonable time requires a GPU, but it is easy to get accuracies above 99 per cent. Indeed, we are getting to a point where the few mistakes of the network may even be queried as to real mistakes. For example, an interesting variant of such networks has been studied by Jürgen Schmitdhuber's lab using a design with several parallel CNN streams that resemble an ensemble method similar to classification forests discussed in Chapter 3. They showed that such a network is able to recognizes all but thirty-two examples. These examples are shown in Fig. 4.8 together with their "correct" label shown in the upper right-hand corner, and the first and second choice produced by the network at the bottom of each image. I leave it to the reader to judge for themselves if these labels are sensible.

4.4.3 More examples of deep networks

We have demonstrated the CNN on the classic MNIST dataset, but it is interesting to note that these networks gained wide recognition in another dataset called ImageNet. ImageNet is a collection of over 1 million pictures from the Internet that have been labeled for over 1,000 classes. This dataset has been used for a competition where some traditional machine learning methods such as SVMs have gained some success. However, the traditional methods stagnated with accuracies remaining in the 80 per cent range. Alex Krizhevsky and colleagues applied CNNs to the problem and won a competition in 2012, starting a trend of improving the performance of models in object

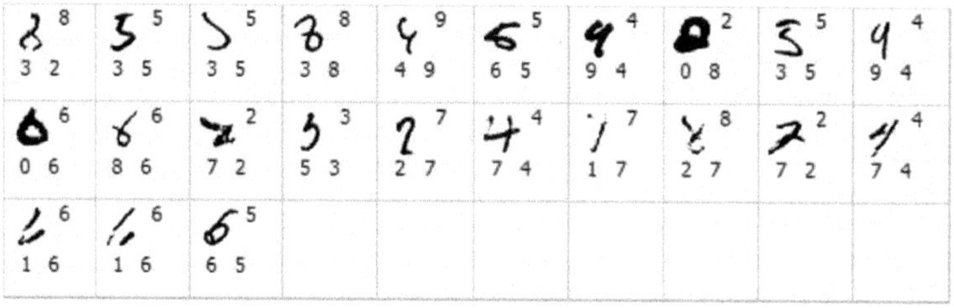

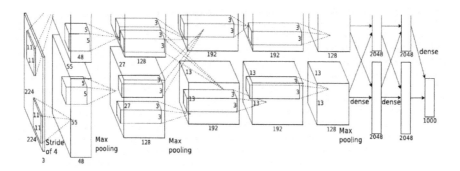

Fig. 4.8 The examples of the MNIST test set that were misclassified in the networks. From Dan Ciresan, Ueli Meier, and Jurgen Schmidhuber, Multi-column Deep Neural Networks for Image Classifcation: Technical Report Number IDSIA, 04–12, p. 4, Figure 2b, © The Authors, 2012.

recognition even further. The so-called **AlexNet** shown in Fig. 4.9 was trained on ImageNet. This network takes 3-dimensional images (e.g. RGB values of pixels) and applies a layer of filters to them. This specific network divided the pathways through the network into a stream in order to facilitate the computation with two GPUs, but at this point it is only necessary to look at one stream. In this example, the inputs are of size 224×224 with three channels (RGB). This input is fed into a convolution layer. The first-level filters are of size 11×11, so that the resulting image is of size 55×55. This layer also consists of forty-eight different filters so that we end up with forty-eight filters. At this stage, the RELU activation function is applied, followed by a max pooling layer. The steps of convolution, applying a gain function, and max pooling are repeated to build a deep convolutional network. At the end, some dense layers are used to gather all the information and make the final classification based on the features extracted by the network.

Fig. 4.9 A famous implementation of a convolutional neural network for image classification called AlexNet which won the ImageNet competition in 2012 (Krizhevsky, Sutskever, Hinton (2017), ImageNet classification with deep convolutional neural networks, Communications of the ACM. 60 (6): 84-{90.) The network was distributed among two GPUs, hence the two pathways with only one interaction before the dense layers to minimize communication overhead.

Convolutional neural networks have become a driving technique behind a lot of progress in computer visions. It is therefore useful to dig a bit deeper into this area in the rest of this chapter. We discussed how CNNs are implementing translation-invariant feature detection, although they are now sometimes used on representations that are not strictly translation invariant. In the detection network above, we switch from a convolutional to a fully connected layer at a specific point, and we could ask ourselves how many convolutional layers we should have before switching to dense layers. In this context, it is good to view a dense network with N nodes as a convolutional layer with N channels and an $i \times j$ kernel (receptive field), where i and j are the width and height of the previous layer that is assumed here to be 2-dimensional besides the channel dimension. So, a dense network is like a convolutional network with large receptive fields added to the previous layer. A more common convolution with small filter sizes can be seen more as a local operation. Such a node can still access a lot of relevant information through the hierarchy of previous representations, and it is possible that during training, the features in previous layers are organized so that they can be accessed locally. Thus, convolutions with small kernels still make sense in a deep network.

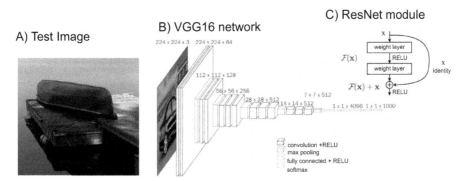

Fig. 4.10 (A) Test image of canoe laying on a dock. (B) Illustration of the network that was implemented by the Oxford Visual Geometry Group called VGG16 which achieved a 92.7 per cent top-five test accuracy in ImageNet for the 2014 VisNet competition (K. Simonyan and A. Zisserman, Very Deep Convolutional Networks for Large-Scale Image Recognition, 2014). (C) Module of a ResNet network with skip connections (From Kaiming He, Xianguy Zhang, Shaoquing Ren, and Jian Sun, Deep Residual Learning for Image Recognition, p. 2, Figure 2 © The Authors, 2015.)

The main focus of many computer vision applications in object recognition which can be seen as a mapping from a high-dimensional sensor space, representing the physical consequences of the appearance of an object, to a lower-dimensional semantic space representing meaning. By using pooling operations it is then common to end up with pyramidal architectures like the one shown in Fig. 4.10A. This architecture from the Oxford Visual Geometry Group (VGG16) was an entry in the ImageNet competition in 2014 and had sixteen layers, hence the name VGG16. It was viewed as a very deep network at this time, although today there are networks in use that have may more layers, even running to the hundreds. Implementing VGG16 is a great exercise. An outline of the architecture is given below. We show here the architecture for the sequential model mode in Keras where we simply add a layer with each add command. The input is thereby inferred from the output of the previous layer. The `summary()` function at the end prints out a summary of the architecture.

Listing 4.10 VGG16Architecture.ipynb

```
from keras import models, Sequential, layers

model = models.Sequential([
layers.Conv2D(64, (3, 3), input_shape=(224, 224, 3),
    padding='same',activation='relu'),
layers.Conv2D(64, (3, 3), activation='relu', padding='same'),
layers.MaxPooling2D(pool_size=(2, 2), strides=(2, 2)),
layers.Conv2D(128, (3, 3), activation='relu', padding='same'),
layers.Conv2D(128, (3, 3), activation='relu', padding='same',),
layers.MaxPooling2D(pool_size=(2, 2), strides=(2, 2)),
layers.Conv2D(256, (3, 3), activation='relu', padding='same',),
layers.Conv2D(256, (3, 3), activation='relu', padding='same',),
layers.Conv2D(256, (3, 3), activation='relu', padding='same',),
layers.MaxPooling2D(pool_size=(2, 2), strides=(2, 2)),
layers.Conv2D(512, (3, 3), activation='relu', padding='same',),
layers.Conv2D(512, (3, 3), activation='relu', padding='same',),
layers.Conv2D(512, (3, 3), activation='relu', padding='same',),
layers.MaxPooling2D(pool_size=(2, 2), strides=(2, 2)),
layers.Conv2D(512, (3, 3), activation='relu', padding='same',),
layers.Conv2D(512, (3, 3), activation='relu', padding='same',),
layers.Conv2D(512, (3, 3), activation='relu', padding='same',),
layers.MaxPooling2D(pool_size=(2, 2), strides=(2, 2)),
layers.Flatten(),
layers.Dense(4096, activation='relu'),
layers.Dense(4096, activation='relu'),
layers.Dense(1000, activation='softmax')
])

model.summary()
```

Training such a network takes time, in this case several weeks on multiple powerful GPUs. However, there are many architectures with published weights. Such pre-trained networks can be used in many ways. Of course they could be used right out of the box on data similar to the data used during training. More importantly, we assume that such systems learn basic filters such as edge detectors and color maps that are useful in other vision system. Using fixed pre-trained layers in other tasks for early layers would make sense for early representations, and training could then concentrate on the higher layers specific to the classes of the new task. This is often advisable as learning more shallow parts of the new network is much more efficient. In Keras there are several pre-trained networks available. As an example, applying the pre-trained VGG16 network on the image of a canoe laying on a dock as shown in Fig. 4.10A is given in the code at Listing 4.11. This codes imports the network that is pre-trained on the ImageNet dataset. It then uses the Keras function to load the test image as this function scales it to the right size by interpolation. Since these networks usually expect batches of figures, we have to add a dimension for the batch size. In our case with one test image, `size=1`. It also uses the function `preprocess_input()` that normalizes the image to the format that is expected by the network. The results of applying this specific test image with the pretrained network is predicting a boathouse with 28 per cent confidence, a dock with 11 per cent confidence, and an ashcan with less than 6 per cent confidence.

Listing 4.11 Recognize.ipynb (part 1) with output

```
from keras.applications.vgg16 import VGG16, preprocess_input,
    decode_predictions
from keras.preprocessing import image
import numpy as np

model = VGG16(weights='imagenet')
img = image.load_img('canoe.jpg', target_size=(224, 224))
plt.imshow(img)
x = image.img_to_array(img)
x = np.expand_dims(x, axis=0)
x = preprocess_input(x)
y = model.predict(x)
print('Predicted:', decode_predictions(y, top=3)[0])

Predicted: [('n02859443', 'boathouse', 0.2774216),
            ('n03216828', 'dock', 0.11578347),
            ('n02747177', 'ashcan', 0.055925433)]
```

We have briefly outlined the basic convolutional network types, specifically that of AlexNet and VGG16, and it is useful to mention at least two more well-known example architectures. The first one is **ResNet**. The important feature introduced by ResNet is to use skip connections where the output of some layers is fed into layers of later stages in additions to the output of the intermediate layers. An example is shown in Fig. 4.11A. The idea behind the improvement in this network is that deep networks are difficult to train. Part of this is the problem of vanishing gradients where the training signal gets smaller and smaller when propagating back the error through the layers to earlier layers. We will later discuss training in more detail. At this point it suffice to mention that shallow networks are easier to train but that such networks usually do not have the representational complexity to describe more detailed features. Skip connections can help in that the shallower network can learn a basic recognition system while the deeper components can learn to represent the residuals, hence the name ResNet. There is a pre-trained ResNet with fifty layers available in Keras, and since this network takes the same input as VGG16, we can simply use the code in Listing 4.12 to try ResNet50 if we ran VGG16 earlier. Applying the picture in Fig. 4.10A to it, ResNet50 guesses labels of canoe with 78 per cent confidence, and much lower confidence level with around 4 per cent confidence for both mailbox and boathouse. Of course, such networks will further evolve. For example, at the time of writing there has been some significant improvements made to ResNet with an architecture called **DenseNet**. Of course, a book such as this can not provide the latest developments in this area, but the above mentioned architectures have contributed much to the development of CNNs.

Listing 4.12 Recognize.ipynb (part 2) with output)

```
from keras.applications.resnet50 import ResNet50

model = ResNet50(weights='imagenet')
y = model.predict(x)
print('Predicted:', decode_predictions(y, top=3)[0])

Predicted: [('n02951358', 'canoe', 0.78379256),
            ('n03710193', 'mailbox', 0.046462867),
            ('n02859443', 'boathouse', 0.041660763)]
```

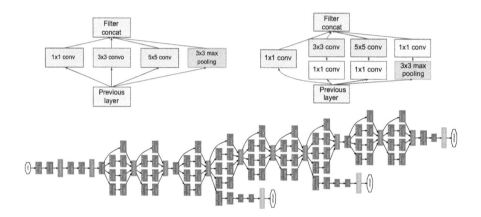

Fig. 4.11 Example of an Inception network that combines filters with different dimensions. From Christian Szegedy, Wei Liu, Yangqing Jia, Pierre Sermanet, Scott Reed, Dragomir Anguelov, Dumitru Erhan, Vincent Vanhoucke, and Andrew Rabinovich, Going Deeper with Convolutions, p. 5., Figure 2 and p. 7, Figure 3, © The Authors, 2014.

Finally, another major architecture idea of deep convolutional networks is the so called GooLeNet, also called an inception network. The idea behind an inception network is the realization that the sizes of objects in pictures can vary quite considerably so that the size of the filters matter. Of course, even with small filter sizes we can cover larger receptive fields (the area covered by a neuron) in later layers in a hierarchical network. However, this brings with it the challenges of training deeper networks. A major component of the inception network is to combine filters with different kernel sizes. For example, 1×1, 3×3, and 5×5 kernels, as shown in Fig. 4.11A. The outcomes of these filters are then concatenated to represent the input for the next layer. The larger the filter the more computationally expensive it is. Therefore, later versions of the inception networks factorize $n \times n$ convolution into a $1 \times N$ and a $N \times 1$ convolution. This is computationally much more efficient. Note that pooling is included as a parallel stream in the inception layer that gets concatenated with the output of the other filters.

Another feature of an inception network shown in Fig. 4.11B is to use a layer of c filters to compress the channels. Note that when we talk about an $n \times n$ convolution we mean the convolution operation in each channel and that we then add together the results of all the channels. Keeping the number of channels small also helps with the computational efficiency of the networks. Finally, the architecture shown in Fig. 4.11C shows another interesting feature, that of using intermediate outputs for training purposes. The idea is to help layers during training to get feedback so that the learning of such deep networks becomes more efficient early during the learning phase. While this last feature has not been as useful in practice as expected, there are several other tricks in later versions of the inception network that help to build even deeper versions. Keras includes the version 3 of the inception networks called InceptionV3, as well as a version that combines these ideas with skip connections called InceptionResNetV2. Since the inception network takes a different size input, we need to load the picture for our test case again as shown below. The InceptionV3 network predicts a dock with 10 per cent confidence, a barrow with 5 per cent and a canoe with 4 per cent.

Listing 4.13 Recognize.ipynb (part 3) with output)

```
from keras.applications.inception_v3 import InceptionV3

model = InceptionV3(weights='imagenet')
img = image.load_img('canoe.jpg', target_size=(299, 299))
plt.imshow(img)

x = image.img_to_array(img)
x = np.expand_dims(x, axis=0)
x = preprocess_input(x)
y = model.predict(x)

print('Predicted:', decode_predictions(y, top=3)[0])
```

4.5 What and where

We have so far only discussed object recognition. In many applications, we want to go further and also tell where the objects are in the picture. For example, for self-driving cars, we want to know where pedestrians are or where the road is. One way of doing this is to place bounding boxes around the objects, as shown in Fig.4.12. A popular architecture for this is called YOLO (You Only Look Once). The idea is thereby to train a network not only on single labels, but also on the location (x, y), the size (w, h) of a bounding box, and its confidence. The network does this by dividing an image into an array of grid cells of size $S \times S$, where S was set to $S = 7$ in the original example. The network makes B predictions of the five numbers mentioned earlier $(x, y, w, h, \text{conf})$ for each bounding box ($B = 2$ in the original example), so that we need $S \times S \times (B * 5 + C)$ output nodes. C is here the number of classes, which was $C = 20$ in the dataset in the original paper, hence the output shape of $7 \times t \times 30$. Training this network then requires a loss function with multiple components, weighting the contribution of classification accuracy, location accuracy, and confidence. There are several other variants of YOLO in the literature, but there are of course also other architectures to estimate bounding boxes.

While such "what-and-where" networks have many applications already, sometimes we need even more precision in the localization of objects. An example is the important area of segmentation, which seeks to outline objects in pictures. An example

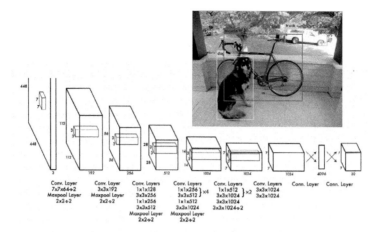

Fig. 4.12 A network called YOLO (You Only Look Once) that predicts bounding boxes for objects and labels them. From Joseph Redmon, Santosh Divvala, Ross Girshick, and Ali Farhadi, You Only Look Once: Unified, Real-Time Object Detection, p. 2., Figure 2 and p. 3, Figure 3, © The Authors, 2016.

is shown in Fig.4.13. This is important when removing objects from pictures or to plan specific manipulations such as a robot grabbing an object. One possible solution to this is classifying each pixel. This seems to be a daunting task, but we will see that there are elegant solutions available with fully convolutional networks. To discuss this further, we go back to the VGG16 network discussed at the end of the last section. We can strip off the top (dense) layers and then add another layer that up-samples the last convolutional layer of the VGG16. This up-sampling can be some form of interpolation, although the filters can also be learned. It is best to think about this up-sampling as the inverse of pooling. In this way we can recover the size of the original image. We can then use a segmented version as a fine-grained label for each pixel and train on the corresponding loss. It is thereby common to drop some of the connections so that only specific regions contribute to training in each iterations. This procedure mimics some form of training on individual objects. We can then combine this coarse semantic information with more fine-grained information from the original input, or also from early layers convolutional layers. This resembles somewhat the skip connections discussed earlier. Needless to say, there are now a variety of new versions of such segmentation networks discussed in the literature.

4.6 More tricks of the trade

We mentioned several networks that have considerably enhanced computer vision capabilities and have thereby enabled a flurry of new applications. Such networks are now in use in commercial applications, and these commercial networks are sometimes even larger than the ones discussed here. Getting these large networks to work appropriately requires a lot of training and, sometimes, additional tricks. Here we mention a few common techniques that are used frequently. It is worthwhile to study these

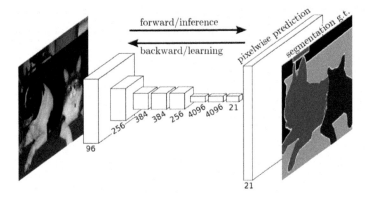

Fig. 4.13 A fully convolutional network (FCN) which consists of layers for recognition as in VGG16 and then uses up-sampling and skip connections to classify each pixel in the image. From Jonathan Long, Evan Shelhamer, and Trevor Darrell, Fully Convolutional Networks for Semantic Segmentation, p. 1, Figure 1 © The Authors, 2015.

further and we will mainly outline some of those techniques here and will have more discussions on some details in later chapters.

Learning appropriately is a major task to make the networks work in applications, and the training algorithms are therefore important to study. We have thus far not talked much about this central aspect of machine learning and we will go into more details later, but most learning algorithms for neural networks are gradient based, which brings with it some challenges. While later we will go through some of the calculations of the gradients in small examples, modern packages include automatic differentiation routines that make the application of gradient learning much simpler. We have used some popular choices earlier, such as the Adam optimizer, which is an adaptive learning rate method.

While learning algorithms have received a lot of attention, a big factor for the success of training a network is the number of training examples we need. Unfortunately, there is no simple rule for how many training examples are necessary. Efficient training depends on many factors such as the training algorithm itself, the right regularization, and, of course, ultimately on the complexity of the problem itself. The only fact that is clear is that a more complex model generally needs more training data. While "big data" has been a buzzword in certain circles, many applications do not have an infinite number of labeled examples, and making deep learning work with limited data is hence a very interesting and quite relevant area in practice. Indeed, it can be argued that the brain is a model that must be able to capture a complex world from limited experience (data) in contrast to some of the AI applications that often target a very narrow application domain with data that are usually out of the reach of individual humans during development. Thus, training with limited data is a major challenge in machine learning. We will later discuss techniques such as unsupervised learning that can help us with pre-training networks to a stage where smaller labeled data can be used. Transfer learning is another hot topic in machine learning that seeks to utilize trained knowledge of similar tasks to learn new tricks quickly. In a hierarchical vision system it is clear that we do not have to learn all layers all over again for new problems.

Learning feature representations in early layers should be to some extent independent of the higher-level tasks. It is therefore common to utilize pre-trained networks in vision and other domains such as natural language processing.

We have already seen and used pre-trained networks in Keras in the last section, where we used a VGG16 network pre-trained on ImageNet. The next step is to use some part of the network, such as the layers before the dense network, as pre-trained feature encoders. We can then build on top of this encoder of the learned latent space of image representations a new network for a new classification task. If we treat the feature encoder as a preprocessing step, then the new network on top of this is just another network that has to be trained. It is also possible to view the whole architecture as a new network and train all of the layers. This can still be beneficial, in contrast to training from scratch, as the initial weight conditions are already contributing to the solution and fine-tuning them to a new application might be beneficial. Using parts of a pre-trained network is easy in Keras as it includes a parameter in the call to the model function to disregard the top layers. The Keras documentation includes example code under Applications to show how to fine-tune pre-trained networks.

In addition to using pretrained networks, preventing overfitting in large networks is often necessary and is a bit of an art. Methods for preventing overfitting are commonly referred to as **regularization** techniques. The name comes from the fact that overfitting usually manifests itself by high variance in generalization, and making such new predictions more "regular" is our aim. The main idea behind regularization is to introduce sensible restrictions so that the effective model is less complex. For example, in overfitting it can happen that some of the weight values are overly large, and a common method is therefore to encourage the optimizer to find solutions in which all parameters are as small as possible. Since the model parameters are now weights, such a procedure is often called **weight decay**. Rather than minimizing each single weight, it is common to restrict only the sum of the weights or the square of the vector norm to be minimized. The latter we have already seen in support vector machine where minimizing the squared norm of the weight vector corresponds to maximizing the margin in classification. Another popular method for deep learning is **dropout**. Dropouts randomly sets the activation of some neurons in a layer to 0 so that this neuron does not contribute to the prediction of the output during learning. This prevents the specialization of single neurons (often called grandmother cells) as then there must be other neurons that also can perform the tasks in conjunction with others. During the employment of the model, this dropout is removed to guarantee maximal performance. We will see later that we can summarize many regularization methods by describing them as **priors** in our model assumptions.

Finally, important techniques that often helps enormously to find good solutions in the model space is **input normalization** and **batch normalization**. We commonly normalize the input by subtracting the mean of the data, either over all the available data, or more commonly over each new batch of the input data, and dividing this by the standard deviation of the data.

$$\mu = \frac{1}{n_B} \sum_{i=1}^{n_B} x_i \qquad (4.13)$$

$$\sigma^2 = \frac{1}{n_B} \sum_{i=1}^{n_B} (x_i - \mu)^2 \tag{4.14}$$

$$x_i \leftarrow \frac{x_i - \mu}{\sqrt{\sigma^2}} \tag{4.15}$$

Sometimes there is a small number added to σ^2 to prevent the fraction in the last equation becoming too large when σ^2 is close to 0. Input normalization will often help the speed of learning, and we will later discuss why this is. If normalization of input data helps, then why not apply it to each layer in the network? This is now common and called batch normalization. One problem with this procedure is that by changing the overall scaling and a possible shift of the data in each batch, then the following network has to unlearn the specific weights. This seems rather counterproductive. Batch normalization therefore includes two separate trainable parameters to absorb the overall effect of the shift and scale,

$$x_i \leftarrow \gamma x_i + \beta. \tag{4.16}$$

With these trainable parameters, the training algorithm itself can adjust the right rate of changes.

There are many other tricks and techniques to make deep neural networks work for some applications, and working with such techniques is not always easy. For example, it is not always the case that batch normalization helps and sometimes it could even worsen the training early in the training process. The same holds for dropout and the choice of the learning rule. As we stressed already several times, at the end it depends on the structure of the problem itself whether the specific model proposed through deep learning is appropriate for this application. This is another reason to understand the principles behind such methods, such as regularization in general, which we will consider in the following chapter.

Part II

Foundations
Regression and probabilistic
modeling

5 Regression and optimization

We have seen that writing machine learning programs is easy with high-level computer languages and with the help of good machine learning libraries. However, applying such algorithms with superior performance appropriately requires considerable experience and a deeper knowledge of the underlying ideas and algorithms. We will now take a step back to consider basic regression in more detail, which in turn will be the foundation for discussing probabilistic models in the next chapters. This chapter includes the discussion of the basis of the learning algorithm though gradient descent.

5.1 Linear regression and gradient descent

Linear regression is usually taught in high school, but my hope is that this book will provide a new appreciation for this subject and associated methods. It is the simplest form of machine learning, and while linear regression seems limited in scope, linear methods still have some practical relevance since many problems are at least locally approximately linear. Furthermore, we use them here to formalize machine learning methods and specifically to introduce some methods that we can generalize later to non-linear situation. Supervised machine learning is essentially regression, although the recent success of machine learning compared to previous approaches to modeling and regression is their applicability to high-dimensional data with non-linear relations, and the ability to scale these methods to complex models. Linear regression can be solved analytically. However, the non-linear extensions will usually not be analytically solvable. Hence, we will here introduce the formalization of iterative training methods that underly much of supervised learning.

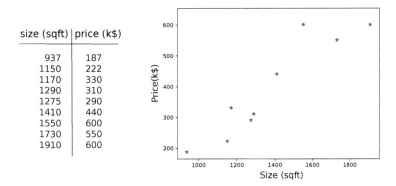

size (sqft)	price (k$)
937	187
1150	222
1170	330
1290	310
1275	290
1410	440
1550	600
1730	550
1910	600

Fig. 5.1 Some example data of house prices and the corresponding size of each house.

Fundamentals of Machine Learning, Thomas P. Trappenberg, Oxford University Press (2020).
© Oxford University Press. DOI: 10.1093/oso/9780198828044.001.0001

To undertake discuss linear regression, we will follow an example of describing house prices. The table on the left in Figure 5.1 lists the size in square feet and the corresponding asking prices of some houses. These data points are plotted in the graph on the right in Figure 5.1. The question is, can we predict from these data the likely asking price for houses with different sizes?

To do this prediction we make the assumption that the house price depend essentially on the size of the house in a linear way. That is, a house twice the size should cost twice the money. Of course, this linear model clearly does not capture all the dimensions of the problem. Some houses are old, others might be new. Some houses might need repair and other houses might have some special features. Of course, as everyone in the real estate business knows, it is also location that is very important. Thus, we should keep in mind that there might be unobserved, so-called **latent** dimensions in the data that might be important in explaining the relations. However, we ignore such hidden causes at this point and just use the linear model over size as our hypothesis.

The linear model of the relation between the house size and the asking price can be made mathematically explicit with the linear equation

$$y(x; w_1, w_2) = w_1 x + w_2, \tag{5.1}$$

where y is the asking price, x is the size of the house, and w_1 and w_2 are model parameters. Note that y is a function of x, and here we follow a notation where the parameters of a function are included after a semi-colon. If the parameters are given, then this function can be used to predict the price of a house for any size. This is the general theme of supervised learning; we assume a specific function with parameters that we can use to predict new data.

The remaining question is what values these parameters should have? For this we need example data, or training data. Also, to evaluate how good some choices of the values for the model parameters are, we must define how we undertake the evaluation of these values. This evaluation is specified in a loss function $\mathcal{L}$. We will start here by using a traditional choice of the mean square error (MSE) function,

$$L(w_1, w_2; x^{(i)}, y^{(i)}) = \frac{1}{2N} \sum_i (w_1 x^{(i)} + w_2 - y^{(i)})^2, \tag{5.2}$$

and we will later discuss when this is a good choice. The superscript i labels the different training examples and we put this into brackets so it is not confused with an exponent. This function considers the square distance between the predicted price values (the linear function) and the actually asking prices. Note that we view this function as a function of the model parameters w_1 and w_2 (the unknowns), and the training data $x^{(i)}$ and $y^{(i)}$ are the parameters of this function that are given. The loss function is central in machine learning and designing the right loss function is an important discussion we need to have. We will see later that this is best archieved using a probabilistic view of machine learning, and we will hence continue here describing the use of a loss function.

We use the loss function to determine the model parameters. More specifically, the values of the model parameters that minimize the loss are considered to result in the best predictor for new data points. To find these values we have to minimize the loss function as functions of the parameters. Since the loss function here is a sum of square

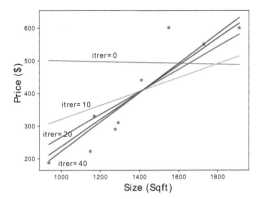

Fig. 5.2 Example of regressing data with a linear model. The data points shown as stars specify some house prices together with the size of the house. The different lines show how a gradient descent with an appropriate choice of parameters would result in a linear regression lines for different numbers of iterations

functions, this can be calculated analytically. We will however use this opportunity to introduce a method called **gradient descent** that is a dominant technique in machine learning. The idea is to start with a random value for each parameter and improve the loss in consecutive steps by changing the values along the negative gradient,

$$\begin{pmatrix} w_1 \\ w_2 \end{pmatrix} \leftarrow \begin{pmatrix} w_1 \\ w_2 \end{pmatrix} - \alpha \nabla L(w_1, w_2; x^{(i)}, y^{(i)}). \tag{5.3}$$

The **hyperparameter** α is called the learning rate, and the Nabla operator ∇ represents the gradient.

$$\nabla L(w_1, w_2; x^{(i)}, y^{(i)}) = \begin{pmatrix} \frac{\partial}{\partial w_1} \\ \frac{\partial}{\partial w_2} \end{pmatrix} L(w_1, w_2; x^{(i)}, y^{(i)}). \tag{5.4}$$

Minimizing the loss function with gradient descent is an important part of machine learning and the basic principle to derive the learning rule for specific models. In our case, calculating the derivative for MSE loss function (5.2) with the linear prediction function (5.1) gives the following learning rules for the two parameters

$$w_1 \leftarrow w_1 - \alpha \frac{1}{N} \sum_i (w_1 x^{(i)} + w_2 - y^{(i)}) x^{(i)} \tag{5.5}$$

and

$$w_2 \leftarrow w_2 - \alpha \frac{1}{N} \sum_i (w_1 x^{(i)} + w_2 - y^{(i)}). \tag{5.6}$$

The results of the regression for different numbers of iterations, together with some further consideration discussed next, is shown in Fig. 5.1. We will now go through some details that will hopefully shed some light on some of the subtleties of this algorithm.

5.2 Error surface and challenges for gradient descent

It is instructive to look at the precise numerical results and details when implementing the whole procedure. We first link our common NumPy and plot routines and then define the data given in the table in Fig. 5.1. This figure also shows a plot of these data.

Listing 5.1 LinearRegression.ipynb (part 1)

```
import numpy as np
import matplotlib.pyplot as plt

hsize=np.array([937,1150,1170,1290,1275,1410,1550,1730,1910])
price=np.array([187, 222, 330, 310, 290, 440, 600, 550, 600])

plt.plot(hsize, price,'*')
plt.xlabel('Size (Sqft)')
plt.ylabel('Price ($)')
plt.show()
```

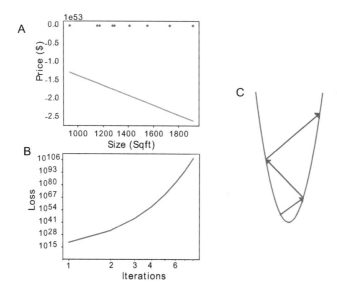

Fig. 5.3 (First attempt to implement a gradient descent learning rule for linear regression.

We now write the regression code as shown in Listing 5.2. First we set the starting values for the parameters w_1 and w_2, and we initialize an empty array to store the values of the loss function L in each iteration. We also set the update (learning) rate α to a small value. We then perform ten iterations to update the parameters w_1 and w_2 with the gradient descent rule. Note that an index of an array with the value -1 indicates the last element in an Python array. The result of this program is shown in Fig. 5.2. The fit of the function shown in Fig. 5.2A does not look right at all. To see what is occurring it is good to plot the values of the loss function as shown in Fig. 5.2B. As can be seen, the loss function gets bigger, not smaller as we would have expected, and the values itself are extremely large.

Listing 5.2 LinearRegression.ipynb (part 2)

```
w1=np.array([-1]); w2=np.array([-1]); L=np.array([])
alpha=0.1

for iter in range(10-1):
y=w1[-1]*hsize+w2[-1]
w1=np.append(w1,w1[-1]-alpha*sum((y-price)*hsize))
w2=np.append(w2,w2[-1]-alpha*sum(y-price))
L=np.append(L,sum((y-price)**2))

plt.plot(hsize,price,'*')
plt.plot(hsize,y)
plt.xlabel('Size_(Sqft)'); plt.ylabel('Price_($)')
plt.show()
plt.loglog(L)
plt.xlabel('Iterations'); plt.ylabel('Loss')
plt.show()
```

The rising loss value is a hint that the learning rate is too large. The reason that this can happen is illustrated in Fig. 5.2C. This graph is a cartoon of a quadratic loss surface. When the update term is too large, the gradient can overshoot the minimum value. In such a case, the loss of the next step can be even larger since the slope at this point is also higher. In this way, every step can increase the loss value and the values will soon exceed the values representable in a computer.

So, let's try it again with a much smaller learning rate of `alpha=0.00000001` which was chosen after several trials to get what look like the best result. The results shown in Fig. 5.2 look certainly much better although also not quite right. The fitted curve does not seem to balance the data points well, and while the loss values decrease at first rapidly, they seem to get stuck at a small value.

To look more closely at what is going on we can plot the loss function for several values around our expected values of the variable. This is shown in Fig. 5.2C. This reveals that the change of the loss function with respect to the parameter w_2 is large, but that changing the parameter w_1 on the same scale has little influence on the loss value. To fix this problem we would have to change the learning rate for each parameter, which is not practical in higher-dimensional models. There are much more sophisticated solutions such as Amari's Natural Gradient, but a quick fix for many applications is to normalize the data so that the ranges are between 0 and 1. Thus, by adding the code

Listing 5.3 LinearRegression.ipynb (part 3)

```
hsize=(hsize-min(hsize))/(max(hsize)-min(hsize))
price=(price-min(price))/(max(price)-min(price))
```

and setting the learning rate to `alpha=0.04`, we get the solution shown in Fig. 5.2. The solution is much better, although the learning path is still not optimal. However, this is a solution that is sufficient most of the time.

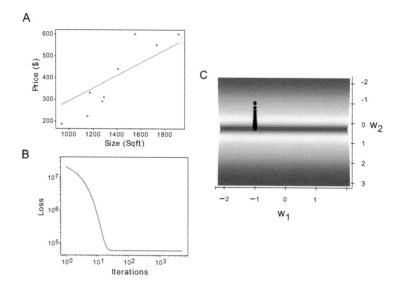

Fig. 5.4 Second attempt to implement a gradient descent learning rule for linear regression with a much smaller learning rate and more iterations.

5.3 Advanced gradient optimization (learning)

Learning in machine learning means finding parameters of the model $\mathbf{w}$ that minimize the loss function. There are many methods to minimize a function, and each one would constitute a learning algorithm. However, the workhorse in machine learning is usual some form of a **gradient descent** algorithm that we encountered earlier. Formally, the basic gradient descent minimizes the sum of the loss values over all training examples, which is called a **batch algorithm** as all training examples build the batch for minimization. Let us assume we have m training data, then gradient descent iterates the equation

$$w_i \leftarrow w_i + \Delta w_i \tag{5.7}$$

with

$$\Delta w_i = -\frac{\alpha}{N} \sum_{k=1}^{N} \frac{\partial \mathcal{L}(y^{(i)}, \mathbf{x}^{(i)} | \mathbf{w})}{\partial w_i}, \tag{5.8}$$

where N is the number of training samples. We can also write this compactly for all parameters using vector notation and the Nabla operator ∇ as

$$\Delta \mathbf{w} = -\frac{\alpha}{N} \sum_{i=1}^{N} \nabla \mathcal{L}^{(i)} \tag{5.9}$$

with

$$\mathcal{L}(y^{(i)}, \mathbf{x}^{(i)} | \mathbf{w}) \tag{5.10}$$

With a sufficiently small learning rate α, this will result in a strictly monotonically decreasing learning curve. However, with many training data, a large number of training

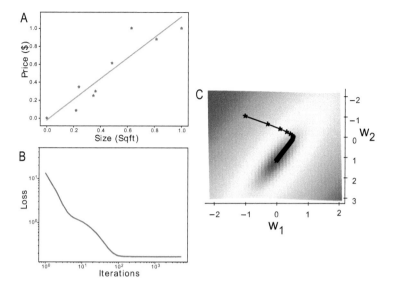

Fig. 5.5 Third attempt which leads to a much better solution by simply normalizing the range of the data to a unitary regime.

examples have to be kept in memory. Also, batch learning seems unrealistic biologically or in situations where training examples only arrive over a period of time. So-called **online** algorithms that use the training data when they arrive are therefore often desirable. The online gradient descent would consider only one training example at a time,

$$\Delta \mathbf{w} = -\alpha \nabla \mathcal{L}^{(i)}, \tag{5.11}$$

and then use another training example for another update. If the training examples appear randomly in such an example-wise training, then the training examples provide a random walk around the true gradient descent. This algorithms is hence called the **stochastic gradient descent (SGD)**. It can be seen as an approximation of the basic gradient descent algorithm, and the randomness has some positive effects on the search path such as avoiding oscillations or getting stuck in local minima. In practice it is now common to use something in between, using so-called mini-batches of the training data to iterate using them. This is formally still a stochastic gradient descent, but it combines the advantages of a batch algorithm with the reality of limited memory capacities.

Gradient descent is known as a very efficient local optimizer. It can often be observed that such an algorithm leads to a steep decline of the loss values before learning seems to slow down. One problem with the algorithm is that it can, strictly speaking, only find local minima as illustrated in Fig. 5.6A. An analogy would be to think about a ball rolling downhill on the loss surface. With the basic gradient descent we are always strictly going downhill. However, with a real ball we would have **momentum** so that the ball could overcome a small hill if the momentum is great enough. To incorporate momentum into the gradient descent algorithm, we can modify the update so that we take some percentage of the previous step into account,

$$\Delta \mathbf{w}(t) = -\alpha \nabla \mathcal{L}(t) + m \Delta \mathbf{w}(t-1). \tag{5.12}$$

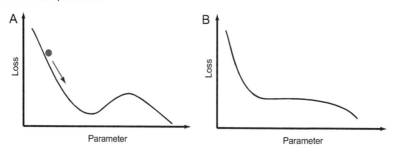

Fig. 5.6 Illustration of gradient descent with a local minima (A) and a saddle point (B).

A momentum term of $m = 0.9$ is a common starting value, but such hyperparameters of the algorithms are of course problem-dependent and need to be evaluated on a case-by-case basis.

Local minima have often been stated as a main difficulty for gradient descent, although true local minima are increasingly difficult to realize in higher dimensions. To be a true local minimum, it is necessary that all changes and all combination of changes of all directions of the parameters lead to larger loss values. It is clear that with increasing dimensions there is therefore an increasing chance to find an "escape route". However, even so, it is now known that true local minima are not likely to be the problem with most high-dimensional learning scenarios, saddle points, or at least shallow areas of the loss functions seem to present a problem in many applications. A momentum term is a common way to help with such shallow areas.

There are additional techniques in common use today. For example, we can change the learning rate based on the history of the learning performance, and such adaptive learning rates are now commonly used. For example, a very popular algorithm is the ADAM optimizer. ADAM stands for adaptive moment estimation which is a slight modification of the momentum method. Instead of strictly using the last entry of the gradient as the momentum, the ADAM method uses a sliding average of the gradient

$$\mathbf{m} \leftarrow \alpha_1 \mathbf{m} + (1 - \alpha_1)\nabla\mathcal{L}^{(i)}, \tag{5.13}$$

as well as the variance of the gradient

$$\mathbf{v} \leftarrow \alpha_2 \mathbf{v} + (1 - \alpha_2)(\nabla\mathcal{L}^{(i)})^2 \tag{5.14}$$

to modulate the update with the gradient. The model parameters are thereby updated according to

$$\mathbf{w} \leftarrow \mathbf{w} - \alpha\frac{\mathbf{m}/(1 - \alpha_1)}{\sqrt{\mathbf{v}/(1 - \alpha_2)} + \epsilon}, \tag{5.15}$$

where the small factor ϵ is added to prevent possible divisions by 0.

There are more advanced variations of gradient descent methods in use. For example, it is possible to take into account higher-order gradient terms that describe the curvature of the loss functions. While this requires the calculation of the higher derivatives or, in general, the Hessian, it will allow much larger learning rate parameters that will speed up learning. One of the best variations of these methods is the natural gradient that tries to keep the improvement in the loss value for each iteration constant by describing the curvature in the weight-loss function spanned by the weight values.

While we are not discussing these advanced methods here in more detail, I would like to close this section by pointing out that gradient methods are of course not the only minimization method that can be applied to machine learning. As an example, let us consider a simple version of a **genetic algorithm**. For this we treat the vector of all model parameters as the "genome" of an individual model, and we consider a pool of such models. Each candidate model is then evaluated by the loss function, and a certain percentage of the best performers are copied into the new pool of individuals in the next generation. These parent individuals are also allowed to reproduce by taking two of these individuals and swapping parts of their genes at a certain transition point, and by changing some of the entries randomly. The first operation is called a crossover, while the second operation is commonly called a mutation. In this way we produce new candidate models that can then be evaluated with the loss function. Such directed search methods have been shown to find solutions, although the cost of such methods are commonly prohibitive.

5.4   Regularization: ridge regression and LASSO

We discussed earlier a linear problem with a one dimensional input x. Machine learning problems often consist of high-dimension problems in the sense that the input is a vector with many dimensions. For example, if we want to undertake image processing, we would represent a gray-scale image as a list of many gray-level values, one for each pixel. Within linear regression this means that we should introduce one parameter for each input dimension. Such a linear model would look like

$$y = w_0 + w_1 x_1 + w_2 x_2 + ... = \mathbf{w}^\mathrm{T} \mathbf{x}. \qquad (5.16)$$

This shows how useful vector notation are in order to summarize all the components. Also, we made a common trick to augment the feature vector with a constant $x_0 = 1$ so that we do not have to treat the y-intercept differently to the other parameters. It is sometimes customary to make the input vector even larger by supplying combinations of input features and higher-order moments of the feature values, such as taken squares and higher powers of the values. The reason for this is to help modeling non-linear relations. The point here is that feature dimensions in the order of thousand or millions are not uncommon in machine learning, and machine learning models have therefore a large number of parameters.

We have discussed earlier that a large amount of parameters relative to the number of data can lead to overfitting, and methods to restrict the parameters to prevent overfitting have played a very important role in machine learning. A common consideration is to include a term in the objective function that keeps the parameters small. For example, we can include a penalty term proportional to the absolute value of the parameters or even the sum of the square values to even more penalize larger weight values. A penalty on the size of the parameter value should keep these values small or even 0 in case they do not contribute sufficiently to the model. To be concrete, we define the L^p norm as

$$||\mathbf{w}||_p = \left(\sum_i |w_i|^p \right)^{\frac{1}{p}}, \tag{5.17}$$

such as the quadratic form of the L^2 norm

$$||\mathbf{w}||^2 = w_1^2 + w_2^2 + ..., \tag{5.18}$$

or the Euclidean distance which is the L^1 norm,

$$||\mathbf{w}|| = \sqrt{w_1^2 + w_2^2 + ...} \ . \tag{5.19}$$

We can then add this penalty term on the parameters to an unregularized loss function

$$\tilde{L}(\mathbf{w}; \mathbf{x}, y) = L(\mathbf{w}; \mathbf{x}, y) + \gamma ||\mathbf{w}||_p^p. \tag{5.20}$$

The loss $L(\mathbf{w}, \mathbf{x}, y)$ is our regular loss function. For example, the previously used MSE objective function can be modified as

$$\tilde{L}(\mathbf{w}; \mathbf{x}^{(i)}, y^{(i)}) = \frac{1}{2N} \sum_i (\mathbf{w}^{\mathrm{T}} \mathbf{x}^{(i)} - y^{(i)})^2 + \gamma ||\mathbf{w}||^2. \tag{5.21}$$

The hyperparameter γ allows us to vary how strongly we should take this constraint into account. The gradient descent of this regularized loss function with a quadratic penalty term is

$$\Delta \mathbf{w} = -\alpha \frac{\mathrm{d}L(\mathbf{w}, \mathbf{x}, y)}{\mathrm{d}\mathbf{w}} - 2\gamma \mathbf{w}. \tag{5.22}$$

which we can also write in the form

$$\mathbf{w} \leftarrow (1 - 2\alpha\gamma)\mathbf{w} - \alpha \frac{\mathrm{d}L(\mathbf{w}, \mathbf{x}, y)}{\mathrm{d}\mathbf{w}}. \tag{5.23}$$

This corresponds to an exponential decay of the weights when the gradient is 0. In other words, this puts pressure on the weights to decay unless they are reinforced by the gradient. This type of regularization is therefore often called **weight decay**. The specific case of this quadratic penalty term is also called **ridge regression** or **Tikhonov regularization**.

Using the L^1 norm,

$$\tilde{L}(\mathbf{w}, \mathbf{x}, y) = L(\mathbf{w}, \mathbf{x}, y) - \gamma ||\mathbf{w}||, \tag{5.24}$$

is related to a technique called **LASSO** (least absolute shrinkage and selection operator), in the case of linear regression with a quadratic loss function. This form of regularization leads to a constant weight decay,

$$\Delta \mathbf{w} = -2\gamma \mathrm{sign}(\mathbf{w}) - \alpha \frac{\mathrm{d}L(\mathbf{w}, \mathbf{x}, y)}{\mathrm{d}\mathbf{w}}. \tag{5.25}$$

There is some argument that L^2 regularization leads to a more sparse representation than ridge regression. For example, it can be shown that such regularization works very well in situations where a few relevant features are embedded in a large and noisy vector with irrelevant features.

It is useful to implement such methods directly from scratch, although we leave this as a useful exercise for the reader to undertake. In the following, we use the routines from sklearn to look at an instructive example. Here, we chose points from the linear model

$$y = 0.5x_1 + 0.5x_2 \tag{5.26}$$

and add some noise in the feature values. Our training points are hence $(x_1, x_2, y) = \{(0, 0, 0), (1, 0.9, 1), (2, 2.1, 2)\}$. The code for test different versions of regularization is given here.

Listing 5.4 RidgeLasso.ipynb (with output)

```python
import numpy as np
from sklearn import linear_model
from mpl_toolkits.mplot3d import Axes3D

fig = plt.figure(); ax = fig.gca(projection='3d')

x = np.array([[0, 0], [1, .9], [2.1, 2]]); y= np.array([0, 1, 2])
ax.plot(x[:,0],x[:,1],y,'*');

reg = linear_model.LinearRegression(); reg.fit(x, y)
print(reg.coef_)
ax.plot([0,2],[0,2],[0,np.dot(reg.coef_,[2,2])]);

reg = linear_model.Ridge(alpha = .5); reg.fit(x, y)
print(reg.coef_)
ax.plot([0,2],[0,2],[0,np.dot(reg.coef_,[2,2])]);

reg = linear_model.Lasso(alpha = 0.1); reg.fit(x, y)
print(reg.coef_)
ax.plot([0,2],[0,2],[0,np.dot(reg.coef_,[2,2])]);
```

This program incidentally shows how to make 3-dimensional plots. The regression lines in this 3-dimensional plot are show in Fig. 5.4. The resulting lines look very similar, but it is instructive to look at the coefficients, which are

$$\{w_1, w_2\}_{\text{reg}} = \{1.82, -0.91\} \tag{5.27}$$

$$\{w_1, w_2\}_{\text{ridge}} = \{0.45, 0.42\} \tag{5.28}$$

$$\{w_1, w_2\}_{\text{lasso}} = \{0.82, 0\}. \tag{5.29}$$

The values of the linear regression without normalization are interesting as the large value for the first parameter is compensated by the large negative value of the second parameter. While this works for the specific training points, generalization with other examples might not work so well. Ridge regression finds much closer values similar to our original model. However, LASSO is also interesting as it finds a much smaller model where it can explain the data with only one parameter. This might be valuable in practical applications.

Regression is an important topic in machine learning, and there are other methods that are actively used. For example, we have already mentioned dropout which includes a certain probability that some of the parameters are set to 0 during the generation of an output during training. This is particularly used in deep neural networks where it is thought to resembles some biological processes as neurons sometimes do not fire

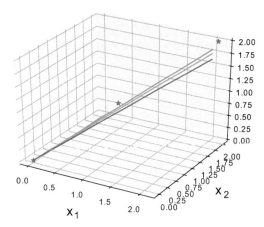

Fig. 5.7 (linear regression without regularization and with regularization using Ridge regression and Lasso.

even with the same stimulus that would activate them at other times. In this way, it is necessary that the model is able to represent specific data points with a combination of other parameters. This prevents that specific parts of the model specialize to specific sample data.

Another solution to the problem is to use lots of data compared to the number of parameters, that will constrain the parameters sufficiently. For the most part we can loosely equate the number of parameters with the complexity of the model. Of course, the specific architecture, such as a hierarchical versus flat representations, is of course also part of the complexity equation; we are thinking here more about a given architecture and ask how we can sufficiently constrain the parameters. Large data collections such as ImageNet have therefore been essential in demonstrating the abilities of deep networks. However, more often than not, we tend not to have enough training data, and **data augmentation** is a common and essential technique even in face of large data sets like ImageNet. Images are actually a good example to see where certain transformations are good candidates for sound data augmentation. Shifting an image should not alter its content, and rotation and some form of stretching does also not alter essential features for classifying the content of the figure. Indeed, even changing individual pixels in a high-resolution image does not have a drastic impact on recognition abilities. Thus, generating more training images with these transformations from the labeled training set is a good way to increase the training data set. Injecting noise either at an input level or at an output level is another example of such data transformations for data augmentation. The data augmentation technique is a good example where we use some expert knowledge to augment the training data set in defining which transformations should not alter the content. However, some caution is in order as such transformations are not necessarily suitable in every situation. To some extent we must already know the data distribution required to generate proper examples, which is of course what we want to model. Thus, this can be a chicken-and-egg situation.

We mentioned **bagging** (bootstrap aggregating) in Chapter 3 as an ensemble method to prevent overfitting. Another basic technique used in neural networks is **early stopping**. In this technique, we simply monitor the difference between the training and validation error and stop training when they diverge. There are many other techniques with the effect of guiding the search in a specific subspace of the parameter space. Unsupervised pre-training or semi-supervised methods can be placed in this category. A good discussion of advanced methods can be found in *Deep Learning* by Ian Goodfellow, Yoshua Bengio, and Aaron Courville.

5.5 Non-linear regression

Linear regression is often applied because many relations in practical application can be at least approximately linear. It is also simple and offers a good starting point forF experimenting with new algorithms. Linear models are therefore still important and should be considered a good first step in modeling data. However, going beyond linear models is one of the gifts of modern machine learning. Allowing non-linear relations in a model opens the modeling space to an infinite number of possible models and hence the possibility of an unbounded number of parameters. Overfitting is thus often an even more pronounced problem in high-dimensional non-linear models. Solving, or at least mediating this problem is therefore strongly tied to the success of the models, such as deep learning.

As a start point for discussing such cases, let us first consider a polynomial of order n;

$$y = w_0 + w_1 x^1 + w_2 x^2 + \ldots + w_n x^n = \sum_{i=0}^{n} w_i x^i. \qquad (5.30)$$

We can fit this function to our house data with a gradient descent rule, noting that the derivative (we only have 1-dimension at the moment) is

$$\frac{\mathrm{d}y}{\mathrm{d}w_i} = x^i. \qquad (5.31)$$

Hence, the learning rule is

$$w_i \leftarrow w_i - \alpha x^i. \qquad (5.32)$$

A fit of the house data with a polynomial of order 12 is shown in Fig. 5.5A, and the corresponding loss values at the end of training in Fig. 5.5B. The loss becomes a little bit better over time, and it might be possible to reduce this further with some more training iterations. The resulting regression curve seems to capture some of the curvature of the data, although it seems unreasonable to assume that larger houses become cheaper after they reach a certain size.

While this polynomial model function is certainly non-linear, it is interesting to note that we can cast the regression problem again into a linear framework. That is, we can create a new feature vector $\mathbf{x}$ with components $x_i = x^i$. We can then rewrite the model as

$$y = \mathbf{w}^{\mathrm{T}}\mathbf{x}, \qquad (5.33)$$

A

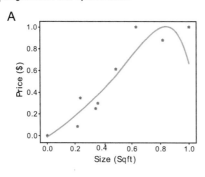

B

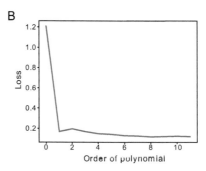

Fig. 5.8 (A) Polynomial regression of the house data with polynomial of order 12. (B) Loss after learning for polynomial models of different order.

which again is a linear model. In other words, we have first applied a non-linear transformation from the feature space of $\mathbf{x}$ into a new feature space of $\mathbf{x}_{\text{new}}$,

$$\mathbf{x}_{\text{new}} = \phi(\mathbf{x}). \tag{5.34}$$

After this transformation we were able to use a linear model in this transformed space. The transformed space was here larger than the original space, but in this transformed space we were able to use a linear regression model. This is sometimes called generalized linear regression. Finding the right transformation function ϕ is not easy and we somewhat transformed the problem into the problem of finding the appropriate non-linear transformation. Deep learning can be seen as learning this transformation from the data.

It is worthwhile to consider another non-linear example function to our house data. For this we choose a series of Gaussian functions,

$$y = \sum_i w_{1,i} e^{-(w_{2,i}-x)^2/w_{3,i}}. \tag{5.35}$$

We have three sets of parameters in this model, and the corresponding learning rules are

$$w_{1,i} \leftarrow w_{1,i} - \alpha(y-\hat{y})e^{-(w_{2,i}-x)^2/w_{3,i}} \tag{5.36}$$

$$w_{2,i} \leftarrow w_{2,i} + \alpha(y-\hat{y})2w_{1,i}e^{-(w_{2,i}-x)^2/w_{3,i}}\frac{-(w_{2,i}-x)^2}{w_{3,i}} \tag{5.37}$$

$$w_{3,i} \leftarrow w_{3,i} - \alpha(y-\hat{y})w_{1,i}e^{-(w_{2,i}-x)^2/w_{3,i}}\frac{-(w_{2,i}-x)^2}{w_{3,i}^2} \tag{5.38}$$

A fit of the data with a single Gaussian is shown in Fig. 5.5A, which looks somewhat similar to the fit with the 12-order polynomial, albeit with only three parameters. However, the reason to bring up this function is to realize that with an increasing number of parameters and hence complexity of the function, we can easily overfit. For example, if we take the number of Gaussians to be equal to the number of training points, we can produce a curve that goes through almost all the training points as shown in Fig. 5.5B. It is clear that this function would only act to generalize as we do not expect that houses outside these training examples cost nothing as predicted by the model. This is a clear demonstration of overfitting.

A

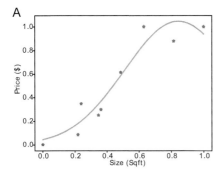

B

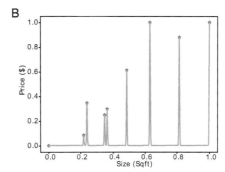

Fig. 5.9 non-linear regression with a sum of Gaussians. On the left is the fit of a single Gaussian, on the right is a fit with many Gaussians equal to the number of points and small variance. The model on the right is clearly overfitting.

5.6 Backpropagation

5.6.1 The sigmoidal perceptron and the delta learning rule

We are now ready to look at applying gradient descent to neural network models. We will start with a simple sigmoidal neuron and then generalize our approach to the multilayer perceptron.

As usual, we have to start with a parameterized model and define an appropriate loss function. In Chapter 4 we started with the threshold perceptron. However, the threshold function is not differentiable and hence this model can not be solved by gradient descent. However, we can instead use a differentiable approximation for the gain function in form of a sigmoid function called the logistic function,

$$g(x; \beta) = \frac{1}{1 + e^{-\beta x}}. \tag{5.39}$$

This is a differentiable approximation of the threshold function in the sense that when the parameter β that describes the slope of the function around $x = 0$ goes to infinity, then the threshold function is recovered. While we argued for this gain function in terms of approximating a threshold function, the logistic perceptron is a specific model or parameterized hypothesis functions in its own right, and we will later see that we can give this gain function a probabilistic interpretation.

The net input to this perceptron is the weighted sum over the input channels

$$h(\mathbf{x}; \mathbf{w}) = \sum_i w_i x_i = \mathbf{w}^T \mathbf{x}, \tag{5.40}$$

and the output is then calculated with the gain function,

$$y(\mathbf{x}; \mathbf{w}) = g(h(\mathbf{x}; \mathbf{w})) \tag{5.41}$$

$$= \frac{1}{1 + e^{-\mathbf{w}^T \mathbf{x}}}, \tag{5.42}$$

where we have absorbed the parameter β as a scaling factor in the parameters $\mathbf{w}$. A graphical representation of this model is shown in Fig. 5.10A. The logistic perceptron

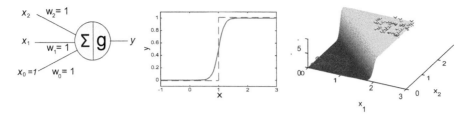

Fig. 5.10 A) Graphical representation of a perceptron with three input channels of which one is constant. B) The logistic function with different slopes and offset parameters. C) Illustration of the logistic regression problem with two input features.

was introduced in the late 1950s by Frank Rosenblatt, biologically inspired learning model, and he later wrote one of the first comprehensive books about perceptrons.

The next step is to find the appropriate parameters from example data. At this point we already know that one solution to the learning problem is a gradient descent on a loss function. We will choose a common function in traditional neural networks by using the mean square error function,

$$E(\mathbf{w}) = \frac{1}{2N} \sum_i \left(y^{(i)} - y(\mathbf{x}^{(i)}; \mathbf{w}) \right)^2. \tag{5.43}$$

Using the $1/2$ in this formula is simple convention. We will later discuss which loss functions are appropriate, arguing that the loss function should be chosen carefully from a probabilistic interpretation. However, at this point it can be seen as a simple example.

To find this minimum we again use gradient descent, and go through these steps as a reviewing exercise. In the gradient descent learning rule, weight values are updated according to

$$w_j \leftarrow w_j - \alpha \frac{\partial E}{\partial w_j}, \tag{5.44}$$

where α is a learning rate parameter. We can now calculate the gradient in order to provide a formula that can be implemented with Python. For this we have to recall two rules from calculus, namely that the derivative of an exponent function is

$$\frac{\mathrm{d}}{\mathrm{d}x} x^n = n x^{n-1}. \tag{5.45}$$

The derivative of the Euler function is

$$\frac{\mathrm{d}}{\mathrm{d}x} e^x = e^x, \tag{5.46}$$

which is an interesting fact in its own right as this means that this function is equal to its slope at every point. This is not coincidental as the functions is actually defined as such. Finally, we need the chain rule

$$\frac{\mathrm{d}}{\mathrm{d}x} f(g(x)) = \frac{\mathrm{d}f}{\mathrm{d}g} \frac{\mathrm{d}g}{\mathrm{d}x}. \tag{5.47}$$

With these rules we get

$$\frac{\partial E}{\partial w_j} = \frac{1}{N} \sum_i \left((y^{(i)} - y(\mathbf{x}^{(i)}; \mathbf{w}))(-1) \frac{\partial y}{\partial w_j} \right).$$ (5.48)

The derivative of our model with respect to the parameters is

$$\frac{\partial y}{\partial w_j} = \frac{\partial}{\partial w_j} \frac{1}{1 + e^{-\sum_i w_i x_i}} = \frac{e^{-\sum_i w_i x_i}}{(1 + e^{-\sum_i w_i x_i})^2} \frac{\partial \sum_i w_i x_i}{\partial w_j}.$$ (5.49)

In the remaining derivative over the sum, only the term survives that contains the w_j. Hence this derivative is x_j. Also, we can write some portion of this equation in terms of the original function to simplify the expression, namely

$$\frac{e^{-\sum_i w_i x_i}}{(1 + e^{-\sum_i w_i x_i})^2} = y(1 - y),$$ (5.50)

and hence

$$\frac{\partial y}{\partial w_j} = y(1 - y)x_j.$$ (5.51)

We can now collect all the pieces and write the whole update rule for the weight values as

$$w_j \leftarrow w_j - \alpha \frac{1}{N} \sum_i \left((y^{(i)} - y(\mathbf{x}^{(i)}; \mathbf{w}))y(\mathbf{x}^{(i)}; \mathbf{w})(1 - y(\mathbf{x}^{(i)}; \mathbf{w}))x^{(i)}_j \right)$$ (5.52)

The first factor within the body of the sum is called the delta term in the following,

$$\delta(\mathbf{x}^{(i)}; \mathbf{w}) = (y^{(i)} - y(\mathbf{x}^{(i)}; \mathbf{w}))y(\mathbf{x}^{(i)}; \mathbf{w})(1 - y(\mathbf{x}^{(i)}; \mathbf{w})),$$ (5.53)

or, if we write this without the arguments to see the structure clearly, this is

$$\delta = (y^{(i)} - y)y(1 - y).$$ (5.54)

We can thus write the learning rule in a generic form

$$w_j \leftarrow w_j + \alpha \frac{1}{N} \sum_i \left(\delta(\mathbf{x}^{(i)}; \mathbf{w})x^{(i)}_j \right).$$ (5.55)

The program implementation of the simple perceptron in Python is shown in Listing 5.5. The program starts with defining the training problem (the training dataset) in feature arrays X and desired label vector Y. The columns of the matrix X correspond to the feature vector of each sample, and the columns therefore represent all the training samples. We then introduce and initialize some variables, specifically the number of input nodes Ni and output nodes No, the weight matrix to the output nodes wo is initialized randomly, dwo are the changes (gradients) of the weights, and do is the delta term of the output node.

Listing 5.5 PerceptronOr.ipynb (part 1)

```
import numpy as np
import matplotlib.pyplot as plt

X=np.array([[0,0,1,1],
                    [0,1,0,1],
                    [1,1,1,1]])
Y=np.array([[0,1,1,1]])

# model specifications
Ni=3; No=1;

#parameter and array initialization
Ntrials=100
wo=np.random.randn(No,Ni); dwo=np.zeros(wo.shape)
error1=np.array([])
error2=np.array([])

for trial in range(Ntrials):
        y=1/(1+np.exp(-wo@X)) #output for all pattern
        do=y*(1-y)*(Y-y)  # delta output
        # update weights with momentum
        dwo=0.9*dwo+do@X.T
        wo=wo+0.5*dwo
        error1=np.append(error1,np.sum((Y-y)**2))
        error2=np.append(error2,np.sum(1-(abs(Y-y)<0.1)))
```

An example learning curve where we show the absolute difference between the desired output and the actual output of the network is shown on the left in Fig. 5.11 by the blue line. Overall, the error is getting smaller, indicating that some learning takes place. The error does not, however, reach 0. This comes from the fact that we use a sigmoid function which approaches a value of 1 only asymptotically. However, we can introduce another post-processing step in which we apply a threshold function. This corresponds to the error that we calculate in the above program. The corresponding learning curve is shown on in orange on the left graph in Fig. 5.11. This demonstrates that this perceptron can solve the Boolean OR function with this post-processing step. The error function such as the loss used for training is somewhat useful as it shows that there is continuous progress during learning even when the thresholded value stays constant, although the values themselves do not tell the whole story. The thresholded values give us some indication of how many patterns are recognized, but it would be better to check every pattern separately, something which we omitted to keep the program short. It is very useful to always calculate error numbers that can be interpreted in terms of the performance that a user is looking for, which is not necessarily the loss function used for the gradient descent.

We have already discussed batch versus online learning in the linear case and it might be good to review this again for backpropagation. We have derived here the learning rule based on the mean square error over all the training points. This corresponds to applying all the training examples and calculating the average gradient before updating the weight values based on this average. This is batch training, since we use the whole batch of training examples for each weight update step. In contrast, we use one training example at a time, $(\mathbf{x}^{(i)}, y^{(i)})$, and calculate the gradient for this point, and use this gradient to update the weight value after the application of each

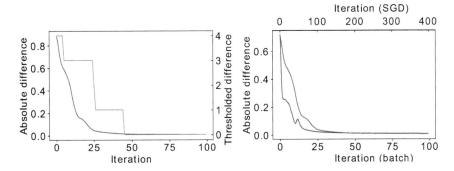

Fig. 5.11 Learning curve of sigmoid perceptron trained on the Boolean OR function. The graph of on the left-hand side shows the learning curve for batch learning. The blue curve shows the absolute difference between the desired output and the sigmoidal activation of the output node. The orange line shows the thresholded difference. The right-hand graph compares the batch learning curve (blue) from the left graph to the SGD learning curve (red).

data point. This is an online learning method since the point is to use each incoming data point for one update and there is no need to store anything. Of course, in reality we want to perform several iterations so that we must keep each training point. In the implementation below, we chose a random sample from the training pattern. If the training patterns are random, then this method is the **stochastic gradient descent (SGD)**. An example of such a learning curve is shown as red line in the right-hand graph of Fig.5.11.

Listing 5.6 PerceptronOr.ipynb (part 2)

```
#parameter and array initialization
Ntrials=400
wo=np.random.randn(No,Ni); dwo=np.zeros(wo.shape)
error=np.array([])

for trial in range(Ntrials):
        i=np.random.randint(0,4)
        y=1/(1+np.exp(-wo@X[:,i])) #output for one pattern
        do=y*(1-y)*(Y[:,i]-y)  # delta output
        # update weights with momentum
        dwo=0.9*dwo+np.outer(do,X[:,i])
        wo=wo+0.5*dwo
        error=np.append(error,np.sum((Y-1/(1+np.exp(-wo@X)))**2))
```

What is the advantage or disadvantage of the different methods? The batch algorithm guarantees that the average training error decreases. So if we plot this curve and see that the training error is increasing we know that there must be something wrong. By contrast, when we change the weights based on the last training example it is expected that the performance of the other training points get worse and we need to reduce the pace of the learning rate. Note that here we showed performance curves in the training set. We must, of course, study the generalization, which is difficult to show in this sized example.

As usual in machine learning, different methods will perform differently in different situations. However, it is now common to have large data sets where an online approach is more appropriate. Also, there are benefits of SGD in that this approach produces stochastic paths through the weight space which might help avoid local minima or shallow areas. This is even more important in the non-linear case as the linear case corresponds to a convex optimization problem with no local minima. Again, it is now common with large datasets to use **mini batches**. This will help in the processing for keeping a smaller dataset in memory before loading new mini batches. Within each mini batch we can still learn in a batch or SGD way.

5.6.2 Multilayer perceptron (MLP)

Let us now consider the XOR function which is $y = 1$ if both arguments are the same and 0 otherwise. It is interesting to try and learn this case using the perceptron program as this does not seem to work. Indeed, this function can not be learned by the perceptron as the XOR function is not linearly separable. This has lead to the demise of perceptrons in the 1970s although it was clear that more elaborate perceptrons with multiple layers could solve this problem. Frank Rosenblatt started to build such networks out of the simple neuron models and wrote a book about them. He even started to build neural computers based on such perceptrons and trained them similar to the algorithm shown below. It seems that due to Rosenblatt's early death and Marvin Minsky's strong opposition to perceptrons that the public realized that learning was problematic with these more elaborate structures. Thus, multilayer perceptrons became popular again only when effective training was rediscovered and made popular in 1986s by Rummelhardt, Hinton, and Williams.

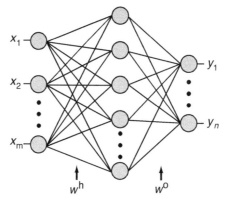

Fig. 5.12 The standard architecture of a feedforward multilayer network with one hidden layer, in which input values are distributed to all hidden nodes with weighting factors summarized in the weight matrix $\mathbf{w}^h$. The output values of the nodes of the hidden layer are passed to the output layer, again scaled by the values of the connection strength as specified by the elements in the weight matrix $\mathbf{w}^o$.

We will now consider networks of simple sigmoidal neurons to build up what are commonly called artificial neural networks since the perceptron is basically just one neuron. We will first consider a network structure as shown in Fig. 5.12. The network has a layer of m input nodes, a layer of h hidden nodes, and a layer of n output nodes.

The input layer merely represent the input values, while the hidden and output layer perform active calculations specified earlier with the sigmoidal neuron (Eqn 5.41). The term hidden nodes comes from the fact that these nodes do not have connections to the external world such as input and output nodes. The network is a graphical representation of a non-linear function of the form

$$\mathbf{y} = g(\mathbf{w}^o g(\mathbf{w}^h \mathbf{x})). \tag{5.56}$$

It is easy to include more hidden layers in this formula. For example, the activation rule for the output of a four-layer network with three hidden layers and one output layer can be written as

$$\mathbf{y} = g(\mathbf{w}^o g(\mathbf{w}^{h3} g(\mathbf{w}^{h2} g(\mathbf{w}^{h1} \mathbf{x})))), \tag{5.57}$$

where each layer uses the same activation function. Let us discuss a special case of a multilayer mapping network where all the nodes in all hidden layers have linear activation functions ($g(x) = x$). Eqn 5.57 then simplifies to

$$\mathbf{y} = \mathbf{w}^o \mathbf{w}^{h3} \mathbf{w}^{h2} \mathbf{w}^{h1} \mathbf{x}$$
$$= \tilde{\mathbf{w}} \mathbf{x}. \tag{5.58}$$

In the last step we have used the fact that the multiplication of a series of matrices simply yields another matrix, which we labelled $\tilde{\mathbf{w}}$. Eqn 5.58 represents a single-layer network as discussed earlier. It is therefore essential to include non-linear activation functions, at least in the hidden layers, to take advantage of the computational advantages of hidden layers that we are about to discuss. Note that it is also possible to build more diverse networks, such as by including connections between different hidden layers, not just between consecutive layers as shown in Fig. 5.12. However, the basic layered structure is sufficient for the following discussions and we will come back to this point later in the book.

Since the perceptron was not able to represent some Boolean functions, we should now ask which functions can be approximated by multilayer perceptrons. The answer is, in principle, any. A multilayer feedforward network is a **universal function approximator**. This means that, given enough hidden nodes, any mapping functions can be approximated with arbitrary precision by these networks. While this can be proven formally, it is also easy to comprehend why this is the case. Each hidden nodes adds another factor with its own free parameters to the function that is represented by the network. For example, with the combination of two sigmoidal nodes that have the opposite weights and different offsets, one can build a local function like the one shown on the left in Fig. 5.13. With such local functions, that can be tunes in size and location of the bump, one can build up arbitrary non-linear functions in as much precision as one wants.

The remaining problems involve knowing how many hidden nodes we need, and finding the right weight values. Also, the general approximator characteristics does not tell us if it is better to use more hidden layers or just to increase the number of nodes in one hidden layer. These are important concerns for practical engineering applications of those networks. These questions are related to the bias-variance trade-off since more nodes will increase the complexity of the model and can hence increase the potential

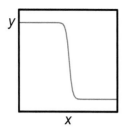 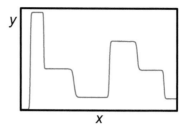

Fig. 5.13 Left: A basis function in form of a sigmoid function. The right-hand function is made up of the basis function by simply adding scaled, shifted, and reflected copies of the basis function.

for high variance (overfitting), while too few terms have the potential to introduce a bias (underfitting).

To train these networks, we consider again minimizing MSE which would be appropriate for Gaussian noisy data around the mean described by the model. The learning rule is then given by a gradient descent on this error function,

$$w_j^l \leftarrow w_j^l - \alpha \frac{\partial E}{\partial w_j^l}, \tag{5.59}$$

with $l \in \{h, o\}$.

Specifically, the gradient of the MSE error function with respect to the output weights is given by

$$
\begin{aligned}
\frac{\partial E}{\partial w_{ij}^o} &= \frac{1}{2} \frac{\partial}{\partial w_{ij}^o} \sum_k (\mathbf{y}^{(k)} - \mathbf{y})^2 \\
&= \frac{1}{2} \frac{\partial}{\partial w_{ij}^o} \sum_k \left(\mathbf{y}^{(k)} - g(\mathbf{w}^o g(\mathbf{w}^h \mathbf{x}^{(k)})) \right)^2
\end{aligned}
\tag{5.60}
$$

Let's call the activation of the hidden nodes $\mathbf{y}^h$,

$$\mathbf{y}^h = g(\mathbf{w}^h \mathbf{x})). \tag{5.61}$$

Then we can continue with our derivative as,

$$
\begin{aligned}
\frac{\partial E}{\partial w_{ij}^o} &= \frac{1}{2} \frac{\partial}{\partial w_{ij}^o} \sum_k \left(\mathbf{y}^{(k)} - g(\mathbf{w}^o \mathbf{y}^h) \right)^2 \\
&= -\sum_k g'(\mathbf{w}^h \mathbf{x}^{(k)})(y_i^{(k)} - y_i) y_j^h \\
&= \delta_i^o y_j^h,
\end{aligned}
\tag{5.62}
$$

Eqn 5.62 is just the delta rule as presented earlier because we have only considered the output layer. The calculation of the gradients with respect to the weights of the hidden layer again requires the chain rule as they are more embedded in the error function. Thus we have to calculate the derivative

$$\frac{\partial E}{\partial w_{ij}^h} = \frac{1}{2} \frac{\partial}{\partial w_{ij}^h} \sum_k (\mathbf{y}^{(k)} - \mathbf{y})^2$$

Table 5.1 Summary of error-back-propagation algorithm

Initialize weights arbitrarily

Repeat until error is sufficiently small

Apply a sample pattern to all input nodes: x_i

Propagate input through the network by calculating the rates of
nodes in successive layers l: $y_i^l = g(\sum_j w_{ij}^l y_j^{l-1})$

Compute the delta term for the output layer:

$$\delta_i^o = g'(y_i^{o-1})(y_i^{\text{desired}} - y_i^o)$$

Back-propagate delta terms through the network:

$$\delta_i^{l-1} = g'(y_i^{l-1}) \sum_j w_{ji}^l \delta_j^l$$

Update weight matrix by adding the term: $\Delta w_{ij}^l = \alpha \delta_i^l y_j^{l-1}$

$$= \frac{1}{2} \frac{\partial}{\partial w_{ij}^{\text{h}}} \sum_k \left(\mathbf{y}^{(k)} - g(\mathbf{w}^o g(\mathbf{w}^{\text{h}} \mathbf{x}^{(k)})) \right)^2. \tag{5.63}$$

After some battle with indices (which can easily be avoided with analytical calculation programs such as MAPLE or MATHEMATICA), we can write the derivative in a form similar to that of the derivative of the output layer, namely

$$\frac{\partial E}{\partial w_{ij}^{\text{h}}} = \delta_i^{\text{h}} x_j, \tag{5.64}$$

when we define the delta term of the hidden term as

$$\delta_i^{\text{h}} = g^{\text{h}\prime}(h_i^{\text{in}}) \sum_k w_{ik}^o \delta_k^o. \tag{5.65}$$

The error term δ_i^{h} is calculated from the error term of the output layer with a formula that looks similar to the general update formula of the network, except that a signal is propagating from the output layer to the previous layer. This is the reason that the algorithm is called the **error-backpropagation algorithm**.

In this derivation we used the MSE over all the training patterns. Since all the training patterns are used at once, this algorithm is again a batch algorithm. Using a batch algorithm is generally a good idea, but it also takes up a lot of memory with large training sets and we have mentioned that an online version when new data points arise in a random order can help with avoiding local minima. The online version of this algorithm is summarized in Table 5.1. Of course, this algorithm is commonly applied to mini batches at a time.

Let us illustrate a basic multilayer perceptron implementation in Python on the XOR problem. As already discussed in the simple perceptron implementation before, the program starts by defining the training problem (the training dataset) in feature arrays X and desired label vector Y. We then introduce and initialize some variables which now include the activation of the hidden nodes h and the weights to the hidden nodes wh, as well as the corresponding gradient dwh and delta term dh.

Listing 5.7 MLPxor.ipynb (part 1)

```
import numpy as np
import matplotlib.pyplot as plt

X=np.array([[0,0,1,1],
[0,1,0,1],
[1,1,1,1]])
Y=np.array([[1,0,0,1]])

# model specifications
Ni=3; Nh=4; No=1;
#parameter and array initialization
Ntrials=1000
wh=np.random.randn(Nh,Ni); dwh=np.zeros(wh.shape)
wo=np.random.randn(No,Nh); dwo=np.zeros(wo.shape)
error=np.array([])

for trial in range(Ntrials):
        h=1/(1+np.exp(-wh@X)) #hidden activation for all pattern
        y=1/(1+np.exp(-wo@h)) #output for all pattern
        do=y*(1-y)*(Y-y)  # delta output
        dh=h*(1-h)*(wo.transpose()@do)  # delta backpropagated

        # update weights with momentum
        dwo=0.9*dwo+do@h.T
        wo=wo+0.1*dwo
        dwh=0.9*dwh+dh@X.T
        wh=wh+0.1*dwh
        error=np.append(error,np.sum(abs(Y-y)))

plot(error)
```

We then iterate over trials. We implemented here the batch version where we propagate forward all samples from the training set and update the weights. This code is very compact, using matrix notations. In general, is it useful to think about the layers of the neural network for performing operations such as building the dot product between the input vector and the weight matrix. This compact formulation helps a great deal with building complex models. However, to clarify the vector notation with a component-wise formulation, we offer and example here for calculating the network output for all patterns.

Listing 5.8 MLPxor.ipynb (part 2)

```
# test all pattern
for pat in range(4):
        x=X[:,pat]
        #calculate prediction
        for ih in range(Nh): #for each hidden node
                sumInput=0
                for ii in range(Ni): #loop over input features
                        sumInput=sumInput+wh[ih,ii]*x[ii]
                        h[ih]=1/(1+exp(-sumInput))
        for io in range(No): #for each output node
                sumInput=0
                for ih in range(Nh): #loop over inputs from hidden
                        sumInput=sumInput+wo[io,ih]*h[ih]
                        y[io]=1/(1+exp(-sumInput))
```

An example learning curve where we show the absolute difference between the desired output and the actual output of the network appears on the left of Fig. 5.14, while on the right is shown the error when using a threshold post-processing as we did with the perceptron. This demonstrates that the MLP can solve the Boolean XOR function.

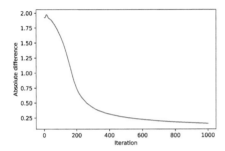 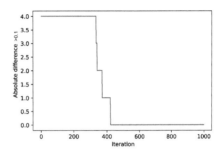

Fig. 5.14 Learning curve of an MLP trained on the Boolean XOR function. The graph on the left-hand side shows the learning curve of the absolute difference between the desired output and the sigmoidal activation of the output node. The graph on the right shows an example of the performance when we use the rounded value of the output node as prediction.

Before leaving this area, it is useful to point out some general observations. Artificial neural networks have certainly been one of the first successful methods for non-linear regression, implementing non-linear hypotheses of the form $h(\mathbf{x}; \mathbf{w}) = g(\mathbf{w}^T x)$.

The corresponding mean square loss function,

$$L \propto \left(y - g(\mathbf{w}^T x)\right)^2 \tag{5.66}$$

is then also a general non-linear function of the parameters. Minimizing such a function is generally difficult. However, we could consider instead hypotheses that are linear in the parameters, $h(\mathbf{x}; \mathbf{w}) = \mathbf{w}^T \phi(\mathbf{x})$, so that the MSE loss function is quadratic in the parameters,

$$L \propto \left(y - \mathbf{w}^T \phi(\mathbf{x})\right)^2. \tag{5.67}$$

The corresponding quadratic optimization problem can be solved much more efficiently. This line of thinking has been further developed in support vector machines that we reviewed earlier. I point this out here to stress that basic neural networks are not always optimal in the way they are commonly implemented and that variations are possible. Also, an interesting and central further issue is how to choose the non-linear function ϕ. This brings us back to non-linear support vector machines and deep learning.

5.7 Automatic differentiation

Calculating the gradients for a multilayer perceptron of simple sigmoid units has already shown to be a bit cumbersome, so we might be worried about how more elaborate networks could be implemented. Fortunately, programing derivatives can be highly automated and such techniques are now commonly used in machine learning toolboxes. We will here briefly outline the idea behind such techniques.

There are four principle methods. One is to work out the algebraic expression of a derivative by hand and then code the result. For example, let's assume we want to find the gradient of the function

$$f(x, y) = \sin(x) + x * y + \ln(y) \tag{5.68}$$

which we can find by applying the analytic differentiation rules to be

$$\begin{pmatrix} \frac{\partial f(x,y)}{\partial x} \\ \frac{\partial f(x,y)}{\partial x} \end{pmatrix} = \begin{pmatrix} \cos(x) + y \\ x + \frac{1}{y} \end{pmatrix}. \tag{5.69}$$

The expressions on the right can also be found with symbolic mathematical manipulations such as implemented in symbolic math tools like Mathematica or Maple. We can then use these expressions to write code for calculating the values of the gradients at specific points x_0 and y_0. For example, the partial derivative of the function in x-direction at $x = 0$ and $y = 1$ is $\frac{\partial f(x,y)}{\partial x}|_{(0,1)} = 2$.

While such methods are exact save manual mistakes, another possibility is to use numeric approximations based on finite difference quotients for the partial derivatives like

$$\frac{\partial f(x, y)}{\partial x} = \frac{f(x + \Delta x, y) - f(x, y)}{\Delta x} \tag{5.70}$$

Such an approximation is easy to implement but introduces numerical errors. For example, with a step width of $\Delta x = 0.1$ we get a value of $\frac{\partial f(x,y)}{\partial x}|_{(0,1)} \approx 1.998$ for our example. While this seems acceptable, in practice such errors can result in such large variations for complex non-linear functions that they are rarely used in machine learning.

The more common way of implementing gradient calculations in machine learning is to represent complicated functions as graphs of basic functions and then use a chain rule to represent their derivatives as a graph of basic derivatives. Backpropagation itself is actually an example of such a strategy. Let us first explain the basic idea with a forward mode for automatic differentiation. We can represent the example function above with the primal graph shown in Fig. 5.15 where

$$v_1 = x \quad (= 0)$$
$$v_2 = y \quad (= 1)$$
$$v_3 = \sin(v_1) \quad (= 0)$$
$$v_4 = \ln(v_2) \quad (= 0)$$
$$v_5 = v_1 * v_2 \quad (= 0)$$
$$v_6 = v_3 + v_4 + v_5 \quad (= 0).$$

This is like a neural network with weights always set to 1 but where every node can have a different gain function. This underlines the fact again that a neural network is mostly a graphical representation of a complex function. In brackets, we show the evaluation of this functions with input $x = 0$ and $y = 1$.

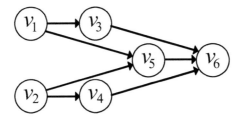

Fig. 5.15 A computational graph for the function $f(x, y) = \sin(x) + x * y + \ln(y)$.

If we want to take the derivative of the function with respect to the inputs, we can apply the chain rule. To simplify the notation, we can write the partial derivative as an operator D. Then we have the derivative graph similar to the primal graph with

$$Dv_1 = Dx \quad (= 1)$$
$$Dv_2 = Dy \quad (= 0)$$
$$Dv_3 = \cos(v_1) * Dv_1 \quad (= 1)$$
$$Dv_4 = \frac{Dv_2}{v_2} \quad (= 0)$$
$$Dv_5 = Dv_1 * v_2 + v_1 * Dv_2 \quad (= 1)$$
$$Dv_6 = Dv_3 + Dv_4 + Dv_5 \quad (= 2).$$

These are again elementary functions nodes that form a graph for the derivative analog to the primary function graph. At this point it is wise to note that such functions are already implemented as code so that this graph represents existing code that can be used to calculate the values of the derivatives at specific points. For example, if we want to calculate the partial derivative with respect to x, then $Dv_1 = 1$ and $Dv_2 = 0$. All other variables are then given or computed by the expressions. We included the corresponding numbers for the example of the derivative in the x-direction at points $x = 0$ and $y = 1$ in brackets in the above equations. This illustrates the basic idea behind automatic differentiations.

While the forward mode of automatic differentiation is easy to implement, there are other algorithms that can be more suited for the gradients we have to calculate in neural networks and show how the backpropagation algorithm is a form of automatic differentiation. The reverse mode algorithm starts with a forward pass though the network. We also define an adjoint variable

$$\bar{v}_i = \frac{\partial f}{\partial v_i} \tag{5.71}$$

which specifies how much the variable v_i contributes to the change in the output value. With these notations we can unravel the chain rule in reverse order

$$\bar{v}_6 \quad (= 1)$$
$$\bar{v}_5 = \bar{v}_6 \frac{\partial v_6}{\partial v_5} = \bar{v}_6 * 1 \quad (= 1)$$
$$\bar{v}_4 = \bar{v}_6 \frac{\partial v_6}{\partial v_4} = \bar{v}_6 * 1 \quad (= 1)$$

$$\bar{v}_3 = \bar{v}_6 \frac{\partial v_6}{\partial v_3} = \bar{v}_6 \quad (= 1)$$

$$\bar{v}_2 = \bar{v}_5 \frac{\partial v_5}{\partial v_2} + \bar{v}_4 \frac{\partial v_4}{\partial v_2} = \bar{v}_5 v_1 + \bar{v}_4 * \frac{1}{v_2} \quad (= 1)$$

$$\bar{v}_1 = \bar{v}_5 \frac{\partial v_5}{\partial v_1} + \bar{v}_3 \frac{\partial v_3}{\partial v_1} = \bar{v}_5 V_2 + \bar{v}_3 cos(v_1) \quad (= 2)$$

and we recover the directional derivatives of the above example as noted in the brackets. Notice that we calculated here the full gradient with the direction derivative in both directions, though we used here a forward pass and a reverse pass. In the forward mode, we would have to do two forward passes through the derivative network. In machine learning the output of the network for training is a cost function, and error-backpropagation then corresponds to automatic differentiation with the reverse mode. Most machine learning packages have implemented such strategies so that in practice, we do not have to undertake the differentiation but simply raise an optimizer on a specific model and cost function.

6 Basic probability theory

Probably the biggest challenge in using data to build models is the nature of uncertainty. This includes the limited knowledge about the world, such as relying on noisy or unreliable sensors. Even just knowing if a sample sets is appropriate to cover the dependencies we want to uncover presents some uncertainty in machine learning. The mathematical description of uncertainty is covered in probability theory, and it should thus not be a surprise that using this language has helped enormously to formalize the areas of machine learning for a deeper understanding.

This chapter provides a refresher in probability theory, in particular with respect to the formulations that build the theoretical language of modern machine learning. Probability theory is the formalization of random numbers, and we outline what these are and how they are characterized by probability density or probability mass functions. We discuss how such functions have traditionally been characterized and provide a review of how to work with such mathematical objects such as transforming density functions and how to measure differences between density function. We then review definitions and basic operations with multiple random variables, including the Bayes law, and end with an outline of some important approximation techniques of so-called Monte Carlo methods.

We are here mainly interested in the language of probability theory rather than statistics that we take here as meaning specific methods for hypothesis testing and related procedures. While machine learning methods can be viewed as a range of advanced statistical methods, our concern here is to learn about the language and tools of probability theory as means for developing machine learning methods.

6.1 Random numbers and their probability (density) function

The main instrument for describing uncertainty and hence the subject of probability theory is **random numbers** and their associated variables. While a regular number has only one specific value, a random number will have different values every time we "look" at it (draw a sample from the distributions). For example, let's think about some data that we acquired using a light sensor. We might think that an ideal light sensor will give us only one reading while holding it to a specific surface. However, the characteristics of the internal electronic circuit might change due to changing temperatures or fatigue in the sensor itself, or since we may move the sensor unintentionally away from the surface. It is hence likely that we get different readings over time. While some people might argue that such causes are mainly unknown (latent) factors, it is of no importance to us why we have uncertainty but rather that we have uncertainty. Consider image recognition; we have a lighter in the shape of a gun so that the functionality of

Fundamentals of Machine Learning, Thomas P. Trappenberg, Oxford University Press (2020). © Oxford University Press. DOI: 10.1093/oso/9780198828044.001.0001

the object is uncertain from its shape. Acknowledging uncertainty instead of denying it or simply trying to avoid it is an important paradigm shift in machine learning.

A common misconception about randomness is that one cannot predict anything about a random variables. While we might not be able to predict a specific value, it is often the case that some values might be more likely than others. Indeed, we might be able to say something about how often a certain number will appear when drawing many examples. We might even be able to state how confident we are with this number, or, in other words, how variable these predictions are. Complete knowledge of a random variable, that is, how likely each value is for a random variable x, is captured by the probability density function $pdf(x)$ in the continuous case and by the probability mass function $P(x)$ in the discrete case. We discuss some specific examples of such functions in the following. In these examples, we assume that such probability functions are know *a priori*, but in many practical applications we must estimate this function. Indeed, estimation of probability functions is in some sense the essence of machine learning. If we would know the "world probability density function", the probability function of all possible events in the world, then we could predict as much as possible in and about this world.

Probability theory is the theory of random numbers. We denote such numbers by capital letters to distinguish them from regular numbers written in lower case. A random variable, X, is a quantity that can have different values each time the variable is inspected, such as in measurements in experiments. This is fundamentally different to a regular variable, x, which does not change its value once it is assigned. A random number is thus a new mathematical concept, not included in the regular mathematics of numbers. A specific value of a random number is still meaningful as it might influence specific processes in a deterministic way. For example, a restaurant owner might be uncertain about how many people will come into the restaurant, but once people are in he should serve this number of people.

Since the value of a random number can change every time it is inspected, it is useful to describe more general properties when drawing samples many times. This frequency is captured by the mathematical construct of a probability. Note that there is often a debate whether random numbers should be defined solely on the basis of a frequency measurement, or if they should be treated as a special kind of object with this inherent property. This philosophical debate between "Frequentists" and "Bayesians" is of minor importance for our applications. We do not ask where the uncertainty is coming from, we simply use the probability construct as a tool to describe uncertainty, and it is of minor importance to us if this is a inherent limitation or simply a lack of knowledge.

We can formalize the idea of expressing probabilities of drawing specific values for random variable with some compact notations. For these notations we sometimes need to distinguish discrete random numbers and continuous random numbers. There is, in principle, not much difference between these two kinds of random variables except that the mathematical formulation has to be slightly different to be mathematically correct. For example, the probability mass function for discrete random numbers,

$$P(x) = P(X = x) \tag{6.1}$$

describes the frequency with which each possible value x of a discrete variable X occurs. Note that x is a regular variable, not a random variable. The value of $P(x)$

predicts the fraction of times we get a value x for the random variable X if we draw many examples of the random variable. Probabilities are sometimes written as a percentage, but here we will stick to the fractional notation. From this definition it follows that the frequency of having any of the possible values is equal to 1, which is an important normalization condition for a probability function,

$$\sum_x P(x) = 1. \tag{6.2}$$

In the case of continuous random numbers, we have an infinite number of possible values x so that the fraction for each number becomes formally infinitesimally small. It is thus necessary to write the probability distribution function as $P(x) = p(x)\mathrm{d}x$, where $p(x)$ is the probability density function (pdf). Note that we have used upper-case and lower-case letters. The sum in Egn 6.2 then becomes an integral, and the normalization condition for a continuous random variable is

$$\int_x p(x)\mathrm{d}x = 1. \tag{6.3}$$

A finite probability value makes then only sense for a certain range of numbers such as

$$P(a < x < b) = \int_{x=a}^{b} p(x)\mathrm{d}x. \tag{6.4}$$

We will formulate the rest of this section in terms of continuous random variables. The corresponding formulae for discrete random variables can easily be deduced by replacing the integrals over the pdf with sums over the probability function. It is also possible to use the delta-function to write discrete random processes in a continuous form. The delta-function $delta(x)$ is a very convenient notation, which is formally a functional since it is only defined within an integral or the limiting case of a function series. One can think of it as a density function that is 0 except for its arguments for which it is infinite, so that

$$\int_{-\infty}^{\infty} \delta(x_1) f(x)\mathrm{d}x = f(x_1). \tag{6.5}$$

The delta function is useful for writing discrete events in a continuous form. For example, we could write the discrete density function for throwing a dice

$$P(x) = \frac{1}{6} \quad \text{for } x = \{1, 2, ..., 6\}, \tag{6.6}$$

as a density function

$$p(x) = \frac{1}{6}\delta(x = x_i) \quad \text{with } x_i = \{1, 2, ..., 6\}. \tag{6.7}$$

Note that we are here only playing with notations in order to introduce a concise language for our purposes.

6.2 Moments: mean, variance, etc.

In the following, we only consider independent random values that are drawn from identical pdfs, often labeled as iid (independent and identically distributed) data. That is, we do not consider cases with different probabilities when given a specific value of a random variable in a previous trial. We assume, mainly for simplicity, that this static probability density function describes all we can know about the corresponding random variable.

Let us consider the arbitrary pdf, $p(x)$, with the following graph:

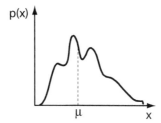

Any curve like this which is strictly positive and where the area under the curve is bounded to one (see Egn 6.3) is a possible probability density function. The specific curve shown can be characterized as multimodal because it has several peaks. It would be useful to have this function parameterized in an analytical format, and we will list some common parameterized density function below. Since we often don't know the probability density function of the quantities of interest in a machine learning setting, we will have to estimate pdfs. This approximation is the learning process in machine learning, and we will later outline specific methods to do this.

Communicating the form of a pdf is difficult, and traditionally it is common to describe random variables with a small set of numbers that are meant to capture some properties of the probability density function. For example, we might ask what the most frequent value is when drawing many examples. This number is given by the largest peak value of the distribution.

$$p^{\mathrm{max}} = \mathrm{argmax}_x p(x). \tag{6.8}$$

Even more common is to ask about the average value of the random sample when drawing many examples. A common quantity to know is thus the expected arithmetic average of those numbers, which is called the mean, expected value, or expectation value of the distribution. This is defined as

$$\mu = \int_{-\infty}^{\infty} x p(x) \mathrm{d}x. \tag{6.9}$$

This formula formalizes the calculation of adding all the different numbers together with their corresponding frequencies.

A careful reader might have noticed a little oddity in our discussion. On the one hand, we are saying that we want to characterize random variables through some simple measurements because we do not know the pdf, yet the last formula seems to assume that we know the pdf $p(x)$. To solve this apparent oddity, we need to be more careful and talk about the true underlying functions and the estimation of such functions. If we know the pdf that governs the random variable X, then Egn 6.9 is the definition of the mean. However, in most applications we do not know the pdf, but we can define an approximation of the mean from measurements. For example, if we measure the frequency p_i of values in certain intervals around values x_i, then we can estimate the true mean μ by

$$\hat{\mu} = \frac{1}{N} \sum_{i=1}^{N} x_i p_i. \tag{6.10}$$

It is a common practice to denote an estimate of a quantity by adding a hat symbol to the quantity's symbol. Also, note that here we have used a discretization procedure to approximate random variables that can be continuous in the most general case.

We could enter again the philosophical debate as we have treated the pdf as fundamental and described the arithmetic average like an estimation of the mean. This should hence be viewed as *Bayesian*. However, we could also be pragmatic and say that we only have a collection of measurements so that the numbers are the "real" thing, and that pdfs are only a mathematical construct. We will continue with a Bayesian description but note that this makes no difference in the end when using the formalism in specific applications.

The mean of a distribution is not the only interesting quantity that characterizes a distribution. For example, we might want to ask what the median value is. The median value is the value for the random variable for which it is equally likely to find a value lower or larger than this value,

$$\int_{-\infty}^{\mathrm{median}(x)} p(x)\mathrm{d}x = \int_{\mathrm{median}(x)}^{-\infty} p(x)\mathrm{d}x. \tag{6.11}$$

The median is equal to the mean in cases of symmetric distribution. However, the median can sometimes be more informative than the mean in cases of asymmetric distributions. For example, the average household income in a nation can be very high if there is a small percentage of very rich people. However, it is usually more telling to know the value for the household income on which half the population has to live on. In extension, we could ask about the numbers in the bottom quarter, and the next quarter, etc. Most telling is, of course, to see the whole distribution of income. The summary statistics like the mean and the median are only a crude approximation of the picture provided by the distribution.

Let's get back to other measurements to characterize the distribution of a random variable. The spread of the pdf around the mean is also very revealing as it gives us a sense of how distributed the values are. This spread is often characterized by the standard deviation (std), or its square, which is called variance, σ^2, and is defined as

$$\sigma^2 = \int_{-\infty}^{\infty} (x - \mu)^2 f(x)\mathrm{d}x. \tag{6.12}$$

This is mathematically called a second moment of the distribution whereas the mean is the first moment. These two moments are generally not enough to characterize the probability function uniquely; this is only possible if we know all moments of a distribution, where the nth moment about the mean is defined as

$$m^n = \int_{-\infty}^{\infty} (x - \mu)^n f(x) \mathrm{d}x. \tag{6.13}$$

Higher moments specify further characteristics of distributions such as terms with third-order exponents (related to the quantity called skewness) or fourth-order (such as a quantity called kurtosis). Knowing all moments of a distribution is equivalent to knowing the distribution precisely, and knowing a pdf is equivalent to knowing everything we could know about a random variable.

In case the distribution function is not given, moments have to be estimated from data. For example, the mean can be estimated from a sample of measurements by the sample mean,

$$\bar{x} = \frac{1}{n} \sum_{i=1}^{n} x_i, \tag{6.14}$$

and the variance from the sample variance,

$$s_1^2 = \frac{1}{n} \sum_{i=1}^{n} (\bar{x} - x_i)^2. \tag{6.15}$$

We discuss later how these estimates are the appropriate maximum likelihood estimates of these parameters. Note that the sample mean is an unbiased estimate while the sample variance of the naive estimate $E(X^2)$ is biased. A statistic is said to be biased if the mean of the sampling distribution is not equal to the parameter that is intended to be estimated. Also, the estimation of the variance is not optimal for small samples. It is therefore common to adjust the estimate with the so-called Bessel's correction for the unbiased sample variance,

$$s_2^2 = \frac{1}{n-1} \sum_{i=1}^{n} (\bar{x} - x_i)^2. \tag{6.16}$$

The difference is small for large sample sizes.

As mentioned earlier, knowing all moments uniquely specifies a pdf. This also implies that an incomplete list of moments does not uniquely define a pdf. Just extracting a list of estimated moments is thus of limited use for generalization without an explicit hypothesis of the underlying density function. While it is common to report the mean and variance of samples, this is specifically useful in case of an assumed Gaussian distributions as all higher moments are 0 for this specific distribution. Thus, in practice it is mostly assumed, often without explicit mention, that the data are Gaussian distributed when reporting mean and variance. In the age of computers with good plotting programs it is easy to a least make some checks about this assumption. For example, plotting a histogram and seeing if this resembles somewhat a bell-shaped function is easy to do. Also, since we can now plot easily many data such as point clouds, the way of summarizing distributions with moments should be seen as a more old-fashioned option. In the same general sense, machine learning can even be seen as a new approach to statistics that is currently making its way into many scientific areas as a data analytics method.

6.3 Examples of probability (density) functions

There is an infinite number of possible pdfs. However, some specific forms have been very useful for describing some specific processes and have thus been given names. The following is a small list of examples with some discrete and several continuous distributions. The list is intended to give an overview of distributions that are often mentioned in scientific work, and some of them will be discussed again in a later chapters. Most examples are discussed as 1-dimensional distributions except the last example, which is a higher-dimensional distribution. Again, we need to keep in mind that machine learning is mostly concerned with high-dimensional cases so that these distributions act merely as a starting point for illustrating some ideas.

6.3.1 Bernoulli distribution

A Bernoulli random variable is a variable from an experiment that has two possible outcomes: success with probability p; or failure, with probability $(1 - p)$.

> Probability function:
> $$P(\text{success}) = p \quad \Rightarrow \quad P(\text{failure}) = 1 - p$$
> mean: p
> variance: $p(1 - p)$.

6.3.2 Multinomial distribution

This is the distribution of outcomes in n trials that have k possible outcomes. The probability of each outcome is thereby p_i.

> Probability function:
> $$P(x_i) = n! \prod_{i=1}^{k} (p_i^{x_i} / x_i!)$$
> mean: np_i
> variance: $np_i(1 - p_i)$.

An important example is the binomial distribution ($k = 2$), which describes the the number of successes in n Bernoulli trials with probability of success p. Note that the binomial coefficient is defined as

$$\binom{n}{x} = \frac{n!}{x!(n-x)!} \tag{6.17}$$

and is given by the Python function `itertools.permutations`.

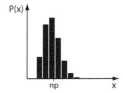

> Probability function:
> $$P(x) = \binom{n}{x} p^x (1 - p)^{n-x}$$
> mean: np
> variance: $np(1 - p)$.

6.3.3 Uniform distribution

Equally distributed random numbers in the interval $a \leq x \leq b$. Pseudo-random variables with this distribution are often generated by routines in many programming languages.

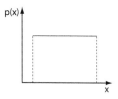

Probability density function:
$$p(x) = \begin{cases} \frac{1}{b-a} & \text{for } a \leq x \leq b, \\ 0 & \text{otherwise.} \end{cases}$$
mean: $(a+b)/2$
variance: $(b-a)^2/12$.

6.3.4 Normal (Gaussian) distribution

The limit of the binomial distribution for a large number of trials depends on two parameters, the mean μ and the standard deviation σ. The importance of the normal distribution stems from the central limit theorem outlined below.

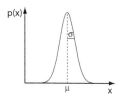

Probability density function:
$$p(x) = \frac{1}{\sigma\sqrt{2\pi}}e^{\frac{-(x-\mu)^2}{2\sigma^2}}$$
mean: μ
variance: σ^2.

6.3.5 Chi-square distribution

The sum of the squares of normally distributed random numbers is chi-square distributed and depends on a parameter ν that is equal to the mean. Γ is the gamma function included in Python as `scipy.stats.gamma`.

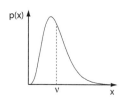

Probability density function:
$$p(x) = \frac{x^{(\nu-2)/2}e^{-x/2}}{2^{\nu/2}\Gamma(\nu/2)}$$
mean: ν
variance: 2ν.

6.3.6 Multivariate normal distribution

We will later consider density functions of a several random variables, $x_1, ..., x_n$. Such density functions are called multivariate. An important example is the multivariate Normal distribution (`scipy.stats.multivariate_normal` in Python) given by

$$p(x_1, ..., x_n) = p(\mathbf{x}) = \frac{1}{\sqrt{2\pi}^n \sqrt{|\mathbf{\Sigma}|}} \exp(-\frac{1}{2}(\mathbf{x} - \mu)^T \mathbf{\Sigma}^{-1}(\mathbf{x} - \mu)). \quad (6.18)$$

This is a straight-forward generalization of the 1-dimensional Gaussian distribution mentioned earlier where the mean is now a vector μ, and the variance generalizes to a covariance matrix $\Sigma = [\mathrm{Cov}[X_i, X_j]]_{i=1,2,\dots,k;j=1,2,\dots,k}$ which must be symmetric and positive semidefinite. An example with mean $\mu = (1\ 2)^T$ and covariance $\Sigma = (1\ 0.5; 0.5\ 1)$ is shown in Fig. 6.1.

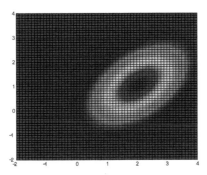

Fig. 6.1 Multivariate Gaussian with mean $\mu = (1\ 2)^T$ and covariance $\Sigma = (1\ 0.5; 0.5\ 1)$.

6.4 Some advanced concepts

6.4.1 Cumulative probability (density) function and the Gaussian error function

We have mainly discussed probabilities of single values as specified by the probability (density) functions. However, in many cases we need to know the probabilities of having values within a certain range. The probability of a specific valuer of a continuous random variable is actually infinitesimally small (nearly zero), and only the probability of a range of values is finite and has a useful meaning of a probability. This integrated version of a probability density function is the probability of having a value x for the random variable X in the range of $x_1 \leq x \leq x_2$ and is given by

$$P(x_1 \leq X \leq x_2) = \int_{x_1}^{x_2} p(x)\mathrm{d}x. \tag{6.19}$$

A common quantity that we often need to calculate is the probability that a normally (Gaussian) distributed variable has values between $x_1 = 0$ and $x_2 = y$. The probability of Eqn 6.19 then becomes a function of y. This defines the **Gaussian error function**

$$\frac{1}{\sqrt{2\pi}\sigma} \int_0^y \mathrm{e}^{-\frac{(x-\mu)^2}{2\sigma^2}} \mathrm{d}x = \frac{1}{2}\mathrm{erf}(\frac{y-\mu}{\sqrt{2}\sigma}). \tag{6.20}$$

The name of this function comes from the fact that this integral occurs when calculating confidence intervals with Gaussian noise and is often abbreviated as erf. This Gaussian error function for normally distributed variables (Gaussian distribution with mean $\mu = 0$ and variance $\sigma = 1$) is commonly tabulated in books on statistics. Mathematical programming libraries usually include routines that return the values for specific arguments. In Python, this is implemented by the routine `scipy.special.erf`, and values for the inverse of the error function are returned by the routine `scipy.special.erfinv`.

Another important general case of Egn 6.19 is when x_1 in the equation is equal to the lowest possible value of the random variable (usually $-\infty$). The integral in Egn 6.19 then corresponds to the probability that a random variable has a value smaller than a certain value, say y. This function of y is called the **cumulative density function** (cdf),[4]

$$P^{\text{cum}}(x < y) = \int_{-\infty}^{y} p(x)\mathrm{d}x, \qquad (6.21)$$

which we will utilize further below.

6.4.2 Functions of random variables and the central limit theorem

A function of a random variable X,

$$Y = f(X), \qquad (6.22)$$

is also a random variable, Y, and we often need to know the pdf of this new random variable. Calculating with functions of random variables is a bit different to calculating with regular functions, something to which we need pay attention. Let us illustrate how to do this with an example. Say we have an equally distributed random variable X, as commonly approximated with pseudo-random number generators on a computer. The probability density function of this variable is given by

$$p(x) = \begin{cases} 1 & \text{for } 0 \le x \le 1, \\ 0 & \text{otherwise.} \end{cases} \qquad (6.23)$$

We are seeking the probability density function $p_Y(y)$ of the random variable

$$Y = e^{-X^2}. \qquad (6.24)$$

The random number Y is **not** Gaussian distributed as we might naïvely think. To calculate the probability density function we can employ the cumulative density function of Egn 6.21 by noting that

$$P(Y \le y) = P(e^{-X^2} \le y) = P(X \ge \sqrt{-\ln y}). \qquad (6.25)$$

Thus, the cumulative probability function of Y can be calculated from the cumulative probability function of X,

$$P(X \ge \sqrt{-\ln y}) = \begin{cases} \int_{\sqrt{-\ln y}}^{1} p(x)\mathrm{d}y = 1 - \sqrt{-\ln y} & \text{for } e^{-1} \le y \le 1, \\ 0 & \text{otherwise.} \end{cases} \qquad (6.26)$$

The probability density function of Y is the the the derivative of this function,

$$p_Y(y) = \begin{cases} 1 - \sqrt{-\ln y} & \text{for } e^{-1} \le y \le 1, \\ 0 & \text{otherwise.} \end{cases} \qquad (6.27)$$

The probability density functions of X and Y are shown below.

---

[4]Note that this is a probability function, not a density function.

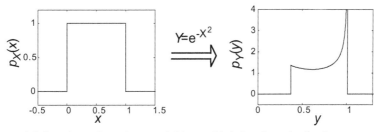

A special function of random variables, which is of particular interest as it can approximate many processes in nature, is the sum of many random variables. Sums of random variables often occur, for example when calculating averages from measured quantities,

$$\bar{X} = \frac{1}{n}\sum_{i=1}^{n} X_i, \tag{6.28}$$

and we are interested in the probability density function of the random variables that represents the mean. This function depends, of course, on the specific density function of the random variables X_i. However, there is an important observation summarized in the **central limit theorem**. This theorem states that the average (normalized sum) of n random variables that are drawn from any distribution with mean μ and variance σ is approximately normally distributed with mean μ and variance σ/n for a sufficiently large sample size n. The approximation is, in practice, even good for relatively small numbers of added variable. For example, the normalized sum of only seven uniformly distributed pseudo-random numbers is shown in Fig. 6.2 that was produced with the code in Listing 6.1.

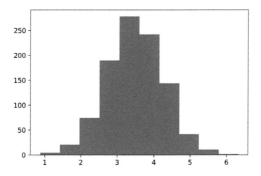

Fig. 6.2 Histogram of 1,000 samples of a random number that is the sum of seven uniformly distributed random numbers.

Listing 6.1 CentralLimit.ipynb

```
import numpy as np
import matplotlib.pyplot as plt

x=sum(np.random.rand(7,1000))
plt.hist(x)
```

6.4.3 Measuring the difference between distributions

An important practical consideration is how to measure the similarity or difference between two density functions, say the density function p and the density function q. Note that such a measure is a matter of definition, similar to distance measures of real numbers or functions where we can come up with a variety of definitions. However, there are some basic properties that we expect from a distance measure $d(a, b)$ between two items, a and b. For example, a distance measure should be 0 if the items to be compared are the same, that is $d(a, a) = 0$. Also, the value should be positive otherwise, $d(a, b) > 0$ for $a \neq b$, and a distance measure should be symmetric, meaning that $d(a, b) = d(b, a)$.

To measure the difference between to distributions we could just plot them on top of each other and measure the difference in area. However, as we will see later, we can define the information content in form of a logarithm of the probability, and the difference of logarithms is equal to the logarithm of the quotient. As common in probability theory, this measure should be weighted itself with the probability of the densities. A popular measure of similarity between two density functions is hence the so-called **Kulbach–Leibler (KL) divergence** that is given by

$$d^{\mathrm{KL}}(p, q) = \int p(x) \log\left(\frac{p(x)}{q(x)}\right) \mathrm{d}x \tag{6.29}$$

$$= \int p(x) \log(p(x)) \mathrm{d}x - \int p(x) \log(q(x)) \mathrm{d}x. \tag{6.30}$$

This measure is 0 if $p = q$ and always larger than 0 if $p \neq q$. However, this measure is not symmetric and is therefore called a divergence instead of a distance. KL is related to the information gain or relative entropy in information theory.

6.5 Density functions of multiple random variables

So far, we have discussed mainly probability (density) functions of single random variables. As mentioned earlier, we use random variables to describe data such as sensor readings in robots, of which there are many. Thus, in many applications we consider multiple random variables. The quantities described by the random variables might be independent, but in many cases they are also related. Indeed, we will later talk about how to describe various types of relations. Thus, in order to discuss situations with multiple random variables, or multivariate statistics, it is useful to know the basic rules.

6.5.1 Basic definitions

Stochastic machine learning models usually contain many random variables In the following we introduce the multivariate concepts for two variables, although these concepts readily generalize directly to an arbitrary number of variables. We start with some essential definitions. The total knowledge about the co-occurrence of specific values for two random variables X and Y is captured by the

joint distribution: $p(x, y) = p(X = x, Y = y)$. $\tag{6.31}$

This is a 2-dimensional functions. The 2 dimensions refers here to the number of variables, although a plot of this function would be a 3-dimensional plot. An example is shown in Fig. 6.3. All the information we can have about a stochastic system is encapsulated in the joint pdf. The slice of this function, given the value of one variable, say y, is the

$$\textbf{conditional distribution:} \quad p(x|y) = p(X = x | Y = y). \tag{6.32}$$

A conditional pdf is also illustrated in Fig. 6.3. If we sum over all realizations of y we get the

$$\textbf{marginal distribution:} \quad p(x) = \int p(x, y) dy. \tag{6.33}$$

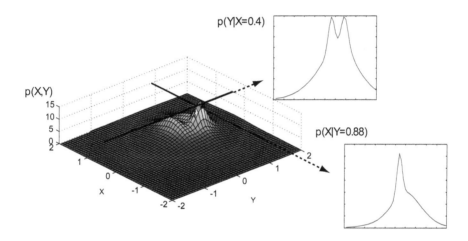

Fig. 6.3 Example of a two-dimensional probability density function (pdf) and some examples of conditional pdfs.

If we know some functional form of the density function or have a parameterized hypothesis of this function, than we can use methods such a maximum likelihood estimation, introduced later, to estimate the parameters as in the 1-dimensional cases. This will be the essence of supervised learning in the probabilistic context and will be discussed in more detail later. If we do not have a parameterized hypothesis function we need to use other methods, such as treating the problem as discrete, and building histograms to describe the density function of the system. This would be a non-parametric approach. Approximating a density function with histograms is a parameter-free method, although the bin size is a hyperparameter of the method. The problem with this method is that it becomes very challenging, or "data hungry", with increasing dimensions. That is, if we use a histogram method to estimate the joined density function where we discretize the space along every dimension into n bins, this will create n^2 bins for a 2-dimensional histogram, and n^d for a d-dimensional problem. This exponential scaling is a major challenge in practice since we also need considerable data in each bin to sufficiently estimate the probability of each bin. This problem has been termed the "curse of dimensionality" by Richard Bellman. We will later discuss that building appropriate models can address this curse.

6.5.2 The chain rule

If we know the joint distribution of some random variables we can make the most predictions of these variables. However, in practice, we often have to estimate these functions, and we can often only estimate conditional density functions. A very useful rule to know is therefore how a joint distribution can be decomposed into the product of a conditional and a marginal distribution,

$$p(x, y) = p(x|y)p(y) = p(y|x)p(x), \tag{6.34}$$

which is an example of a **chain rule**. Note the two different ways in which we can decompose the joint distribution. This is easily generalized to n random variables by

$$p(x_1, x_2, ..., x_n) = p(x_n|x_1, ...x_{n-1})p(x_1, ..., x_{n-1}) \tag{6.35}$$
$$= p(x_n|x_1, ..., x_{n-1}) * ... * p(x_2|x_1) * p(x_1) \tag{6.36}$$
$$= \Pi_{i=1}^n p(x_i|x_{i-1}, ...x_1), \tag{6.37}$$

but note that there are also different decompositions possible. We will learn more about this and useful graphical representations in the next chapter.

Estimations of processes are greatly simplified when random variables are independent. A random variable X is independent of Y if

$$p(x|y) = p(x). \tag{6.38}$$

Using the chain rule Eqn 6.34, we can write this also as

$$p(x, y) = p(x)p(y); \tag{6.39}$$

that is, the joint distribution of two independent random variables is the product of their marginal distributions. Similarly, we can also define conditional independence. For example, two random variables, X and Y, are conditionally independent of random variable Z if

$$p(x, y|z) = p(x|z)p(y|z). \tag{6.40}$$

Note that total independence does generally not imply conditionally independence, and visa versa, although this might hold true for some examples.

6.6 How to combine prior knowledge with new evidence

6.6.1 Bayes rule

One of the most common tasks we will encounter in the following is the integration of prior knowledge with new evidence. For example, we might have a robot that estimates its current position at certain values and then get new (noisy) sensory data that adds some suggestions for different positions. This is also a common task in fusion of data from different sensors. In general, we assume that we already have a model that we built from previous data, and now we want to refine this model with new data. The general question we have to solve is how to weight the different evidence in light of the reliability of this information. Solving this problem is easy in a probabilistic framework and is one of the main reasons that so much progress has been made with the application of probabilistic machine learning.

How prior knowledge should be combined with prior knowledge is an important question. Luckily, we already know how to do it best in a probabilistic sense. Namely, if we divide the chain rule (Eqn 6.34) by $p(y)$, which is possible as long as $p(y) > 0$, we get the identity

$$p(x|y) = \frac{p(y|x)p(x)}{p(y)}, \tag{6.41}$$

which is called **Bayes rule** after the inventor Thomas Bayes. This theorem is important because it tells us how to combine **prior** knowledge over a random variable we want to estimate, $p(x)$, with the **likelihood** $p(y|x)$ of data y given x. The likelihood can often be measured in some way, for example by measuring some sensors reading y when controlling the state x. The **posterior** distribution, $p(x|y)$, which is the new knowledge of the distribution with the new data, can then be calculated by multiplying the likelihood with the prior for x and normalizing this properly by the marginal distribution of having such data, $p(y)$, also called **evidence**. We will see that, in practice, knowing the marginal of the data is difficult, but we will also see that the non-normalized version is useful in some applications such as classification, as discussed later.

Bayes rule in conjunction with the chain rule and the rule of total probability are basically all the rules you need to do probabilistic inference. Probabilistic inference is to use these rules together with the known or estimated density functions to derive probabilistic statements. For example, let us calculate how likely it is to rain if a meteorologist is predicting rain,

$$p(X = r|Y = r) = ?. \tag{6.42}$$

The random variable X stands for the "actual condition," and r means rain, and the random variable Y stands for "predicted condition." Let us assume we know the following factors that we can measure easily. Let us assume that it rains in 30 per cent of the days,

$$p(X = r) = 0.3, \tag{6.43}$$

which we just calculated from past data by taking the ratio of days on which it rained. Since there are only two choices, it follows that the probability of no rain, which we write as $\not{r}$, is

$$p(X = \not{r}) = 1 - p(X = r) = 0.7. \tag{6.44}$$

Furthermore, from past predictions we know that the meteorologist predicts correctly that it is raining 90 per cent.

$$p(Y = r|X = r) = 0.9. \tag{6.45}$$

This number is again derived from previous data. From this we might conclude that it should be raining with a 90 per cent probability, but we also need to take the prior knowledge into account which should bias our prediction downwards because it is less likely to rain than not to rain. To apply Bayes rule, we also need to know how the meteorologist performs predicting no rain, and let's assume that she is slightly better at predicting when it is not raining as she gets this right 95 per cent of the times. That is

$$p(Y = \not{r}|X = \not{r}) = 0.95. \tag{6.46}$$

The last equations also implies that she predicts rain in 5 per cent of the cases when it does not rain,

$$p(Y = r|X = \not{r}) = 0.05. \tag{6.47}$$

We now have all the components we need to find a solution to the above question using Bayes theorem, namely

$$
\begin{aligned}
p(X = r|Y = r) &= \frac{p(Y = r|X = r)p(X = r)}{p(Y = r|X = r)p(X = r) + p(Y = r|X = \not{r})p(X = \not{r})} \\
&= \frac{0.9 * 0.3}{0.9 * 0.3 + 0.1 * 0.7} \\
&\approx 0.8.
\end{aligned}
\tag{6.48}
$$

Thus, we see that the actual probability that it is not raining if the meteorologist predicts it is less than we might have thought.

Taking the prior into account is an essential part in Bayesian reasoning. This will become clear in classification. For example, if we have a binary classification problem in which the positive is highly unlikely, say 99 per cent, then always predicting the positive outcome would give us an accuracy of 0.99. Even though that seems good, a real success of a prediction system should considerable outperform this naïve prediction.

This is already an example of Bayesian modeling. We actually made a model of two Bernoulli random variables

$$P(X = r) = p_{xr} \quad \text{and} \quad P(Y = r) = p_{yr}. \tag{6.49}$$

and the conditional distributions

$$P(X = r|Y = r) = p_{xryr} \quad \text{and} \quad P(X = r|Y = \not{r}) = p_{xry\not{r}}. \tag{6.50}$$

and estimated the parameters p_{xr}, p_{yr}, p_{xryr}, and $p_{xry\not{r}}$ from data. Estimating the parameters for data is the learning part, and we will derive the procedure of using the ratio of previous events that is appropriate for this model. We then used this model with the rules of probability theory, specifically Bayes rule and the rule of total probability, to make predictions. This last step is sometimes called making a statistical inference. We will formalize the process of how to learn the parameters of the model in the next chapter, and we will discuss the process of Bayesian modeling with associated tools in Chapter 8.

Let us discuss a second example that should help us to appreciate the usefulness and difficulty with Bayes rule. Let us assume we have a robot for which we want to estimate the distance to a wall from sensor readings. For example, we might know from the integration of our previous path that we are a distance of $\hat{x}$ away from a wall with a probability that is Gaussian with variance σ_1 around this estimated point. That is, our prior knowledge is

$$p(x) = \mathcal{N}(\hat{x}, \sigma_1). \tag{6.51}$$

We then invoke a distance sensor. We have tested this sensor before and derived form it the likelihood that we get a reading y if the sensor is a distance x from the wall. Let us assume that this is also Gaussian around x with variance σ_2^2,

$$p(y|x) = \mathcal{N}(x, \sigma_2). \tag{6.52}$$

The question now is: if we get a sensor reading of y, what is the estimate of the distance x to the wall given a sensor reading of y, the posterior $p(x|y)$? Note that this is not only one answer but gives is the probability for each possible distance. We might then choose the point estimate with the highest probability, but the advantage in having a full probabilistic view enables advanced probabilistic reasoning.

We are lucky here, since both the prior and the likelihood are Gaussian distributed, and one can show that the product of two Gaussian distributions is again Gaussian distributed where the mean and variance is a weighted sum over the contributing Gaussians, namely

$$\mu = \frac{\sigma_2^2 \hat{x} + \sigma_1^2 x}{\sigma_1^2 + \sigma_2^2} \tag{6.53}$$

and

$$\sigma = \frac{\sigma_1^2 \sigma_2^2}{\sigma_1^2 + \sigma_2^2} \tag{6.54}$$

Furthermore, and most importantly, since we know that the resulting distribution is a Gaussian, we also know how to normalize this distribution so that we do not have to calculate the denominator $p(y)$ which depends on movements of the robot and all corresponding sensor measurements that we do not know. Therefore, in this situation we can calculate the posterior analytically, which is given by

$$p(x|y) = \mathcal{N}(\mu, \sigma). \tag{6.55}$$

We wanted to show here that the posterior of a Gaussian likelihood with a Gaussian prior is tractable. Unfortunately, for most other distributions, we can not calculate the denominator analytically, which is a major problem for applying Bayesian inference analytically. The next section introduces a numerical sampling method that can be used in a general cases to estimate posteriors. The next section introduces a method that can be used in general cases to sample posteriors.

6.6.2 Markov chain Monte Carlo (MCMC)

A techniques that is commonly mentioned and used in machine learning papers is Markov chain Monte Carlo (MCMC). We will introduce here the idea behind this technique with an example of generating random variables from an arbitrary density function.

While many computer programs include methods to generate random numbers from a handful of well-defined density functions, we sometimes need a way to sample from density functions that are not already defined in a computer library. Let's say we have a density function of the form

$$p(x) = \begin{cases} x & \text{for } 0 \leq x \leq 2, \\ 0 & \text{otherwise,} \end{cases} \tag{6.56}$$

as illustrated in Fig. 6.6.2a which was generated with the code.

Listing 6.2 MCMC.ipynb (part 1)

```
import numpy as np
import matplotlib.pyplot as plt

x=np.arange(0,2.1,0.1); y=x/2
x=np.append(x,2); y=np.append(y,0)
plt.plot(x,y)
plt.axis([-1,3,0,1.1])
plt.show()
```

To generate random numbers from this distribution we can just chose some random sample points and then chose with the probability specified by our function to accept or reject this this sample. The histogram of 1000 proposal samples produced with the code

Listing 6.3 MCMC.ipynb (part 2)

```
sample=np.array([])
nsample=1000
x=2*np.random.rand(nsample)
y=np.random.rand(nsample)
for i in range(nsample):
    if y[i] < x[i]/2:
        sample=np.append(sample,x[i])
plt.hist(sample)
sample.shape
```

is shown in the middle pannel of Fig. 6.6.2. While this works, we have only produced around 500 true samples as we had to reject many of them. This is a fairly good ratio with this chosen uniform distribution for potential sample points since we build in not to produce sample proposals outside the range $0 < x < 2$. This method is clearly wasteful in areas with low probability.

A better methods is to use more samples in areas of high probability. This is called importance sampling, and there are useful ways to do this called Markov chain Monte Carlo (MCMC) method. For these, we produce a chain of proposal points by taking a step from a current position. For example, we can just add a symmetric random step to the current position. We then accept or reject this proposal according to the ratio of the current position and the proposed position. This is implemented in the following code.

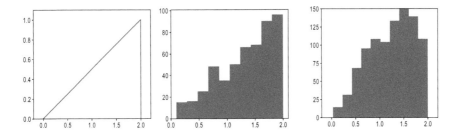

Fig. 6.4 Example of probability function (left) and corresponding uniform samples (middle) and MCMC samples (right).

Listing 6.4 MCMC.ipynb (part 3)

```
current = 1
sample=np.array([])

for i in range(nsample):
    flag = 1
    while flag == 1:
        proposal = current + 0.4*np.random.rand()-0.2
        if (proposal > 0 and proposal < 2): flag=0
    if np.random.rand() < proposal/current:
        current=proposal
        sample=np.append(sample,proposal)
plt.hist(sample)
sample.shape
```

We choose thereby arbitrarily the first current position at $x = 1$. We then produce a proposal position by taking a random step. This formally builds a Markov chain as the new position only depends on the current position. We chose in this example a uniform distribution between -0.2 and 0.2 for the step. We could have taken other steps. For example, the Metropolis algorithm that we describe here traditionally takes a Gaussian distributed step, and some modern algorithms consider even better choices for specific problem classes. The important next step of the algorithm is to accept the proposal if a uniform random number is smaller than the ratio of the probability of the proposal versus the probability of the current position, namely

$$p(\text{accept}) = \frac{p(\text{proposal})}{p(\text{current})}. \qquad (6.57)$$

If the probability of the proposal is larger than the probability of the current sample, then we will always accept the proposal. This in itself is a hill-climbing algorithm. However, we also sometimes need to take the other direction, and this ratio guarantees that for long chains this random walk converges to the target distribution. In this example, we also restricted the proposal values to the range between 0 and 2 in order to compare the results directly with the previous case, although this method would rarely produce proposals far outside this range. This method produced around 950 valid samples. In practice, one should always run this algorithm for a while first so that the dependence on the initial conditions is minimized. Furthermore, the step width and samples should be chosen so that they are independent. For this, it is a good practice to study the correlation coefficient between samples in the chain.

We have introduced the MCMC method with a simple example of generating random variables. This method is very important as it can be used to calculate general posteriors. More specifically, the MCMC is a method to calculate posterior distributions without the need to evaluate the denominator, also called the partition function, which is usually intractable. That is,

$$p(x|y) \sim \frac{p(x_{\text{proposal}}|y)}{p(x_{\text{current}}|y)} \tag{6.58}$$

$$= \frac{\frac{p(y|x_{\text{proposal}})p(x_{\text{proposal}})}{p(y)}}{\frac{p(y|x_{\text{current}})p(x_{\text{current}})}{p(y)}} \tag{6.59}$$

$$= \frac{p(y|x_{\text{proposal}})p(x_{\text{proposal}})}{p(y|x_{\text{current}})p(x_{\text{current}})}. \tag{6.60}$$

Thus, the intractable denominator cancels out in this ratio. The only problem with this method is that it can take considerable computational resources so that other methods might be considered such as building generative models as discussed later in this book.

7 Probabilistic regression and Bayes nets

We discussed a linear model and linear regression in Chapter 5, and we will now revise this method to include a description of uncertainty in the data. This will show us how modern probabilistic machine learning can be formulated. We follow first a simple stochastic generalization of the linear regression example to introduce the formalism. This leads to the important maximum likelihood principle on which we will base learning. We later generalize this idea to non-linear problems in higher dimensions and relate this to Bayes nets. After this, we will discuss how such a probabilistic approach is related to deep learning.

7.1 Probabilistic models

We again consider supervised learning where examples of input–output relations are given and our goal is to make a model that can make predictions of previously unseen data. The main difference is that we do not only want to make a prediction of a value, but we would also like to know how probable different values are. Let us consider an example from robotics where we want to model how far a terrestrial robot is moving when the wheels are turning for a given number of seconds after activating the corresponding motors with a certain power. Figure 7.1A shows a Lego Mindstorm robot that has two motorized wheels and an ultrasonic distance motor attached to it. We want to model (or predict) how far this robot moves when both motors are driven for a certain amount of time.

The i-th training data are denoted by the pairs $(x^{(i)}, y^{(i)})$, where the feature inputs $x^{(i)}$ is the time in seconds we let both motors run, and the outputs or labels y is the distance that the robot traveled. The true distance traveled has to be provided by the teacher, most likely in the form of measurements such as from using a ruler or as sensor that measures distance such as a laser range-finder or an ultrasonic sensor. To automate the collection of data we use an ultrasonic sensor to measure the distance to a wall while driving the robot for different amounts of times forward and backward. The ultrasonic data are now the teacher feedback, and the teacher's data are considered the ground truth and will not be questioned here. The point is that later we do not need the teacher (ultrasonic sensor) to predict how far the robot travels.

Figure 7.1B shows several measurements of the distance traveled for different times the motors are activated. The data clearly reveal some systematic relation between the time of running the motor and the distance traveled, the general trend being that the traveled distance increases with increasing running time of the motors. While there seems to be some noise in the data, the outliers and the noise cannot hide a linear trend

Fundamentals of Machine Learning, Thomas P. Trappenberg, Oxford University Press (2020).
© Oxford University Press. DOI: 10.1093/oso/9780198828044.001.0001

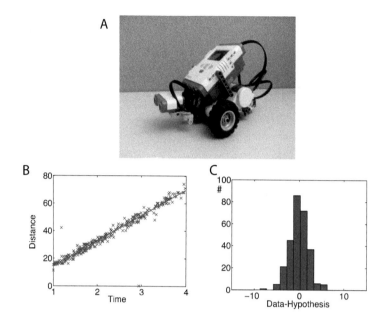

Fig. 7.1 (A) A terrestrial robot build with Lego Mindstorm with an ultrasonic sensor at the front. (B) Measurements of distance travelled by a robot when running the motor for different numbers of milliseconds with a given power. (C) Corresponding histogram of differences between data and a line that is fitted by minimizing the the mean square error between the data points and the line.

for most of the data. Let us therefore run a linear regression as discussed in Chapter 5 with the model,

$$\hat{y}(x; \mathbf{w}) = w_0 + w_1 x. \tag{7.1}$$

We only considered one input variable x above, but we can easily generalize this to higher-dimensional problems where more input attributes are given. For example, another factor that influences the distance traveled is the power setting of the motor. Of course, the distance traveled within a certain time does depend on the power and it is not just an independent additive effect on the travelled distance. Results of the experiment for different power settings and different travel times are show in Fig. 7.2. Fig. 7.2A also includes a fit to Eqn 7.2. However, these data are better described by a bi-linear hypothesis,

$$\hat{y}(\mathbf{x}; \mathbf{w}) = w_0 + w_1 x_1 x_2. \tag{7.2}$$

The corresponding fit of the data is also shown in Figure 7.2A. Sometimes we do not know all the factors. For example, we might not be given the power settings of the motors in this experiment so that the data look as shown in Figure 7.2C. These data look more noisy than the previous data, although we know that this is not really noise but, rather, unknown factors. The point of including this example is basically that it does not really matter if this randomness may come from an **irreducible indeterminacy**; that is, true randomness in the world that can not be penetrated by further knowledge, or this noise might represent **epistemological limitations** such as the lack of knowledge of hidden processes or limitations in observing states directly. The only important fact for us is that we have to live with these limitations. The inclusion of describing uncertainty has helped to make large progress in machine learning.

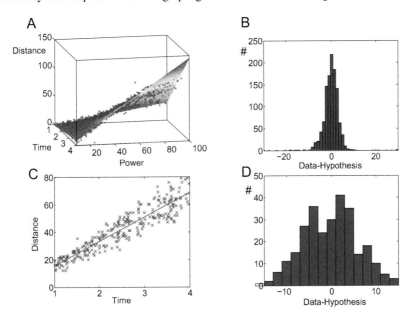

Fig. 7.2 (A) Measurements of distance travelled by the robot when running the motor for different number of milliseconds and various power settings. Fit according to Eqn 7.2 (B) Histogram of differences between data and hypothesis. (C) The same data as shown in (A) when collapsed across the power setting. The corresponding distribution shown in (D) is much wider than the histogram shown in Fig. 7.1.

We have so far basically ignored the fluctuations in the data with the functional regression procedure, and we now investigate more the fluctuations around this trend. Fig. 7.1C, 7.2B, and 7.2D are plots of the histogram of the differences between the actual data and the (linear) functional hypothesis of the above regressions. The histograms look a lot like a Gaussian distribution. This is not so surprising since according to the central limit theorem, a Gaussian can be expected as a result result of a variety of independent noise sources and this distribution is hence often observed in nature.

In the following, we will assume that the input values $\mathbf{x}$ are given and hence that they are not random variables. However, all the following derivations are easily modified if we treat these variables also at random. In this case we would use for the data the density function

$$p(\hat{y}, \mathbf{x}|\boldsymbol{w}) = p(\hat{y}|\mathbf{x}; \boldsymbol{w})p(\mathbf{x}). \tag{7.3}$$

In this example, we have actually chosen the x-values from a uniform distribution so that the factor $p(x)$ would be a constant or 0 so that it would not matter anyhow. It therefore does not really matter in the following example. We only mention this fact here as many textbooks on Bayesian statistics consider density functions of data given parameters, $p(D|\mathbf{w})$, and we just want to highlight that we will maintain consistent notation although we use the more common model in machine learning where we only consider the predicted value as random.

Of course, as with the deterministic case, we have to come up with a specific parameterized function, a density function with parameters $\mathbf{w}$. Let us do this for this robot example. Guided by the form of the "noise" in the above robot example, we assume here that the mean of the data follow our previous deterministic model $\hat{y}(\mathbf{x};\mathbf{w})$ with additive Gaussian noise, or with other words, that the data in Fig. 7.1C are Gaussian distributed with a mean $\mu = \hat{y}(x)$ that depends linearly on the value of x,

$$p(\hat{y}|x;\mathbf{w},\sigma) = N(\mu = \mathbf{w}^T\mathbf{x},\sigma) \tag{7.4}$$

$$= \frac{1}{\sqrt{2\pi}\sigma}\exp\left(-\frac{(\hat{y}-\mathbf{w}^T\mathbf{x})^2}{2\sigma^2}\right). \tag{7.5}$$

This functions specifies the likelihood (probability) of values for $\hat{y}$, given an input x and the model with parameters $\mathbf{w}$ and σ. In the following, we keep the parameter σ at a specific value so that we only consider the variables $\mathbf{w}$ as free. This simply helps to keep the formulae manageable for illustration purposes, though including a possible variable variance it is also possible.

Specifying a model with a density function is an important step in modern modelling and machine learning. In this type of thinking, we treat data from the outset as fundamentally stochastic. That is, data can be different even in situations that we have identical inputs. We have just specified a specific probabilistic model for the example robot data.

7.2 Learning in probabilistic models: Maximum likelihood estimate

We will now turn to the important principle that will guide our learning process. Learning means, of course, determining the parameters of the model from example data. Here we introduce the important **maximum likelihood principle**. This principle states that we choose the parameters in a probabilistic model in the following way:

> Given a parameterize hypothesis function $p(y,\mathbf{x}|\mathbf{w})$, we will chose as parameters the values which make the training data $\{y,\mathbf{x}\}$ most likely under the assumption of the model.

The MLE principle is stated here again in its most general form for all random data. In our case, we start with a model of the form $p(y|\mathbf{x};\mathbf{w})$ which specifies a probabilistic regression model for given input data. This is why the input data appear on the right side of the horizontal bar. However, we will see shortly that in MLE we replace all the data at some point with the training data so that we end up with a function (the likelihood function) that is a function of the parameters. Hence, in this case it does not matter if we treat the input data as given or as random variables themselves.

Let us illustrate this on the Gaussian example above with the parameterized model (Eqn 7.5). We are considering the 1-dimensional case with one feature value, x. Given parameters w_0, w_1, and assuming that $\sigma = 1$ to simplify the discussions, and the feature value for the first data point $x^{(1)}$, then the prediction of the probability of the corresponding label is

$$p(Y_1 = y^{(1)}|x^{(1)}; w_0, w_1) = \frac{1}{\sqrt{2\pi}} \exp\left(-\frac{(y^{(1)} - w_0 - w_1 x^{(1)})^2}{2}\right). \qquad (7.6)$$

Now we invoke the maximum likelihood principle and ask which parameters we should choose so that the observed data would be most likely under the model with these parameters. That is, we can maximize the probability so that $y = y^{(1)}$. This can be achieved by choosing values

$$w_1 = \text{arbitrary} \qquad (7.7)$$
$$w_0 = y^{(1)} - w_1 x^{(1)}. \qquad (7.8)$$

This is our first **maximum likelihood estimate (MLE)** of the parameters w_0 and w_1. Of course, since we have more parameters than data points there is a whole manifold of solutions and it is clear that we need more than one data point to make better predictions. In order to do this, we need to know the probability of a combination of data points. For example, let's say we have two data points $(x^{(1)}, y^{(1)})$ and $(x^{(2)}, y^{(2)})$. We then need to know the joint distribution of having the values for two labels with specific values. We have not specified a model for this until now. We can do this by making the assumption that the data points are conditionally independent; that is

$$p(Y_1 = y^{(1)}, \ Y_2 = y^{(2)}|x^{(1)}, x^{(2)}; w_0, w_1) =$$
$$p(Y_1 = y^{(1)} \ |x^{(1)}, x^{(2)}; w_0, w_1) p(Y_2 = y^{(2)}|x^{(1)}, x^{(2)}; w_0, w_1). \qquad (7.9)$$

In general, if we have m samples, and if we assume that the observation are all conditionally independent, the joint probability of several observations is the product of the individual probabilities,

$$p(Y_1 = y^{(1)}, Y_2 = y^{(2)}, ..., Y_m = y^{(m)}|\mathbf{x}_1, \mathbf{x}_2, ..., \mathbf{x}_m; \boldsymbol{w}) = \Pi_i^m p(y_i|\mathbf{x}_i; \boldsymbol{w}). \qquad (7.10)$$

We have written this formula again for a general case where all the parameters are collected in the vector $\mathbf{w}$, and y_i is a short form of $Y_i = y^{(i)}$. We can now insert the specific observations (training data) into the resulting function. We then arrive at a function that is a function of the parameters, no longer a probability function for random variables. This function is equivalent to the functional form Eqn 7.6, but this is now a function of the parameters that estimates the probability from the data. This function is called the **likelihood function**

$$L(\boldsymbol{w}) = \Pi_i^m p(\boldsymbol{w}; y^{(i)}, \mathbf{x}^{(i)}). \qquad (7.11)$$

Since this function it is not a probability density function, we replaced the notation of the vertical bar "|" with the semi-colon ";".

We are nearly done. Instead of evaluating this large product, it is common to use the logarithm of the likelihood function, so that we can use the sum over the training examples,

$$l(\boldsymbol{w}) = \log L(\boldsymbol{w}) = \sum_i^m \log(p(\boldsymbol{w}; y^{(i)}, \mathbf{x}^{(i)})). \qquad (7.12)$$

The logarithmic function increases monotonically. Hence, the maximum of L is also the maximum of l. The maximum (log-)likelihood can thus be calculated from the training data as

$$w^{\text{MLE}} = \text{argmax}_{\boldsymbol{w}} l(\boldsymbol{w}; x^{(1)}, ..., x^{(m)}). \tag{7.13}$$

Of course, we still have to find the maximum in practice. We might be able to calculate this analytically or use one of the search algorithms to find a maximum from this function like a gradient ascent.

Let us apply this to the Gaussian model of the robot example. The log-likelihood function of our hypothesis function for this example is

$$l(\mathbf{w}) = \log \Pi_{i=1}^{m} \frac{1}{\sqrt{2\pi}} \exp\left(-\frac{(y^{(i)} - \mathbf{w}^T \mathbf{x}^{(i)})^2}{2}\right) \tag{7.14}$$

$$= \sum_{i=1}^{m} \left(\log \frac{1}{\sqrt{2\pi}} - \frac{(y^{(i)} - \mathbf{w}^T \mathbf{x}^{(i)})^2}{2}\right) \tag{7.15}$$

or

$$l(\mathbf{w}) = -\frac{m}{2} \log 2\pi - \sum_{i=1}^{m} \frac{(y^{(i)} - \mathbf{w}^T \mathbf{x}^{(i)})^2}{2}. \tag{7.16}$$

Here you can see why the log is a good choice as we can look at a sum instead having a long product of potentially very small numbers. Since the first term in the expression in Eqn 7.16, $-\frac{m}{2} \log 2\pi$, is independent of $\mathbf{w}$, maximizing the log-likelihood function is equivalent to minimizing (because of the minus sign) a quadratic error term

$$E = \frac{1}{2}(y - h(\mathbf{x}; \mathbf{w}))^2 \iff p(y|\mathbf{x}; \mathbf{w}) = \frac{1}{\sqrt{2\pi}} \exp(-\frac{(y - h(\mathbf{x}; \mathbf{w}))^2}{2}). \tag{7.17}$$

This is the square-error loss function, or least mean square (LMS) error if we consider a batch algorithm and divide the value by the number of examples in the batch. This loss function has long been the choice for linear regression. It has also been dominant in machine learning approaches such as multilayer perceptrons for a long time. In terms of our probabilistic view, the LMS regression is equivalent to MLE for Gaussian data with linear dependence of the mean and a constant variance.

However, these assumptions may or may not hold in different applications. The data themselves might not be Gaussian, and even if they are, than the variance might be different for different feature inputs. In this case we would need to minimize Eqn 7.16 with a sigma in the denominator instead. Also, the mean itself might vary in a non-linear way with the parameters. Thus, the point here is the following: a Gaussian model of noise is clearly a good general choice due to the central limit theorem. However, it is possible that there are better choices for specific applications that can result in superior predictions.

We have discussed Gaussian distributed data in most of this section, but one can similarly find corresponding loss functions for other distributions. For example, a **polynomial loss function** correspond more generally to a density model of the form

$$E = \frac{1}{p}||y - h(\mathbf{x}; \mathbf{w})||^p \iff p(y|\mathbf{x}; \mathbf{w}) = \frac{1}{2\Gamma(1/p)} \exp(-||y - h(\mathbf{x}; \mathbf{w})||^p). \tag{7.18}$$

As mention in the discussion of support vector regression, there it is common to use the ε-**insensitive loss function**, where errors less than a constant ϵ do not contribute to the error measure, only errors above this value. The corresponding probabilistic models in this case is

$$E = ||y - h(\mathbf{x}; \mathbf{w})||_\epsilon \Longleftrightarrow p(y|\mathbf{x}; \mathbf{w}) = \frac{p}{2(1 - \epsilon)} \exp(-||y - h(\mathbf{x}; \mathbf{w})||_\epsilon). \quad (7.19)$$

We only mention these examples to show that probabilistic regression can be seen as regressing a deterministic model with an appropriate loss function that depends on the nature of the noise.

7.3 Probabilistic classification

We have already encountered classification methods such as support vector machines and decision trees. We now argue that classification can be seen as an important special case of probabilistic regression. In classification, features are mapped to a finite number of possible categories. We now discuss binary classification again, which is the case of only two target classes where the target function (y-values) might have two possible values such as 0 and 1. Later, we can easily generalize the ideas to more classes. We start here by describing a binary random variable.

7.3.1 MLE of the Bernoulli model

An important probabilistic model of a binary random variable is the Bernoulli model. In this model, a random number which takes the value of 1 with probability ϕ, and the value 0 with probability $1 - \phi$ (the probability of being either of the two choices has to be 1.). That can be nicely combined in the formula,

$$p(y) = \phi^y (1 - \phi)^{1-y}. \quad (7.20)$$

Such a random variable is called Bernoulli distribution. A Bernoulli distribution is hence characterized by one parameter, ϕ. Tossing a coin is a good example of a Bernoulli process (a process of generating such random numbers). We can use maximum likelihood estimation, MLE, to estimate the parameter ϕ from such trials. That is, let us consider m tosses in which h heads have been found. The log-likelihood of such m trials is

$$l(\phi) = log \prod_i \phi^{y^{(i)}} (1 - \phi)^{1-y^{(i)}} \quad (7.21)$$

$$= \log(\phi^h (1 - \phi)^{m-h}) \quad (7.22)$$

$$= h \log(\phi) + (m - h) \log(1 - \phi). \quad (7.23)$$

To find the maximum with respect to ϕ we set the derivative of l with repect to the parameters ϕ to 0,

$$\frac{\mathrm{d}l}{\mathrm{d}\phi} = \frac{h}{\phi} - \frac{m - h}{1 - \phi} \quad (7.24)$$

$$= 0 \tag{7.25}$$

$$\rightarrow \quad \phi = \frac{h}{m}. \tag{7.26}$$

As one might have expected, the maximum likelihood estimate of the parameter ϕ is the fraction of heads in m trials.

7.3.2 Logistic regression

In machine learning we usually consider the case of classification when the parameter ϕ, depends on an attribute x. We can thus write down a probability model like

$$p(y = 1|\mathbf{x}; \mathbf{w}) = f(\mathbf{x}; \mathbf{w}) \tag{7.27}$$

$$p(y = 0|\mathbf{x}; \mathbf{w}) = 1 - f(\mathbf{x}; \mathbf{w}), \tag{7.28}$$

where $f(\mathbf{x}; \mathbf{w}$ is a specific hypothesis function that we need to specify further. We can combine the probabilities into one expression,

$$p(y|\mathbf{x}; \mathbf{w}) = (f(\mathbf{x}; \mathbf{w}))^y (1 - f(\mathbf{x}; \mathbf{w}))^{1-y} \tag{7.29}$$

The corresponding log-likelihood function is

$$l(\mathbf{w}) = \sum_{i=1}^{m} y^{(i)} \, log(f(\mathbf{x}; \mathbf{w})) + (1 - y^{(i)}) \, log(1 - f(\mathbf{x}; \mathbf{w})). \tag{7.30}$$

To find the corresponding maximum we can use the gradient ascent algorithm, which is like the gradient descent algorithm with a changed sign,

$$\mathbf{w} \leftarrow \mathbf{w} + \alpha \nabla_{\mathbf{w}} l(\mathbf{w}). \tag{7.31}$$

To calculate the gradient we can calculate the partial derivative of the log-likelihood function with respect to each parameters,

$$\frac{\partial l(\mathbf{w})}{\partial w_j} = \left(y \frac{1}{f} - (1 - y) \frac{1}{1 - f} \right) \frac{\partial f(\mathbf{w})}{\partial w_j} \tag{7.32}$$

where we dropped indices for better readability.

Let us apply this to logistic regression. An example of 100 sample points of two classes (crosses and stars) are shown in Fig. 7.3. The data suggest that it is far more likely that the class is $y = 0$ for small values of x and that the class is $y = 1$ for large values of x, and the probabilities are more similar in between. Thus, we put forward the hypothesis that the transition between the low and high probability region is smooth and qualify this hypothesis as parameterized density function known as a logistic function or sigmoid function

$$f(\mathbf{x}; \mathbf{w}) = \frac{1}{1 + \exp(-\mathbf{w}^T \mathbf{x})}. \tag{7.33}$$

As before, we can treat this density function as function of the parameters $\mathbf{w}$ for the given data values (likelihood function), and use maximum likelihood estimation to

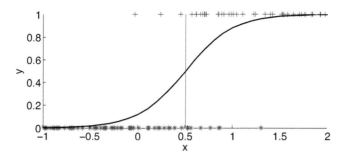

Fig. 7.3 Binary random numbers (stars) drawn from the density $p(y=1) = \frac{1}{1+\exp(-w_1 x - w_0)}$ (solid line).

estimate values for the parameters so that the data are most likely. The density function with sigmoidal offset $w_0 = 2$ and slope $w_1 = 4$ is plotted as solid line in Fig. 7.3.

We can now calculate the derivative of the hypothesis function f with respect to the parameters for the specific choice of the logistic functions. This is given by

$$\frac{\partial f}{\partial w} = \frac{\partial}{\partial w}\frac{1}{1+e^{-wx}} \tag{7.34}$$

$$= \frac{1}{(1+e^{-wx})^2}e^{-wx}(-x) \tag{7.35}$$

$$= \frac{1}{(1+e^{-wx})}(1 - \frac{1}{(1+e^{-wx})})(-x) \tag{7.36}$$

$$= -f(1-f)x \tag{7.37}$$

Using this in Eqn 7.32 and inserting it into Eqn 7.31 with the identity

$$\left(y\frac{1}{f} - (1-y)\frac{1}{1-f}\right)f(1-f) = y(1-f) - (1-y)f \tag{7.38}$$

$$= y - yf - f + yf \tag{7.39}$$

$$= y - f \tag{7.40}$$

gives the learning rule

$$w_j \leftarrow w_j + \alpha\left(y^{(i)} - f(\mathbf{x}^{(i)};\mathbf{w})\right)x_j^{(i)} \tag{7.41}$$

This is an interesting result since this learning rule for logistic regression is similar to the learning rule for linear regression on Gaussian data. Also, logistic regression is equivalent to a simple neural network called a perceptron for which this learning rule was proposed on heuristic grounds in the 1950s, and it is usually called the perceptron learning rule. Our derivation shows that this old heuristic learning rule relates to assumptions of a probabilistic model.

How can we use the knowledge (estimate) of the density function with parameters given after learning to do classification? The obvious choice is to predict the class with the higher probability, given the input attribute. This **Bayesian decision point**, x^t, or dividing hyperplane in higher dimensions, is given by

$$p(y = 1|x^t) = p(y = 0|x^t) = 0.5 \rightarrow x^t \mathbf{w}^T \mathbf{x^t} = 0. \qquad (7.42)$$

We have here considered binary classification with linear decision boundaries as logistic regression, and we can also generalize this method to problems with non-linear decision boundaries by considering hypothesis functions with different functional forms. As already stressed earlier, neural networks are a common way to specify more complex hypothesis functions.

7.4 Maximum a posteriori (MAP) and regularization with priors

Before moving to more complex multivariate models,this is a good opportunity to discuss regularization again within a Bayesian framework. Maximum likelihood estimation is the workhorse of probabilistic supervised learning, though it is useful to put this even into a wider context of probabilistic modeling. In the probabilistic sense, choosing parameters values, given data, should be based on a model of the parameters themselves,

$$p(\mathbf{w}|\mathbf{x}, y). \qquad (7.43)$$

Let us assume we can know this conditional distribution. For example, let us assume it looks like the 1-dimensional example shown in Fig. 7.4. If we know this distribution we can pick a parameter value that we like. For example, we could pick the value w_1, which is the most probable value given the specific data. This is called the **maximum a posteriori (MAP)**

$$\mathbf{w}^{\mathrm{MAP}} = \mathrm{argmax}_{\mathbf{w}} p(\mathbf{w}|\mathbf{x}, y). \qquad (7.44)$$

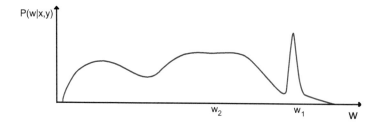

Fig. 7.4 Example of a possible probability distribution of a parameter w given some data.

The main difficulty with MAP or using another procedure based on the distribution $p(\boldsymbol{w}|\mathbf{x}, y)$ is that we usually do not know this distribution a priori. Instead, our approach has been to formulate a probabilistic model in the form of a parameterized density function like

$$p(y|\mathbf{x}; \mathbf{w}). \qquad (7.45)$$

We will now discuss the relation of these density functions. To start with, in the probabilistic model of Eqn 7.45, we assumed that the feature data are magically given, but we could also consider how we select data values in a randomized fashion so that we can again consider the more general case

$$p(y, \mathbf{x}|\mathbf{w}) = p(y|\mathbf{x}; \mathbf{w})p(\mathbf{x}|\mathbf{w}) \tag{7.46}$$

Again, if we pick the training data uniformly, so that the marginal distribution over the features is just a constant, then

$$p(y, \mathbf{x}|\mathbf{w}) \propto p(y|\mathbf{x}; \mathbf{w}). \tag{7.47}$$

Next, we can use Bayes theorem to relate the posterior $p(\mathbf{w}|\mathbf{x}, y)$ to the data model, namely

$$p(\mathbf{w}|\mathbf{x}, y) = \frac{p(y, \mathbf{x}|\mathbf{w})p(\mathbf{w})}{\int_{\mathbf{w}' \in W} p(\mathbf{x}, y|\mathbf{w}')p(\mathbf{w}')\mathrm{d}\mathbf{w}'}, \tag{7.48}$$

where W is the domain of the possible parameter values.

This expression can be used to estimate the most likely values for the parameters. For this we should notice that the denominator, which is called the **partition function**, does not depend on the parameters $\mathbf{w}$ as we are integrating (summing) over all possible values. The most likely values for the parameters can thus be calculated without this term and are given by the maximum a posteriori (MAP) estimate,

$$\boldsymbol{w}^{\mathrm{MAP}} = \mathrm{argmax}_{\mathbf{w}} p(\mathbf{x}, y|\boldsymbol{w})p(\boldsymbol{w}). \tag{7.49}$$

The name of the method comes from the fact that we modify our prior knowledge of parameters, which is summarized as prior distribution $p(\boldsymbol{w})$ by combining this to measurements $(\mathbf{x}, y)$ from specific realizations of the parameters, which is given by the likelihood function $p(\mathbf{x}, y|\boldsymbol{w})$. The resulting posterior distribution should then be a better estimate of the probability of values for the parameters. The function $\mathrm{argmax}_x(f(x))$ picks the argument x for which the function $f(x)$ is maximal. The argument of the function is the set of parameters that is, in a Bayesian sense, the most likely value for the parameters, where, of course, we now treat the probability function as a function of the parameters (e.g., a likelihood function). For a uniform prior, $p(\mathbf{w}) = const$, we get

$$\mathbf{w}^{\mathrm{MAP}} = \mathbf{w}^{\mathrm{MLE}}. \tag{7.50}$$

While a uniform prior of the parameters has been an easy first choice, we can think of other priors. Indeed, this can give us a great insight into regularization from a probabilistic perspective. In section 5.4 we introduced L^p regularization by introducing a bias in the parameters. In the probabilistic models we can do this very elegantly by providing a prior for the parameters that encapsulate the bias in the choice of parameter as argued previously. For example, let us assume that the values of the parameters should more likely be small than large. More specifically, let's assume that we think they should be normal distributed around 0. Then we can write the MAP estimate (Eqn 7.49) as

$$\boldsymbol{w}^{\mathrm{MAP}} = \mathrm{argmax}_{\mathbf{w}} p(\mathbf{x}, y|\boldsymbol{w})\mathcal{N}(0, \sigma^2). \tag{7.51}$$

As usual, we maximize the logarithm of the corresponding likelihood functions instead, which leads to

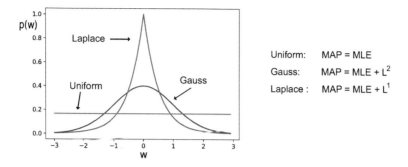

Fig. 7.5 Three distribution commonly used as priors for the parameters when learning together with a maximum likelihood estimate.

$$\boldsymbol{w}^{\mathrm{MAP}} = \mathrm{argmax}_{\mathbf{w}} \log(p(\mathbf{x}, y|\boldsymbol{w})) + \alpha||w||^2, \qquad (7.52)$$

with

$$\alpha = \log \frac{1}{2\sigma^2}. \qquad (7.53)$$

Thus, our previously discussed L^2 regularization corresponds to a Gaussian prior on the weights. Similarly, L^1 regularization correspond to a prior of a isotropic Laplace distribution

$$p(\mathbf{w}) = \frac{1}{2\,b} \exp\left(-\frac{|\mathbf{w}|}{b}\right), \qquad (7.54)$$

which is more peaked towards 0 as can be seen by a comparison of these distributions in Fig. 7.5. Hence the L^1 regularization forces more weights towards 0 compared to the L^2 regularization. This is another example showing how a probabilistic interpretation sheds some light on techniques that have been originally introduced more heuristically. A simple summary of the three priors and their resulting equivalence between MLE and MAP is shown in the table on the right of the figure.

Finally, while we have discussed the common quantities of MAP and MLE in machine learning, it is good to realize that both learning methods only give us a **point estimate**, a single answer for the most likely values of the parameters given a specific data set from which this likelihood has to be estimated. A point estimate is commonly used to make decisions about which actions to take. However, it is possible that other sets of parameter values might only have a little smaller likelihood value, and the situation could quickly change with a few more data points. It is therefore much more prudent to consider also other values. For example, looking again at the example in Fig. 7.4, another strategy might be to pick a weight value in a range where variations in this value would not change the probability considerably in some range, such as values around w_2.

Moreover, in a Bayesian sense, all other choices should be taken into account with their corresponding likelihood. This is particularly true when estimating our confidence for an estimation. In a Bayesian sense, we need to combine all possible estimates with their likelihood. Thus, a limit of the maximum estimation methods discussed earlier, which are dominating much of the current practices in machine learning applications, is that they do not take distribution of answers into account. Some people thus distinguish machine learning from more advanced probabilistic programming. While such advanced probabilistic modeling techniques can give us answer to much deeper questions, the machine learning methods discussed in this book with point estimates are commonly easier to apply to high-dimensional problems.

7.5 Bayes nets: multivariate causal modeling

7.5.1 Causal models

In the previously discussed probabilistic regression examples, we mainly considered models for one random variable, or at most two. We now consider more complex models with many more factors described by random variables. Probability theory nicely generalizes to multiple random variables. Multivariate cases are simply described by a joint probability as outlined in the review of probability theory.

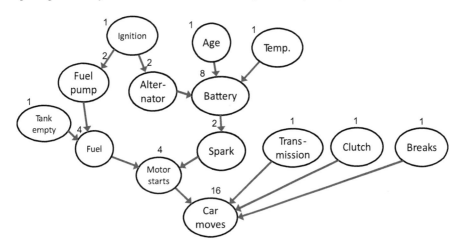

Fig. 7.6 Example of a causal model to diagnose car starting problems (adapted from Sebastian Thrun, MOOC on AI, 2011). While the joint density function of this model has 16,383 parameters, the corresponding causal model has only 45 parameters.

An example adapted from Sebastian Thrun of a model to diagnose when a car is not starting is shown in Fig. 7.6. This example is reasonably sized, although real-world problems would probably be even larger than this. This model considered fourteen random numbers to determine possible causes if the car does not start (the variable "car does not start" is not a random number as we are using this model when we already know that the car is not starting). The random numbers themselves could have two possible outcomes (such as if there is gas in the tank), or even multiple possible values (such as the age of the battery). Now time let us simplify the model by only considering binary values. That is, the age of the battery would only be specified as new or old. The joined probability table for the 14 variables would then have $2^{14} - 1 = 16383$ entries. These parameters have to be estimated (learned) from examples using MAP or MLE.

In addition to the sheer explosion of parameters with increasing model complexity, there is another reason why the joined probability function is not exactly what we need to know. The joint density functions of multiple variables describe the co-occurrence of specific values of the random variables. For example, the joint probability function $p(X, Y)$ is symmetric in its arguments,

$$p(X, Y) = p(Y, X). \tag{7.55}$$

What we really want to do is to a model to reason about the world, or specifically, to reason about possible events. For this, we want to add knowledge or hypotheses about **causal relations**. For example, a fire alarm should be triggered by a fire, although there is some small chance that the alarm will not sound when the unit is defective. However, it is (hopefully) unlikely that the sound of a fire alarm will trigger a fire. It is useful to illustrate such casual relations with graphs such as

In such **graphical models**, the nodes represent random variables, and the links between them represent causal relations with conditional probabilities, $p(A|F)$. Since we use arrows on the links, we discuss here **directed graphs**, and we also restrict our discussions here to graphs that have no loops, so called **acyclic graphs**. **Directed acyclic graphs** are also called **DAGs**.

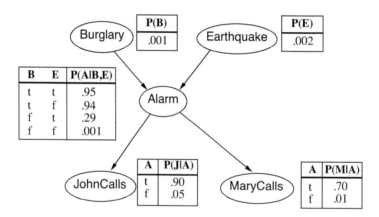

Fig. 7.7 Example of causal model.

Graphical causal models have been advanced largely by Judea Pearl, and the following example is taken from his book.[5]. The model is shown in Fig. 7.7 Each of the five nodes stands for a random binary variable (Burglary B={yes,no}, Earthquake E={yes,no}, Alarm A={yes,no}, John calls J={yes,no}, Mary calls M={yes,no}) The figure also include **conditional probability tables (CPTs)** that specify the conditional probabilities represented by the links between the nodes.

---

[5] Judea Pearl, *Causality: Models, Reasoning and Inference*, Cambridge University Press 2000, 2009.

The joint distribution of the five variables can be factored in various ways following the chain rule mentioned earlier (Eqn 6.35), for example as

$$p(B, E, A, J, M) = P(B|E, A, J, M)P(E|A, J, M)P(A|J, M)P(J|M)P(M).$$
(7.56)

However, the causal model represents a specific factorization of the joint probability functions, namely

$$p(B, E, A, J, M) = P(B)P(E)P(A|B, E)P(J|A)P(M|A),$$
(7.57)

which is much easier to handle. For example, if we do not know the conditional probability functions, we need to run many more experiments to estimate the various conditions ($2^4 + 2^3 + 2^2 + 2^1 + 2^0 = 31$) instead of the reduced conditions in the causal model ($1 + 1 + 2^2 + 2 + 2 = 10$). It is also easy to use the casual model to undertake inference (drawing conclusions), for specific questions. For example, say we want to know the probability that there was no earthquake or burglary when the alarm rings and both John and Mary call. This is given by

$$P(B = f, E = f, A = t, J = t, M = t)$$
$$= P(B = f)P(E = f,)P(A = t|B = f, E = f)P(J = t|A = t)P(M = t|A = t)$$
$$= 0.998 * 0.999 * 0.001 * 0.7 * 0.9$$
$$\approx 0.00062.$$

Although we have a casual model where parent variables influence the outcome of child variables, we can also use child evidence to infer some possible values of parent variables. For example, let us calculate the probability that the alarm rings, given that John calls, $P(A = t|J = t)$. For this, we should first calculate the probability that the alarm rings as we need this later. This is given by

$$P(A = t) = P(A = t|B = t, E = t)P(B = t)P(E = t) + ...$$
$$P(A = t|B = t, E = f)P(B = t)P(E = f) + ...$$
$$P(A = t|B = f, E = t)P(B = f)P(E = t) + ...$$
$$P(A = t|B = f, E = f)P(B = f)P(E = f)$$
$$= 0.95 * 0.001 * 0.002 + 0.94 * 0.001 * 0.998 + ...$$
$$0.29 * 0.999 * 0.002 + 0.001 * 0.999 * 0.998$$
$$= 0.002516442.$$

We can then use Bayes rule to calculate the required probability,

$$P(A = t|J = t) = \frac{P(J = t|A = t)P(A = t)}{P(J = t|A = t)P(A = t) + P(J = t|A = f)P(A = f)}$$
$$\approx \frac{0.9 * 0.0025}{0.9 * 0.0025 + 0.05 * 0.9975}$$
$$\approx 0.0434.$$

We can similarly apply the rules of probability theory to calculate other quantities, but these calculations can get cumbersome with larger graphs. It is therefore useful to use numerical tools to perform such inference. A Python toolbox for Bayesian networks is introduced in the next section.

While inference is an important application of causal models, inferring causality from data is another area where causal models revolutionize scientific investigations. Many traditional methods evaluate co-occurrences of events to determine dependencies, such as a correlation analysis. However, such a correlation analysis is usually not a good indication of causality. Consider the example in Fig. 7.7. When the alarm rings, it is likely that John and Mary call, but the event that John calls is mutually independent of the event that Mary calls. Yet, when John calls it is also statistically more likely to observe the event that Mary calls. Sometimes we might just be interested in knowing about the likelihood of co-occurrence, for which a correlation analysis can be a good start, but if we are interested in describing the causes of the observations, then we need another approach. Some algorithms have been proposed for **structural learning**, such as an algorithm called **inferred causation (IC)**, which deduces what the most likely causal structure behind given data is.

7.5.2   Discrete probabilistic modeling in Python using LEA

There are several tools for working with probabilistic models and Bayesian graphical models. A very prominent general probabilistic programming toolbox is Stan (<http://mc-stan.org>), but we will here give an example using the LEA3 (<http://bitbucket.org/piedenis/lea>) which is a simpler tool for working with discrete probabilities in Python. In particular, LEA has direct support for Bayesian models. This brief section is not meant to be a thorough introduction to this tool but merely to give an example in order to demonstrate the usefulnnes of such tools. We will show an example program for the burglary/earthquake example.

The main part of the program is to define the graph structure and the associated conditional probability tables. The corresponding code is fairly self-explanatory.

Listing 7.1 LeaExample.ipynb (part 1)

```
import lea

burglary   = lea.event(0.001)
earthquake = lea.event(0.002)
alarm = lea.joint(burglary,earthquake).switch({(True ,True ): lea.
    event(0.950),
        (True ,False) : lea.event(0.940),
        (False,True ) : lea.event(0.290),
        (False,False) : lea.event(0.001) })
johnCalls = alarm.switch({True: lea.event(0.90),
                          False: lea.event(0.05) })
maryCalls = alarm.switch({True: lea.event(0.70),
                          False : lea.event(0.01) })
```

This notation includes the specification of the discrete probabiity tables, and it contains the relations between the variables so that there is no need for a separate specification of the network graph.

Once the graph is specified it is possible to use some inference engines that build the heart of such tools. We have seen earlier that the continuous application of Bayes rule for variable elimination leads to the analytic answer for specific queries. Such exact computations for variable elimination can be implemented so that inference can be achieved by simple function calls. For example, if we want to know what the probability is that Mary calls given that there is an alarm, we ca write in LEA

Listing 7.2 LeaExample.ipynb (part 2)
```
P( maryCalls . given ( alarm ) )
```

The answer is 0.7, which can, of course, be directly read off the conditional probability table. A less obvious example is the probability of an alarm when John calls,

Listing 7.3 LeaExample.ipynb (part 3)
```
P( alarm . given ( johnCalls ) )
```

which recovers the 4 per cent that we calculated analytically in the last section. An even more advanced query of a joint probability is

Listing 7.4 LeaExample.ipynb (part 4)
```
P(˜burglary & ˜earthquake & alarm & johnCalls & maryCalls)
```

which is only a small probability of around 0.6 percent.

While exact methods for Bayesian inference are possible, a known factor is that these methods are slow and scale very badly for larger Bayesian networks. There are therefore various approximate inference techniques such as believe propagation, which is based on some message between the nodes in the graph and a minimization of the consistency of the samples. This discussion is, however, beyond the scope of this book.

7.6 Probabilistic and stochastic neural networks

7.6.1 Neural networks as probabilistic regression

As argued earlier, coming up with a parameterized model is often the hard part in machine learning. Up until this point we have tried to specify causal models with and explicit analytic expression for its components to specify a multinomial density function. In Chapter 4 we saw how we can use neural networks as a tool to specify complex functional models. The question now is how we can reconcile neural networks with the probabilistic view of modeling. We will here touch on three aspects of this discussion: that of generalistic versus specific models, that of representing probability functions, and that of stochastic models.

Let us start with the first issue: that of building specific functional descriptions for a specific problem that we want to model versus using neural networks that seem to offer a generic solution. We already discussed Wolpert's "No free lunch" theorem, and it is clear that we should not expect that high-dimensional machines are optimal compared to models that are close to the true underlying world model. However, in practice there is the problem of finding this specific model, and building a very general machine is one way of moving forward. Our strategy is thereby to use data and good regularizations based on useful priors to restrict the model from data. The recent success of deep learning is a testimony that this strategy can work in conjunction with "big data." However, the challenge of using this approach is greater in situations where there is a limited supply of data. Bayesian models and neural networks are often seen as extreme poles in a modeling apporach; here we try to reconcile these views.

Let us now move to the second important subject: how neural networks compare with our desire to build probabilistic models. This connection can be made easily when viewing a perceptron as an implementation of a logistic regression, as outlined in this chapter. The essence there was that a logistic function describes the probability that a data point belongs to one class versus another. In the same way, we are now treating the neural network itself as a function that calculates for each output node a value that represents the probability $p(class = true|x; w)$. For this we need to adapt a one-hot representation of training data in a multiclass problems where each class is represented by a single output node. The value of each output node of the neural network is then assumed to represent the probability that the input is from the corresponding class. We argue that the computational layers leading up to this output layer represent a transformations of features that is necessary to lead to the probabilistic function on which we can base our decision of class membership in classification.

In order to train the network we have already introduced the log-likelihood principle. We are now taking the opportunity to show an alternative way of deriving the learning rule of a neural network which is equivalent to maximum likelihood estimation but which is a more common derivation in the neural network community. Indeed, we will take this opportunity to relate this to several common formulations: that of minimizing the log-likelihood, maximizing the cross-entropy, and of minimizing the Kulback–Leibler divergence.

We start by assuming that the true nature of data is governed by the unknown density function

True data distribution: $q(y|\mathbf{x})$.

(7.58)

The neural network model represents the probability

Model distribution: $p(y|\mathbf{x}; \mathbf{w})$,

(7.59)

which we hope to be a good approximation of $q(y|\mathbf{x})$. The negative log-probability of the given label under the current model is then given by

$$H(p, q) = -\sum_{y} p(y) \log q(y),$$
(7.60)

where we omitted writing some arguments to see the structure more clearly. This quantity is called the **cross-entropy**. The term $p \log q$ is in essence the same as the log-likelihood estimate, which we want to maximize. That is, we want to maximize the log probability of the data given the labels. Since the cross-entropy is the negative of this, maximizing the log-probability of the data given the labels is equivalent of minimizing the cross-entropy. Furthermore, since

$$p \log(q) = p \log \frac{q}{p} + p \log p$$
(7.61)

and $p \log \frac{q}{p}$ is the Kullback–Leibler (KL) divergence, we can relate this the cross-entropy to the entropy of the distribution p an the KL divergence,

$$H(p,q) = H(p) + KL(p||q). \tag{7.62}$$

$$KL(p||q) = \int p(x) \log \frac{p(x)}{q(x)} dx. \tag{7.63}$$

Since changing model parameters does not effect the true data, minimizing the cross-entropy is equivalent to minimizing the KL divergence. This has an interesting interpretation as we can see the learning principle as looking for the parameters that minimize the distribution give by the data and the distribution given by the model. There are therefore many ways to derive the learning rule in neural network, and we hope it became apparent that they are equivalent and that these are closely related to the maximum (log-) likelihood principle.

Let us apply this to a binary classification model which is described by Bernoulli variables that take the value 0 or 1. For this density function, the cross-entropy is given by

$$H(p,q) = -p(y=0|\mathbf{x};\mathbf{w}) \log q(y=0|\mathbf{x}) - p(y=1|\mathbf{x};\mathbf{w}) \log q(y=1|\mathbf{x}) \tag{7.64}$$

or

$$H(p,q) = -p \log q - (1-p) \log (1-q) \tag{7.65}$$

for short, if we consider that p stands for $p(y = 0|\mathbf{x};\mathbf{w})$. We now assume again a sigmoidal function for the probability of the class membership around a decision point,

$$p(\hat{y} = 0|\mathbf{x};\mathbf{w}) = \frac{1}{1 + e^{-\mathbf{xw}}} \tag{7.66}$$

$$1 - p(\hat{y} = 0|\mathbf{x};\mathbf{w}) = \frac{1 + e^{-\mathbf{xw}} - 1}{1 + e^{-\mathbf{xw}}} = \frac{1}{1 + e^{\mathbf{xw}}}. \tag{7.67}$$

Hence, minimizing the cross-entropy between the network output $p(\hat{y})$ and the given labels y is given by minimizing the Loss function

$$L = -y \log p(\hat{y}) - (1-y) \log(1 - p(\hat{y})) \tag{7.68}$$

$$= y \log(1 + e^{-\mathbf{xw}}) + (1-y) \log(1 + e^{\mathbf{xw}}). \tag{7.69}$$

The derivative of the function is

$$\frac{dL}{d(\mathbf{xw})} = y \frac{-e^{-\mathbf{xw}}}{1 + e^{-\mathbf{xw}}} + (1-y) \frac{e^{\mathbf{xw}}}{1 + e^{\mathbf{xw}}} \tag{7.70}$$

$$= -y \frac{1}{1 + e^{\mathbf{xw}}} + (1-y) \frac{1}{1 + e^{-\mathbf{xw}}} \tag{7.71}$$

$$= -y(1 - p(\hat{y})) + (1-y)p(\hat{y}) \tag{7.72}$$

$$= -y + yp(\hat{y}) + p(\hat{y}) - yp(\hat{y}) \tag{7.73}$$

$$= p(\hat{y}) - y, \tag{7.74}$$

from which we can derive the gradient we need for the learning rule

$$\frac{dL}{d(\mathbf{w})} = \frac{dL}{d(\mathbf{xw})} \frac{d\mathbf{xw}}{d(\mathbf{w})} = (p(\hat{y}) - y)\mathbf{x}. \tag{7.75}$$

This expression has again the now familiar form of the perceptron learning rule.

For multi-class problems, the equivalent of the sigmoid is the **softmax function**

$$p(\hat{y} = i | \mathbf{x}; \mathbf{w}) = \frac{e^{\mathbf{x}\mathbf{W}_i}}{\sum_{j=1}^{N} e^{\mathbf{x}\mathbf{W}_j}}, \tag{7.76}$$

where N is the number of classes. You can easily see the equivalence to the sigmoid in the case of having two classes where one of them has input 0,

$$p(\hat{y} = 0) = \frac{e^0}{e^0 + e^{\mathbf{x}\mathbf{w}}} = \frac{1}{1 + e^{\mathbf{x}\mathbf{w}}} = 1 - \frac{1}{1 + e^{-\mathbf{x}\mathbf{w}}}$$
$$p(\hat{y} = 1) = \frac{e^{\mathbf{x}\mathbf{w}}}{e^0 + e^{\mathbf{x}\mathbf{w}}} = \frac{e^{\mathbf{x}\mathbf{w}}}{1 + e^{\mathbf{x}\mathbf{w}}} = \frac{1}{1 + e^{-\mathbf{x}\mathbf{w}}}$$

The derivation of the gradient for this multi-class case works out the same as the binary classification,

$$\frac{dL}{d(\mathbf{x}\mathbf{W})} = p(\hat{\mathbf{y}}) - \mathbf{y} \tag{7.77}$$

$$\frac{dL}{d\mathbf{x}} = (p(\hat{\mathbf{y}}) - \mathbf{y})\mathbf{W}^T \tag{7.78}$$

$$\frac{dL}{d\mathbf{W}} = \mathbf{x}^T(p(\hat{\mathbf{y}}) - \mathbf{y}) \tag{7.79}$$

Thus, in summary. A neural network, regardless of having many or few layers, is in this case an implementation of a probabilistic model for classification or logistic regression when the output layer is chosen to be a softmax function and the loss function is the negative cross-entropy. This concludes the discussion of our second point, how neural networks are related to probabilistic regression.

7.6.2 Stochastic and Bayesian neural networks

We have outlined how we can use a neural network as parameterized function approximator $y = f(\mathbf{x}; \mathbf{w})$. We have used this to approximate a probability function $p(y|\mathbf{x}; \mathbf{w})$ where we determined the parameters from a learning rule such as maximum likelihood estimation. In a Bayesian inference we usually want to go a step further where we want not just to use a point estimate of the parameters but know the posterior probability of all kind of values of the parameters that could have generated the training data, $p(\mathbf{w}|\mathbf{x}; \mathbf{y})$. With this function we could make true estimates of the probability of predictions of the label y^0 for a new data point $\mathbf{x}^0$,

$$p(y^0|\mathbf{x}^0; \mathbf{w}) = \int p(y|\mathbf{x}^0; \mathbf{w})p(\mathbf{w}|\mathbf{x}; \mathbf{y})d\mathbf{w} \tag{7.80}$$

Unfortunately, the posterior $p(\mathbf{w}|\mathbf{x}; \mathbf{y})$ is usually not tractable, and approximate techniques like variational inference have to be used. While a detailed discussion is beyond the scope of this book, we recommend work by David McKay, Radford Neal, and Zoubin Ghahramani for further studies.

Another way of looking into this is to consider the neurons themselves as stochastic so that the neural network forms a Bayesian network itself. For example, we could change the gain function of the artificial neuron to a stochastic rule, like

$$p(y = 1|\mathbf{x}; \mathbf{w}) = \frac{1}{1 + e^{-\mathbf{x}\mathbf{w}}}. \tag{7.81}$$

While this looks equivalent to Eqn 7.66, the difference now is that the output of the neuron is $y = 1$ only with a certain probability and $y = 0$ with the complementary probability. Hence, this neuron is a binary neuron with only binary states, on and off. This seems better to resemble the spiking nature of real neurons.

Networks of probabilistic neurons have been studied briefly earlier, in particular within bi-directional recurrent neural networks that we will review in Chapter 9. If the neurons are stochastic nodes in a network, then we can view this network itself as an undirected Bayesian network where the weights represent some form of conditional probability to influence the firing of the receiving neuron. We will get back to this point in Chapter 9.

There is strong evidence that real neurons are stochastic in nature, and there is also a lot of evidence of the stochastic nature of synapses. While it is sometimes argued that noise in synaptic processes should be expected as this is a biological system, Enoki and Fine showed that the probabilities of neurotransmitter releases can be modulated with classical synaptic plasticity experiments. This area is still largely unexplored.

8 Generative models

This chapter is an introduction to the important topic of building generative models. These are models that are aimed at understanding the variety of a class such as cars or trees. A generative mode should be able to generate feature vectors for instances of the class they represent, and such models should thus be able to characterize the class with all its variations. We discuss this subject both in a Bayesian and in a deep learning context, and also within a supervised and unsupervised context. This area is related to important algorithms such as k-means clustering, expectation maximization (EM), naïve Bayes, generative adversarial networks (GANs), and variational autoencoders (VAE) that are discussed in this chapter.

8.1 Modeling classes

In the previous sections we introduced the idea that understanding the world should be based on a probabilistic model of the world. For example, building a good recognition system means estimating a large density function about the probability of labels of objects given sensory data. What we have done so far is to use classification models as a discriminative recognition model that take feature values $\mathbf{x}$ and make a prediction of an output (label) y. In the probabilistic formulation, the models were formulated as parameterized functions that represent the conditional probability $p(y|\mathbf{x}; \theta)$. A model that discriminates between classes based on the feature values is called a **discriminative model**. Building a discriminative model directly from example data can be a daunting task as we have to learn how each item is distinguished from every other possible item. It worked on some examples earlier because we have mainly used simple models in low dimensions to illustrate the ideas. However, many real-world problems have much larger dimensions.

We will now outline a different strategy: that of learning first about the nature of specific classes and then using this knowledge to infer a classification prediction. We therefore first have to learn a **generative models**,

$$p(\mathbf{x}|y; \theta), \tag{8.1}$$

and then use an inference mechanism to use this knowledge for decision-making. Such a learning strategy seems to resemble human learning closely. Generative models can be used to "generate" examples of class objects. The generative models can be used with an inference engine to solve diverse tasks such as classification. For example, we might first learn about chairs, and independently about tables, and when we are shown pictures with different furnitures we can draw on this knowledge to classify them.

Let's talk briefly about the inference engine. In order to use probabilistic generative models as in Eqn 8.1 for classification, we need to ask how we can combine the

Fundamentals of Machine Learning, Thomas P. Trappenberg, Oxford University Press (2020).
© Oxford University Press. DOI: 10.1093/oso/9780198828044.001.0001

knowledge about different classes to undertake classification. Of course, the answer is provided by Bayes' theorem, so that in this case we can use the rules of probability theory as inference engine. This is the ideal situation in a probabilistic setting. In the following, we show some examples where we can use Bayes rule. In practice, there are situations where undertaking inference analytically with Bayes rule is difficult. Complete or approximate numerical implementations of Bayes rules is thus an important topic. There are good examples where scientists have shown that humans make Bayesian decisions in specific experiments, although there is of course no evidence that such humans use direct calculations based on Bayes theorem.

In order to make a discriminative model from the generative models using Bayes theorem, we need to know the **class priors**, such as what the relative frequencies of the classes is. We can then calculate the probability that an item with features $\mathbf{x}$ belong to a class y as

$$p(y|\mathbf{x};\theta) = \frac{p(\mathbf{x}|y;\theta)p(y)}{p(x)}. \tag{8.2}$$

A decision can be made directly based on this conditional probability. The Bayesian decision criterion of predicting the class with the largest posterior probability is

$$\arg\max_y p(y|\mathbf{x};\theta) = \arg\max_y \frac{p(\mathbf{x}|y;\theta)p(y)}{p(x)} \tag{8.3}$$

$$= \arg\max_y p(\mathbf{x}|y;\theta)p(y), \tag{8.4}$$

where we have used the fact that the denominator does not depend on y and can thus be ignored. In the case of binary classification, this reads:

$$\arg\max_y p(y|\mathbf{x};\theta) = \arg\max_y (p(\mathbf{x}|y=0;\theta)p(y=0), p(\mathbf{x}|y=1;\theta)p(y=1).$$
$$\tag{8.5}$$

While using generative models for classification seem to be much more elaborate, we will see later that there are several arguments which make generative models attractive for machine learning. To start with, it seems much easier and efficient to learn to generalize from similar objects than to learn from possibly difficult discrimination examples.

8.2 Supervised generative models

8.2.1 1D Gaussian example

Classification with generative models have been used for some time. We will be discussing an example here which is related to a method called **linear discriminant analysis** that goes back to a paper by Fisher in 1936. This is the same Fisher who collected the iris dataset that we discussed in Chapter 2. We will start by outlining the idea in a 1-dimensional Gaussian model before deriving the more general case with more attributes and more classes in the next subsection.

An example of the distribution of an attribute x for two classes is shown in Fig. 8.1. As can be seen, these classes are not fully discriminated by this attribute value as the attribute values are overlapping. Thus, a good lesson to learn is that 100 per cent classification is not always possible. However, we can still predict with some high confidence in some cases. A good choice, and indeed the best possible choice, is to predict the blue class on the left for attribute values less than 1 and the red class on the right for attribute values above 1.

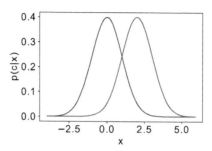

Fig. 8.1 Two overlapping classes with Gaussian distributions of the attribute values x.

Let us formalize this for the specific example of two Gaussian distributions as shown in Fig. 8.1 that were generated with the following distribution function.

$$p(x|y = c_1) = \frac{1}{\sqrt{2\pi}\sigma} e^{-\frac{x^2}{2\sigma^2}} \tag{8.6}$$

$$p(x|y = c_2) = \frac{1}{\sqrt{2\pi}\sigma} e^{-\frac{(x-\mu)^2}{2\sigma^2}} \tag{8.7}$$

In the particular example of the figure, we used the parameters $\mu = 2$ and $\sigma = 1$. The Bayesian decision point as outlined earlier is given by the point where the posteriors are equal, namely

$$e^{-\frac{x_D^2}{2\sigma^2}} p(c_1) = e^{-\frac{(x_D-\mu)^2}{2\sigma^2}} p(c_2), \tag{8.8}$$

where $p(c_1)$ and $p(c_2)$ the marginal class probabilities. This equation is easily be solved by

$$x_D = -\frac{1}{2}\mu + \frac{\sigma^2}{\mu} \log\left(\frac{p(c_2)}{p(c_1)}\right). \tag{8.9}$$

While this decision point is optimal, we will make some error that we can calculate for this example. To do this we need to calculate the area under the curve for the class with the wrong classification. For example, we predict class c_1 wrongly for $x > x_D$ in the following fraction of cases,

$$e_{c1} = \frac{1}{\sqrt{2\pi}\sigma} \int_{x_D}^{\infty} e^{-\frac{x^2}{2\sigma^2}} dx\, p(c_1). \tag{8.10}$$

The integral over a Gaussian is provided by the error function, so that we can write this as

$$e_{c1} = \left(1/2 - 1/2 \operatorname{erf}(\frac{x_D}{\sqrt{2}\sigma})\right) p(c_1). \tag{8.11}$$

Similar, the error for $x < x_D$ is

$$e_{c2} = \left(1/2 - 1/2 \, \mathrm{erf}(\frac{x_D}{\sqrt{2}\sigma})\right) p(c_2). \tag{8.12}$$

Thus, in the case illustrated in Fig. 8.1 with equivalent priors $p(c_1) = p(c_2) = 1/2$, unit variance $\sigma^2 = 1$, and a separation of $\mu = 2$, the best achievable accuracy is

$$\mathrm{Acc} = (1 - \mathrm{erf}(\frac{1}{\sqrt{2}}))/2 \approx 0.84. \tag{8.13}$$

As can be seen, the maximal possible accuracy of a classifier is not always 100 per cent.

8.2.2 Linear discriminant analysis

We now carry the same idea to the more general case of k classes, and we assume that each class has members which are Gaussian distribution over n attribute values. An example for $n = 2$ is shown in Fig. 8.2A. The following is a direct generalization of the 1-dimensional case.

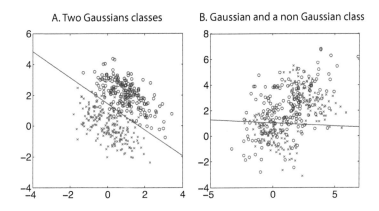

Fig. 8.2 Linear discriminant analysis on a two-class problem with different class distributions.

Each of the classes has a certain class prior

$$p(y = k) = \phi_k, \tag{8.14}$$

and each class itself is multivariate Gaussian distributed, generally with different means, μ_k, and variances, Σ_k,

$$p(\mathbf{x}|y = k) = \frac{1}{\sqrt{2\pi}^n \sqrt{|\Sigma_0|}} e^{-\frac{1}{2}(\mathbf{x}-\mu_k)^T \Sigma_k^{-1}(\mathbf{x}-\mu_k)}. \tag{8.15}$$

$$\tag{8.16}$$

Since we have supervised data with examples for each class, we can use maximum likelihood estimation to estimate the most likely values for the parameters

$\theta = (\phi_k, \mu_k, \Sigma_k)$. For the class priors, this is simply the relative frequency of the training data,

$$\phi_k = \frac{|K|}{m}, \tag{8.17}$$

where K is the set of examples of class k and $|K|$ is the number of examples is this set. Thus we estimated the parameter ϕ_k with the maximum likelihood for this Bernoulli random variable, and we omitted the "hat" to indicate that it is an estimate since this should now be clear from the context. The estimates of the means and variances within each class are given by the corresponding maximum likelihood estimates for the Gaussian parameters,

$$\mu_k = \frac{1}{|K|} \sum_{i \in K} \mathbf{x}^{(i)} \tag{8.18}$$

$$\Sigma_k = \frac{1}{|K|} \sum_{i \in K} (x^{(i)} - \mu_{y^{(i)}})(x^{(i)} - \mu_{y^{(i)}})^T. \tag{8.19}$$

With these estimates, we can calculate the optimal (in a Bayesian sense) decision rule, $G(x; \theta)$, as a function of $\mathbf{x}$ with parameters θ, namely

$$G(x) = arg\max_k p(y = k|\mathbf{x}) \tag{8.20}$$

$$= arg\max_k [p(\mathbf{x}|y = k; \theta)p(y = k)] \tag{8.21}$$

$$= arg\max_k [log(p(\mathbf{x}|y = k; \theta)p(y = k))] \tag{8.22}$$

$$= arg\max_k \left[-log(\sqrt{2\pi}^n \sqrt{|\Sigma_0|}) - \frac{1}{2}(\mathbf{x} - \mu_k)^T \Sigma_k^{-1}(\mathbf{x} - \mu_k) \right.$$
$$\left. + log(\phi_k) \right] \tag{8.23}$$

$$= arg\max_k [-\frac{1}{2}\mathbf{x}^T \Sigma_k^{-1}\mathbf{x} - \frac{1}{2}\mu_k^T \Sigma_k^{-1}\mu_k + \mathbf{x}^T \Sigma_k^{-1}\mu_k + log(\phi_k)], \tag{8.24}$$

as the first term in Eqn 8.23 does not depend on k and we can multiply out the other terms. With the maximum likelihood estimates of the parameters, we have all we need to make this decision.

In order to calculate the decision boundary between classes l and k, we make the common additional assumption that the covariance matrices of the classes are the same,

$$\Sigma_k =: \Sigma. \tag{8.25}$$

The decision point between the two classes with equal class priors is then given by the point where the probabilities for the two classes (Eqn 8.24) is the same. This gives

$$log(\frac{\phi_k}{\phi_l}) - \frac{1}{2}(\mu_k - \mu_l)^T \Sigma^{-1}(\mu_k + \mu_l) + \mathbf{x}\Sigma^{-1}(\mu_k - \mu_l) = 0. \tag{8.26}$$

The first two terms do not depend on x and can be summarized as constant $\mathbf{a}$. We can also introduce the vector

$$\mathbf{w} = \Sigma^{-1}(\mu_k - \mu_l). \tag{8.27}$$

With these simplifying notations is it easy to see that this decision boundary is a linear,

$$\mathbf{a} + \mathbf{wx} = 0. \tag{8.28}$$

As this is a linear equation, this method with the Gaussian class distributions with equal variances is called **linear discriminant analysis (LDA)**. The vector $\mathbf{w}$ is perpendicular to the decision surface. Examples are shown in Fig. 8.2. If we do not make the assumption of equal variances of the classes, then we have a quadratic equation for the decision boundary, and the method is then called **quadratic discriminant analysis (QDA)**. With the assumptions of LDA, we can calculate the contrastive model directly using Bayes rule.

$$p(y = k|\mathbf{x}; \theta) = \tag{8.29}$$

$$\frac{\phi_k \frac{1}{\sqrt{2\pi}^n \sqrt{|\Sigma|}} e^{-\frac{1}{2}(\mathbf{x}-\mu_k)^T \Sigma_k^{-1}(\mathbf{x}-\mu_k)}}{\phi_k \frac{1}{\sqrt{2\pi}^n \sqrt{|\Sigma|}} e^{-\frac{1}{2}(\mathbf{x}-\mu_k)^T \Sigma_k^{-1}(\mathbf{x}-\mu_k)} + \phi_l \frac{1}{\sqrt{2\pi}^n \sqrt{|\Sigma|}} e^{-\frac{1}{2}(\mathbf{x}-\mu_l)^T \Sigma_l^{-1}(\mathbf{x}-\mu_l)}}$$

$$= \frac{1}{1 + \frac{\phi_l}{\phi_k} e^{-\theta^T x}}, \tag{8.30}$$

where θ is an appropriate function of the parameters μ_k, μ_l, and Σ. Thus, the contrastive model is equivalent to logistic regression discussed in the previous chapter, although we use different parameterizations and the two methods will therefore usually give different results on specific datasets. So, which method should be used? In LDA we made the assumption that each class is Gaussian distributed. If this is the case, then LDA is the best method we can use. Discriminant analysis is also popular since it is easy to apply and often works well even when the classes are not strictly Gaussian. However, as can be seen in Fig. 8.2B, it can produce quite poor results if the data are multimodal distributed. Logistic regression is somewhat more general since it does not make the assumption that the class distributions are Gaussian. However, as ;long as we consider only linear models, logistic regression would have also problems with the data shown in Fig. 8.2B.

Finally, we should note that Fisher's original method was slightly more general than the examples discussed here since he did not assume Gaussian distributions. Instead considered within-class variances compared to between-class variances, something which resembles a signal-to-noise ratio. In **Fisher discriminant analysis (FDA)**, the separating hyperplane is defined as

$$\mathbf{w} = (\Sigma_k + \Sigma_l)^{-1}(\mu_k - \mu_l), \tag{8.31}$$

which is the same as in LDA in the case of equal covariance matrices.

8.3 Naïve Bayes

In the previous example, we used 2-dimensional feature vectors to illustrate the classification problems with 2-dimensional plots. However, most machine learning applications work with high-dimensional feature vectors. We will now discuss an important method with generative models which is called **naïve Bayes** that is often used with high-dimensional data. We will discuss this method with an example of text processing, following an example from Andrew Ng of making a spam filter that classifies email messages as either spam ($y = 1$) or non-spam ($y = 0$) emails. To do this, we first need a method to represent the problem in a suitable way. We choose here to represent a text (email in this situation) as a **vocabulary** vector. A vocabulary is simply the list of all possible words that we consider. A text can be represented by a vector with entries 1 if the word can be found in the text or an entry 0 if not, for example:

$$\mathbf{x} = \begin{pmatrix} 1 \\ 0 \\ 0 \\ \cdot \\ \cdot \\ \cdot \\ 1 \\ \cdot \\ \cdot \\ 0 \end{pmatrix} \quad \begin{matrix} \text{a} \\ \text{aardvark} \\ \text{aardwolf} \\ \cdot \\ \cdot \\ \cdot \\ \text{buy} \\ \cdot \\ \cdot \\ \text{zygmurgy} \end{matrix} \tag{8.32}$$

We are here only considering values 0 and 1 instead of, for example, counting how often the corresponding word appears. The later is usually called a "bag of words". The difference of our simplified example to a bag of words is that each entry is a binomial random variable instead of a multinomial in the bag of words. We chose the simpler case here for illustration purposes, although the methods generalizes directly to the other case. In any case, this is a lossy representation where we loose the positions of the words in the text which might be considered essential in text comprehension. Natural language processing has recently made much progress with models such as recurrent neural networks that we will discuss in Chapter 9, but for the basic task discussed in the following it turns out that naïve Bayes yield fairly good results. An interesting part of this example is that we are now considering a very high-dimensional feature vector.

Let us consider here that our vocabulary has 50,000 word, which is a typical size of common languages even though most language have many more words. We now want to build a discriminative model from some training examples. That is, we want to model

$$p(\mathbf{x}|y) = p(x_1, x_2, ..., x_{50000}|y). \tag{8.33}$$

This is a very high-dimensional density function which has $2^{50,000} - 1$ parameters (the -1 comes from the normalization condition). We can factorize this conditional density function with the chain rule

$$p(x_1, x_2, ..., x_{50000}|y) = p(x_1|y)p(x_2|y, x_1)...p(x_{50000}|y, x_1, ..., x_{49999}). \tag{8.34}$$

While the right-hand side has only $50,000$ factors, there are still $2^{50,000} - 1$ parameters we have to learn. We now make a strong assumption, namely that all the words are conditionally independent in each text; that is,

$$p(x_1|y)p(x_2|y, x_1)...p(x_{50000}|y, x_1, ..., x_{49999}) = p(x_1|y)p(x_2|y)...p(x_{50000}|y). \tag{8.35}$$

This is conditional independent, giving the class y, $p(x_1, x_2|y) = p(x_1|y)p(x_2|y)$, which is different from independence like $p(x_1, x_2) = p(x_1)p(x_2)$. The conditional independence in this probabilistic model is called the the **naïve Bayes (NB) assumption**. The corresponding Bayesian network is shown in Fig. 8.3. With the naïve Bayes assumption, we can write the conditional probability as a factor of terms with $50,000$ parameters

$$p(\mathbf{x}|y) = \prod_{j=1}^{50000} p(x_j|y). \tag{8.36}$$

To estimate these parameters we can apply maximum likelihood estimation, which gives

$$\phi_{j,y=1} = \frac{1}{|\{y=1\}|} \sum_{i \in \{y=1\}} x_j^{(i)} \tag{8.37}$$

$$\phi_{j,y=0} = \frac{1}{|\{y=0\}|} \sum_{i \in \{y=0\}} x_j^{(i)} \tag{8.38}$$

$$\phi_y = \frac{|\{y=1\}|}{m}. \tag{8.39}$$

The first equation is the probability that the word j appears in a spam text, the second equation is that the word j appears in a non-spam text, and the third equation specifies the frequency of spam examples in the data set.

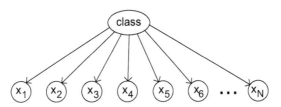

Fig. 8.3 The graphical representation of a naïve Bayes classifier.

With these parameters we can now calculate the probability that email $\mathbf{x}$ is spam as

$$p(y=1|\mathbf{x}) = \frac{\prod_{j=1}^{50.000} \phi_{j,y=1}\phi_{y=1}}{\prod_{j=1}^{50.000} \phi_{j,y=1}\phi_{y=1} + \prod_{j=1}^{50.000} \phi_{j,y=0}\phi_{y=0}}. \tag{8.40}$$

This big advantage of this naïve Bayes model is that the number of parameters are fairly small compared to more complex causal models. There are many examples where the naïve Bayes model works quite well which are, of course, cases where the naïve Bayes assumption is appropriate. Of course, words in a text should be highly correlated, but the gist here is that the pure frequency of words has some correlates with the type of text.

Before we leave this model it is important to note that in practice there is often a slight problem. If some of the words, say word x_{100}, are not part of the training set we have a 0 count that produces a problem as we would divide by 0, $\phi_{100,y=1} = 0$ and $\phi_{100,y=0} = 0$, and hence $p(y=1|x) = \frac{0}{0}$. A common trick, called **Laplace**

smoothing is to add one occurrence of this word in every case, which will insert a small probability proportional to the number of training examples to the estimates,

$$\phi_{j,y=1} = \frac{\sum_{i=1}^{m} 1\{x_j^{(i)} = 1 \wedge y^{(i)} = 1\} + 1}{\sum_{i=1}^{m} 1\{y^{(i)} = 1\} + 2} \tag{8.41}$$

$$\phi_{j,y=0} = \frac{\sum_{i=1}^{m} 1\{x_j^{(i)} = 1 \wedge y^{(i)} = 0\} + 1}{\sum_{i=1}^{m} 1\{y^{(i)} = 0\} + 2}. \tag{8.42}$$

It is interesting to compare the naïve Bayes classification with other classification methods. This would be a recommended exercise.

8.4 Self-supervised generative models

8.4.1 k-means clustering

In the previous learning problems we had training examples with feature vectors $\mathbf{x}$ and labels $\mathbf{y}$. We now discuss an example of unsupervised learning in which no labels are given. Such data are widespread. For example, it is easy to take pictures with a digital camera and hence get huge numbers of pictures. What usually takes time is to label the pictures, as in the ImageNet dataset, or even to segment particular objects in the picture. We can thus not use the supervised training methods we have discussed so far.

However, samples of unlabeled collections still have interesting information embedded in them, and self-supervised learning has important applications. In particular, we can glean some structure from the data which can help in representational learning and hence speed up supervised learning. Self-supervised or unsupervised does not mean that the learning is not guided at all; the learning follows specific principles that are used to guide the organization of the data itself.

We start here by discussing a widespread use of such methods for **data clustering**. In this problem domain, we are given unlabeled data described by a set of features and asked to put them into k categories. In the first example of such clustering, we categorize the data by proximity to a mean value. That is, we assume a model that specifies a mean feature value of the data and classifies the data based on the proximity to the mean value. Of course, we do not know this mean value for each class. The idea of the following algorithm is that we start with a guess for this mean value and label the data accordingly. We then use the labeled data from this hypothesis to improve the model by calculating a new mean value, and repeat these steps until convergence is reached. Such an algorithm usually converges quickly to a stable solution.

More formally, let us consider a training set of data points $\{x^{(1)}, x^{(2)}, ..., x^{(m)}\}$ and a hypothesis of the number of clusters, k, for the k-means clustering algorithm. The algorithm starts by just choosing random initial means for each of the k classes. The next two steps are then iterated. Given the means, we can choose the class label of each data points according to the class label of the closest mean. Then, giving these calculated labels we can now update the mean according to these data. These steps are iterated until convergence. This algorithm is summarized in Table 8.1. An example of the initial state and two iterations of this algorithm is shown in Fig. 8.4. The figure was produced with the following program.

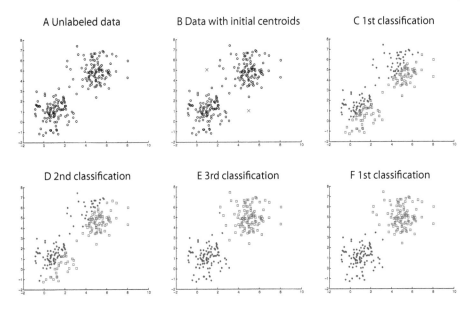

Fig. 8.4 Example of k-means clustering with two clusters.

Listing 8.1 kmeans.ipynb

```
import numpy as np
import matplotlib.pyplot as plt

# Choose 100 Gaussian data with means with mean (1,1) and (5,5)
n=100; x = np.random.randn(2*n,2);  x[:n,:]+=1; x[n:,:]+=5
plt.plot(x[:,0],x[:,1],'ko') # plot points
mu1=[5,1]; mu2=[1,5] # initial centers (arbitrary)

plt.plot(mu1[0],mu1[1],'rx',markersize=12)
plt.plot(mu2[0],mu2[1],'bx',markersize=12)
plt.show()


# repeat this block
y = ((x-mu1)**2).sum(1) < ((x-mu2)**2).sum(1) # expectation
x1=x[y>0.5];   x2=x[y<0.5];
plt.plot(x1[:,0],x1[:,1],'rs');
plt.plot(x2[:,0],x2[:,1],'b*');
mu1=x1.mean(0);   mu2=x2.mean(0); # maximization
plt.plot(mu1[0],mu1[1],'kx',markersize=12)
plt.plot(mu2[0],mu2[1],'kx',markersize=12)
plt.show()
```

In the listing above we did not really start the means randomly but chose a particular difficult start in order to see the effect of the algorithm better. It is a good idea to play around with different configuration of this program such as changing the initial conditions to a random start or the shape of the data distribution.

Table 8.1 k-means clustering algorithm

1. Initialize the means $\mu_1, ... \mu_k$ randomly.
2. Repeat until convergence: {
      Model prediction:
         For each data point i, classify data to class with closest mean
$$c^{(i)} = arg\min_j \|x^{(i)} - \mu_j\|$$
      Model refinement:
         Calculate new means for each class
$$\mu_j = \frac{1\;\mathbb{1}(c^{(i)}=j)x^{(i)}}{1\;\mathbb{1}(c^{(i)}=j)}$$
} convergence.

8.4.2 Mixture of Gaussian and the EM algorithm

We can now extend the idea of k-means clustering to the more rigorous case of assuming a specific generative model for each class. We will again use Gaussian models here as the example, but it should be clear that we can use any form of model for the in-class distribution. Here we assume that we have k Gaussian classes, where each class is chosen randomly from a multinomial distribution,

$$p(z^{(i)} = j) \propto \text{multinomial}(\Phi_j) \tag{8.43}$$

$$p(x^{(i)}|z^{(i)} = j) \propto N(\mu_j, \Sigma_j). \tag{8.44}$$

This is called a **Gaussian mixture model**. The corresponding log-likelihood function is

$$l(\Phi, \mu, \sigma) = \sum_{i=1}^{m} \log \sum_{z^{(i)}=1}^{k} p(x^{(i)}|z^{(i)}; \mu, \Sigma)p(z^{(i)}; \Phi). \tag{8.45}$$

Since here we consider unsupervised learning, we are given input data $\mathbf{x}$ without labels. We therefore use now as labels the symbol z for the labels that we assume to be latent random variables $z^{(i)}$. Not knowing the labels makes the problem harder than the supervised Gaussian model discussed earlier. If were given the class membership, than the log-likelihood would be

$$l(\Phi, \mu, \sigma) = \sum_{i=1}^{m} \log p(x^{(i)}; z^{(i)}, \mu, \Sigma), \tag{8.46}$$

which we could use to calculate the maximum likelihood estimates of the parameter (see Eqns 8.17–8.19),

$$\phi_k = \frac{1}{m}\sum_{i=1}^{m} \mathbb{1}(z^{(i)} = j) \tag{8.47}$$

$$\mu_k = \frac{\sum_{i=1}^{m} \mathbb{1}(z^{(i)} = j)\mathbf{x}^{(i)}}{\sum_{i=1}^{m} \mathbb{1}(z^{(i)} = j)} \tag{8.48}$$

$$\Sigma_k = \frac{\sum_{i=1}^{m} \mathbb{1}(z^{(i)} = j)(x^{(i)} - \mu_j)(x^{(i)} - \mu_j)^T}{\sum_{i=1}^{m} \mathbb{1}(y^{(i)} = k)}. \tag{8.49}$$

The indicator function $\mathbb{1}(x = y)$ is simply 1 if $x = y$ and zero otherwise. Therefore, when put into a sum it simply counts the number of cases in which condition is true.

While we do not know the class labels, we can follow a similar strategy to the k-means clustering algorithm and just propose some labels and use them to estimate the parameters. We can then use the new estimate of the distributions to find better labels for the data, and repeat this procedure until a stable configuration is reached. In general, this strategy is called the **EM algorithm** for expectation-maximization. The algorithm is outlined in Fig. 8.5. In this version we do not hard-classify the data into one or another class, but we take a more soft classification approach that considers the probability estimate of a data point belonging to each class.

1. Initialize parameters ϕ, μ, Σ randomly.
2. Repeat until convergence: {

    E step:

        For each data point i and class j (soft-)classify data as
$$w_j^{(i)} = p(z^{(i)} = j | x^{(i)}; \phi, \mu, \Sigma)$$

    M step:

        Update the parameters according to
$$\phi_j = \frac{1}{m} \sum_{i=1}^{m} w_j^{(i)}$$
$$\mu_j = \frac{\sum_{i=1}^{m} w_j^{(i)} x^{(i)}}{\sum_{i=1}^{m} w_j^{(i)}}$$
$$\Sigma_k = \frac{\sum_{i=1}^{m} w_j^{(i)} (x^{(i)} - \mu_j)(x^{(i)} - \mu_j)^T}{\sum_{i=1}^{m} w_j^{(i)}}.$$

} convergence.

Fig. 8.5 EM algorithm with weighted membership.

An example is shown in Fig. 8.6. In this simple world, data are generated with equal likelihood from two Gaussian distributions, one with mean $\mu_1 = -1$ and standard deviation $\sigma_1 = 2$, the other with mean $\mu_2 = 4$ and standard deviation $\sigma_2 = 0.5$. These two distributions are illustrated in Fig. 8.6A with dashed lines. Let us assume that we know that the world consists only of data from two Gaussian distributions with equal likelihood, but that we do not know the specific realizations (parameters) of these distributions. The pre-knowledge of two Gaussian distributions encodes a specific **hypothesis** which makes up this **heuristic model**. In this simple example, we have chosen the heuristics to match the actual data-generating system (world); that is, we have explicitly used some knowledge of the world.

Learning the parameters of the two Gaussians would be easy if we had access to the information about which data point was produced by which Gaussian; that is, which cause produced the specific examples. Unfortunately, we can only observe the data without a teacher label that could supervise the learning. We therefore choose a self-supervised strategy, which repeats the following two steps until convergence:

E-step: we make assumptions of training labels from the current model (expectation step).

M-step: use this hypothesis to update the parameters of the model to maximize the probability of the observations (maximization step).

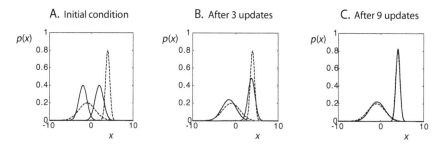

Fig. 8.6 Example of the expectation maximization (EM) algorithm for a world model with two Gaussian distributions. The Gaussian distributions of the world data (input data) are shown with dashed lines. (A) The generative model, shown with solid lines, is initialized with arbitrary parameters. In the EM algorithm, the unlabelled input data are labelled with a recognition model, which is, in this example, the inverse of the generative model. These labelled data are then used for parameter estimation of the generative model. The results of learning are shown in (B) after three iterations, and in (C) after nine iterations .

Since we do not know appropriate parameters yet, we just choose some arbitrary values as the starting point. In the example shown in Fig. 8.6A we used $\mu_1 = 2$, $\mu_2 = -2$, $\sigma_1 = \sigma_2 = 1$. These distributions are shown with solid lines. Comparing the generated data with the environmental data corresponds to hypothesis testing.

The results are not yet very satisfactory, but we can use the generative model to express our expectation of the data. Specifically, we can assign each data point to the class which produces the larger probability within the current world model. Thus, we are using our specific hypothesis here as a recognition model. In the example we can use Bayes' rule to invert the generative model into a recognition model as detailed in the simulation section below. If this inversion is not possible, then we can introduce a separate recognition model, Q, to approximate the inverse of the generative model. Such a recognition model can be learned with similar methods and interleaved with the generative model. Of course, the recognition with the recognition model early in learning is not expected to be exact, but estimation of new parameters from the recognized data in the M-step to maximize the expectation can be expected to be better than the model with the initial arbitrary values. The new model can then be compared to the data again and, when necessary, be used to generate new expectations from which the model is refined. The distributions after three and nine such iterations, where we have chosen new data points in each iteration, are shown in Figs 8.6B and C.

8.5 Generative neural networks

8.5.1 Generative adversarial network (GAN)

We have so far assumed specific functional forms of generative models to discuss generative models in the Bayesian context. We are now going back to deep neural networks which are useful to learn more complex models from data when specific causal models are not known. There are several approaches to building generative models of which we want to mention two, namely generative adverserial networks and the variational autoencoders. The basic idea behind generative adversarial networks

(GANs) is to train a generator neural network model so that the generated examples are able to fool a discriminator network which is itself trained to discriminate between network-generated examples and real example. The overall architecture is outlined in Fig. 8.7. The basic components are a generator network and a discriminator network, but the main idea is how to use them. The discriminator network is typically a deep recognition network such as the convolutional networks we used for MNIST or Ima-geNet. It is either fed a real input or a fake input. So this network is like an forgery expert that needs to distinguish real from fake, a simple binary decision. This discriminator network is trained on a combination of real and fake images where the fake images are generated by the generator network. This is done by providing a random input to this network which can be viewed as a random example from a latent space of the objects that should be generated.

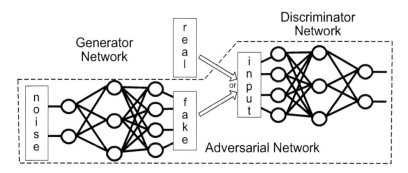

Fig. 8.7 Outline of a generative adversarial network (GAN).

At the beginning the generated objects are certainly not very good, but neither is the discriminator. Once the discriminator gets better we can then use the information learned by the discriminator to make the generator better. This is done by combining the generator and discriminator network with a large adversarial network where the weights of the discriminator part are fixed and the weights of the generator are adjusted with the label of "real" to make the generator output more similar to inputs that would be categorized as real by the discriminator network. The use of the network is hence a bit different to regular deep networks in that the target function moves. The better the generator gets, the more the discriminator has to adjust, and this information in turn drives necessary changes in the generator. In practice, it is not so easy to implement these networks, and many tricks are commonly used. In particular, it is recommended to use both tanh or leaky linear units (LLU), to adjust carefully the learning rates, and to monitor the progress of each network. However, it has been shown that good results can be achieved with such networks after learning.

8.5.2 Variational autoencoder (VA)

We have already discussed the autoencoder in section 4.7 which can be seen as an encoder into a latent space and a decoder from this latent space back into the feature space. Previously we also labelled this latent space as semantic as we assume that this lower-dimensional space represents some meaning. If we vary the latent activation we could generate outputs with the decoder so that such autoencoders could be seen as generative models. However, the question is how to generate this variation in a way in order to generate novel examples which still represent the expected distribution of a target class. We usually do not know much about the structure of the latent space which prevents us from making systematic variations.

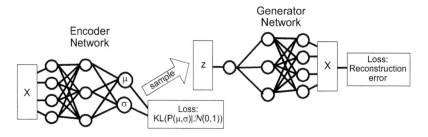

Fig. 8.8 Outline of the idea behind a variational autoencoder (VAE). However, the sampling step in the middle is not a discrete operation through which we cannot backpropagate.

Variational autoencoders have recently addressed these problems in a systematic way. The basic idea is to impose a distribution of latent variables, which is commonly assumed to be a normal distribution

$$P(\mathbf{z}) = \mathcal{N}(0, 1). \tag{8.50}$$

From this the decoder can generate targets X with the target distribution $P(X)$. This is shown on the right in Fig. 8.8. In order to generate the encoding we use a deep network which generates outputs for the mean and variance. We will then sample a point from a Gaussian with the corresponding mean and variance that becomes the input to the decoder. Overall, we train this network as autoencoder while minimizing the Kulback–Leibler distance between the encoder and the assumed normal distribution.

A remaining problem is, however, that the sampling in the middle of this network is a discrete function that cannot be differentiated. Hence, this step would prevent us from backpropagating the reconstruction error to the encoder. However, we can implement the sampling in the following way. We chose a random number

$$\epsilon \sim \mathcal{N}(0, 1), \tag{8.51}$$

which we then multiply with the variance and add the mean from the encoder output. These operations are differentiable. This implementation is illustrated in Fig. 8.9. Hence, this network is basically still an autoencoder with some immediate input and which is trained not only on the reconstruction error, but also on the minimization of the Kulback–Leibler distance between the encoder output and a normal distribution. The latter part of the loss function can also be seen as a regularizer for the latent space which enforces a desirable latent representation.

In the following, we show a minimal MNIST example implementation with Keras following basically the excellent implementation of Francois Chollet. This version is an attempt to minimize the example so that it can be run without GPU. However, implementing deeper networks and training on more example, will give even better results.

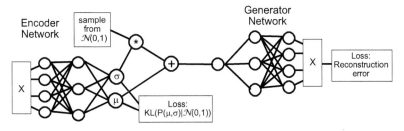

Fig. 8.9 Implementation of a variational autoencoder (VAE) with an additional small random input that approximates the sampling so that the network is fully differentiable.

After importing the necessary libraries, we start by defining the encoder model. We use here three convolution layers with 3×3 kernels. In the second layer we use a stride that eliminates the need for the max pooling that we used in Chapter 4. We save the shape of the output after the convolutional layers as we need this later to up-sample in the inverse way. We then flatten the output so that we can feed into a dense layer with thirty-two nodes and finally to two output layers, one representing the mean and the other the variance of an n-dimensional Gaussian. The dimensions n is here the dimension of the latent space, set to 2 in this example as this will be a useful dimension to visualize later.

Listing 8.2 VAE.ipynb (part 1)

```
import numpy as np
import matplotlib.pyplot as plt
from keras import models, layers, optimizers, datasets, utils, losses
    , metrics
from keras import backend as K

# encoder model
input_img = layers.Input(shape=(28, 28, 1,))
latent_dim = 2
x = layers.Conv2D(32,3,padding='same',activation='relu')(input_img)
x = layers.Conv2D(64,3,padding='same',activation='relu',strides=(2,2)
    )(x)
x = layers.Conv2D(64,3,padding='same',activation='relu')(x)
    shape_before_flattening = K.int_shape(x)
x = layers.Flatten()(x)
x = layers.Dense(32, activation='relu')(x)

z_mean = layers.Dense(latent_dim)(x)
z_log_var = layers.Dense(latent_dim)(x)
```

We then implement the sampling from the Gaussian that is specified by the output of the decoder. Since every operation in Keras has to be implemented as a layer, we need to show here a useful technique. As a simple way to implement an arbitrary expression as Keras layer is to use the layer wrapper called Lambda. We can define a functions which we then pass to this wrapper layer so that the output of this layer becomes the sample which we need as input to the decoder. The decoder then simply uses reshaping and transpose convolutions to generate images with the original image size.

Listing 8.3 VAE.ipynb (part 2)

```
def sampling(args):
z_mean, z_log_var = args
epsilon = K.random_normal(shape=(K.shape(z_mean)[0], latent_dim),
    mean=0., stddev=1.)
return z_mean + K.exp(z_log_var) * epsilon

# generate input for decoder
z = layers.Lambda(sampling)([z_mean, z_log_var])

# Decoder model
decoder_input = layers.Input(K.int_shape(z)[1:])
x = layers.Dense(np.prod(shape_before_flattening[1:]), activation='
    relu')(decoder_input)
x = layers.Reshape(shape_before_flattening[1:])(x)
x = layers.Conv2DTranspose(32, 3,padding='same', activation='relu',
    strides=(2, 2))(x)
x = layers.Conv2D(1, 3, padding='same', activation='sigmoid')(x)
decoder = models.Model(decoder_input, x)
output_img = decoder(z)
```

Training this architecture requires combining a loss function for the autodecoder, for example, the reconstruction error in terms of the cross-entropy of each pixel, with the Kulback–Leibler distance of the output of the decoder from the desired normal distribution of the latent space. The following code shoes how this can be achieved.

Listing 8.4 VAE.ipynb (part 3)

```
class CustomLossLayer(layers.Layer):

def call(self, inputs):
   x = K.flatten(inputs[0])
   y = K.flatten(inputs[1])
   xent_loss = metrics.binary_crossentropy(x, y)
   kl_loss = -5e-4 * K.mean(1 + z_log_var - K.square(z_mean) - K.exp(
       z_log_var), axis=-1)
   loss=K.mean(xent_loss + kl_loss)
   self.add_loss(loss, inputs=inputs)
   return x # return value not used

output = CustomLossLayer()([input_img, output_img])
```

We are now ready to apply this model to the MNIST data as shown in Listing 8.5. We load the MINST data set with Keras as we have previously done in Chapter 4. If you are running this program without GPU acceleration, then we recommend that you try the program first on a smaller data set such as just using 10 per cent of the data as indicated in the commented lines.

Finally, we want to visualize the learned latent space of the VAE. We do this by initializing the decoder with values on a grid in the latent space and then show the generated images with corresponding positions in Fig. 8.10. The intriguing result is that the space has some continuous structure relating the objects. For example, the first line in this example shows how a 9 can be transformed to become a 8 and then a 1. Going downward on the left, the rightmost column shows examples that seem to interpolate smoothly between examples of classes 1, 8 5, 6, and maybe 0. It is possible to see the emergence of this behaviors with less training examples such as only training on 1000 training data and testing on 500 test images. However, the examples might look a bit more fuzzy.

Listing 8.5 VAE.ipynb (part 4)

```
from keras.datasets import mnist

(x_train, _), (x_test, _) = datasets.mnist.load_data()
x_train = x_train.reshape(60000, 28, 28, 1)/255
#x_train = x_train[:6000,:,:,:]
x_test = x_test.reshape(10000, 28, 28, 1)/255
#x_test = x_test[:1000,:,:,:]

vae = models.Model(input_img, output)
vae.compile(optimizer='rmsprop', loss=None)
vae.summary()

vae.fit(x=x_train, y=None, shuffle=True, epochs=10, batch_size=16,
    validation_data=(x_test, None))
```

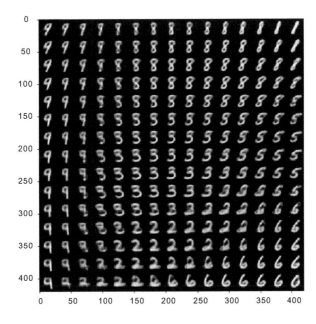

Fig. 8.10 Results of the variational autoencoder on MNIST data. The figure illustrates the structure of the latent space by showing the results of initializing the decoder with values in a grid of the latent space.

Part III

Advanced learning models

9 Cyclic models and recurrent neural networks

We have discussed several directed models with a simple directed consecutive flow of information, including feed-forward neural networks and directed acyclic graphs for Bayesian networks. A more general form of models can include cyclic dependencies where model components that receive information can influence model components from such sending nodes. There are two principle architectures we will discuss in turn in this chapter.

The first principle architecture of cyclic graphs is shown on the left in Fig. 9.1. These types of models are directed graphs similar to the Bayesian networks discussed in Chapter 7, except that we now consider possible loops in the directed graph. We will discuss such models in the context of recurrent neural networks where the network nodes are model neurons as commonly used in neural networks but which now allow feedback connections. We consider such recurrent neural networks in their common setting with deterministic neurons, although it is possible to generalize the architectures to the stochastic case. However, even with deterministic neurons, such architectures can change neuron activations in an ongoing way even with constant input. Formally, such networks represent dynamical systems in the wider context and do therefore represent some form of temporal modeling. The topic of temporal modeling will thus be at the center of the following discussions. Note that the shown network has two input neurons and two output neurons. Such neurons are commonly called visible. In contrast, the neurons that are not connected to the outside worls are called the hidden neurons.

A. Network with feedback connections   B. Network with bidiretinal connections

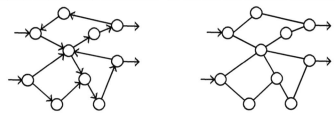

Fig. 9.1 Illustration of two principle cyclic networks with (A) directed graphs and (B) graphs with bi-directional links.

The second type of models that we discuss in this chapter is of the form shown in Fig. 9.1B. The connections between the neurons in such networks are thereby bi-directional. Examples of such neural networks are architectures with lateral connections in the context of layered neural networks and bi-directional connections

Fundamentals of Machine Learning, Thomas P. Trappenberg, Oxford University Press (2020).
© Oxford University Press. DOI: 10.1093/oso/9780198828044.001.0001

between layers in layered neural networks. These types of networks will be discussed in the context of stochastic units in the second half of this chapter. Undirected models of stochastic variables are often called Markov random fields (MRF). The example shown in Fig. 9.1B has input and outputs. If the input represent features $\mathbf{x}$ and the output represents probabilities of labels $\mathbf{y}$, then this graph represents the conditional distribution $p(\mathbf{y}|\mathbf{x})$. This special form of a MRF is commonly called a conditional random field (CRF). This is a very interesting area of modeling with probabilistic models who technical details are somewhat beyond the scope of this book. However, we will specifically discuss some basic bi-directional neural networks that have been instrumental in the development of this area, even getting deep learning off the ground.

9.1 Sequence processing

Our examples of neural network applications have focused on a tasks where an output (label) should be predicted from one input vector. Another common application domain that we will discuss now is that of processing sequences. There are many types of sequence task such as forecasting the stock market or the weather from past observations, or the modeling of progress of patients improvements due to medical interventions. While it is common to have naturally sequential data, there are even reasons to process static data in a sequential form such as searching large images in patches to look for specific objects. Doing this is more memory efficient. Even the human visual system uses sequence processing as scenes are commonly explored by a series of eye movements called saccades. We will start discussing such sequence processing with the basic tasks of temporal predictions where a value of a sequence at position t is to be predicted from previous data points,

$$x(t) = f(x(t-1), x(t-2), ...). \tag{9.1}$$

In general, we should talk about a sequence position, though we commonly view a sequence as a time series. It is hence common to use the symbol t for the index of a sequence position.

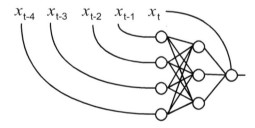

Fig. 9.2 Example of a tabbed delay line to represent temporal sequences to a neural network.

We will now consider several architectures of systems for such temporal processing. The first one we should consider is to use a regular feed-forward network to do sequence prediction from a finite number of previous sequence data. For example, we can place sequence values of n previous values of the sequence into an input vector

$$\mathbf{x} = \begin{pmatrix} x(t-1) \\ \dots \\ x(t-1-n) \end{pmatrix}, \qquad (9.2)$$

and then do a one-step-ahead prediction of the value $s(t)$ as the output,

$$y = x(t). \qquad (9.3)$$

In Fig. 9.2, we visualized the generation of the input vector by tabbing the input sequence with delay lines of different lengths. Representing a finite portion of a sequence in this spatial way is thus sometimes called a tabbed delay line. With such a representation of a time sequence we can immediately apply a deep neural networks for the sequence forecasting. An example of such a simple network with one hidden layer is also shown in Fig. 9.2.

For the following discussion, let's simplify this network with only one hidden node as shown in Fig. 9.3A. We can generalize this easily again to more hidden nodes and many layers of hidden nodes; we have just choosen this simple version for the illustration purposes. With this reduced figure it becomes clear that we assume that the values of the inputs at different times can have different influences on the sequence prediction as we allow the weights to the hidden node to have different values that of course must be learned. This is the most general case, at least for a fixed length of the input sequence. However, if we are looking for a specific pattern in the input sequence which could occur at any position, then we can again use a convolution over the input vector to search for this pattern. For example, in text processing of the sentence "You should take an umbrella because it is raining," the word "umbrella" is highly predictive of the word "raining", although the relative position is variable. Convolutional neural networks have smaller filters compared to dense networks. This will save us parameters as we already discussed for position invariant feature detection in images. The 1-dimensional convolutional solution is illustrated in Fig. 9.3B. A model with fewer parameters will usually require less training examples to learn, and convolution makes sense in many cases.

We can reduce the network complexity even further if we assume that the previous time steps only influence the current time point in a transient or diminishing way. This is often a good assumption. For example, it is well known that the probability of a sunny day is higher following a sunny day than a rainy day. We can describe a situation where the current value influences future time points at $t + u\delta t$ of the activation of the hidden nodes with

$$\mathbf{h}(t) = \mathbf{v}x(t) + \mathbf{u}\mathbf{v}x(t-1) + \mathbf{u}^2\mathbf{v}x(t-2) + \dots, \qquad (9.4)$$

where u are weights with value less then 1. We can then simplify this network with the architecture shown in Fig. 9.3C where we represent the exponentially decaying memory of the input by a delayed input to the hidden node of its previous value. Mathematically, we are only replacing a diminishing sum with a recursive form,

$$\mathbf{h}(t) = \mathbf{v}x(t) + \mathbf{u}\left(\mathbf{v}x(t-1) + \mathbf{u}\mathbf{v}x(t-2) + \dots\right) \qquad (9.5)$$
$$= \mathbf{v}x(t) + \mathbf{u}\mathbf{h}(t-1), \qquad (9.6)$$

which is illustrated in Fig. 9.3C. Since this includes the re-entry of the information through the backward connections, this is called a recurrent neural network (RNN).

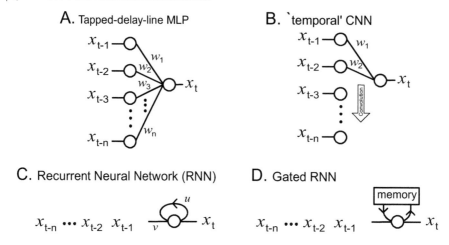

Fig. 9.3 Different ways of sequence processing with neural networks. The illustrations just show one example hidden note, but these networks should be considered with multiple nodes and commonly more layers. (A) A standard feed-forward network (MLP) where the input represents a vector of previous sequence data. (B) A "temporal" convolutional neural network (CNN). (C) A basic recurrent neural network (RNN). (D) A gated recurrent neural network (gRNN) with explicit memory.

In this way we are not longer restricted in building networks for a finite sequence with the tabbed delay line approach. Compared to separate weights for inputs at different times, we introduced here a form of weight sharing in the sense that only the relative times of the sequence is important. This assumption is similar to the position invariance assumption in convolutional networks, and building in this assumption in our architecture will reduce parameters.

The assumption of a diminishing influence from previous time steps has the form of an exponential decay, which is not always appropriate. For example in natural language processing it is common that a given word has relations to other distant words. We can overcome this problem with explicit memory, as illustrated in Fig. 9.3D. We will shortly explore how we can implement such a memory in neural networks, for example with gated networks.

To finalize this simplest form of a recurrent neural network, we include a non-linearity in the layer. For example, the equations for a recurrent layer with a $\tanh(x)$ activation function is,

$$\mathbf{h}(t) = \tanh\left(\mathbf{w}\{\mathbf{x}(t), \mathbf{h}(t-1)\}\right). \tag{9.7}$$

We have thereby used a concatenation notation in the second line, $\{\mathbf{x}, \mathbf{h}\}$ for the vectors $\mathbf{x}$ and $\mathbf{h}$, and we have also concatenated the weight vectors $\mathbf{v}$ and $\mathbf{u}$ into the vector $\mathbf{w}$.

A useful way to visualize this simple RNN is shown in Fig. 9.4, which is an adaptation from the popular blog by Chris Olah. This way of representing the recurrent network will help us to discuss some advanced forms of RNNs later. The illustration shows the computational graph for three time steps, so it shows the unrolling the network in time. This solves a big question you might have about how to train such

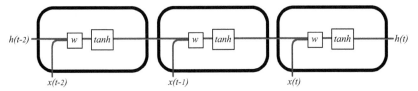

Fig. 9.4 Illustration of a basic RNN unrolled in time (adapted from Chris Olah's blog).

networks, given that the values of the activation of nodes depend on the activations at previous time steps. With the unfolding in time for a certain number of time steps we see that the networks is basically equivalent to a deep feed-forward network, albeit with shared weights in the different (time)-layers. It is therefore possible to use backpropagation learning on these networks, which is called **backpropagation-through-time**.

So, by the end, what have we gained? We simplified the graph of a feed-forward network and replaced it with a recursive version, only to unfold it in time again in order to train it. However, note that we have to do the unrolling only during training (which is not optimal). We also have also a form of weight sharing that makes sense similar to convolutional layers when we look for similar operations at different times in a sequence. Models with shared weights are somewhat easier to train than the ones with more independent weights and do not tend to overfit as easily. The exponential form of the memory limits the usefulness of such networks. The next section addresses this issue.

9.2 Basic sequence processing with multilayer perceptrons and recurrent neural networks in Keras

In the following we demonstrate the implementation of sequence processing with a very simple example. The sequence data are thereby generated from a sine wave at ten discrete equidistant time points within one period

$$x(t) = \sin(\frac{2\pi}{10}t) \quad \text{for} \quad t = 0, ..., 9. \tag{9.8}$$

These data points are shown in Fig. 9.5A with crosses that have been generated using the following program.

Listing 9.1 sinSequence.ipynb (part 1)

```
import numpy as np
import matplotlib.pyplot as plt
from keras import models,layers,optimizers,datasets,utils,losses

# Sine data with 10 steps/cycle
seq = np.array([np.sin(2*np.pi*i/10) for i in range(10)])
print(seq)
```

We then prepare a data set for the specific learning tasks. The first learning tasks will be the one to predict the values of $y = x(t + 1)$ from the value at the previous

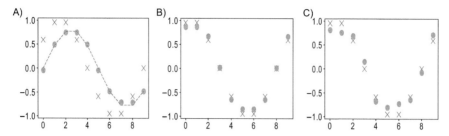

Fig. 9.5 Results of sequence predictions from a sequence that is produced by a sine function. (A) Prediction of the consecutive value in the sequence. The blue crosses show the true value and the orange dots show the results of a simple MLP. The dashed line shows the average of data points with the same value of the preceding data point. (B) Prediction of the consecutive value in the sequence from the two previous values where the predictions are from a simple MLP. (C) Same as (B) except that the predictions are made by a simple RNN.

time step, $x(t)$. Thus, the training set is created by choosing a random example of the sequence points as feature value for the input and uses the next point in the sequence as the target.

Listing 9.2 sinSequence.ipynb (part 2)

```
Num_sequences=200
x_train=np.array([])
y_train=np.array([])
for i in range(Num_sequences):
    ran=np.random.randint(10)
    x_train = np.append(x_train,seq[ran])
    y_train = np.append(y_train,seq[np.mod(ran+1,10)])

x_test=np.array(seq)
y_test=np.array(np.roll(seq,-1))
```

Here we used the modulo function to code the periodic conditions of this time series. We then set up a MLP as we did in Chapter 4 to predict the labels after training.

Listing 9.3 sinSequence.ipynb (part 3)

```
#MLP1
inputs = layers.Input(shape=(1,))
h = layers.Dense(10, activation='relu')(inputs)
outputs= layers.Dense(1, activation='tanh')(h)
model = models.Model(inputs, outputs)

model.compile(loss='mean_squared_error', optimizer='adam')
print(model.summary())
model.fit(x_train, y_train, epochs=1000, batch_size=100, verbose=0)

# evaluate
y_pred = model.predict(x_test, batch_size=10, verbose=1)
plt.plot(y_test,'x')
plt.plot(y_pred,'o')
a = np.array([i for i in range(10)])
b = np.roll( np.flip(a,0),-4)
plt.plot(((y_test[a]+y_test[b])/2),'—')
```

Here we used a single hidden layer with ten nodes. The plot is shown in Fig. 9.5A. This function to be learned is of course ill-defined as there are always two places in one period with the same function values that are either followed by a larger or a smaller value. This is reflected in the results of this experiment. For example, take the first point for which the input is $x = 0$. The correct next value in the sequence should be around $y \approx 0.6$. The next time the input value is around 0, at the sixth point in the sequence, the corresponding next value in the sequence is around $y \approx -0.6$. Hence, the network seems to learn to average over these responses and comes up with a predicted response around 0. The predictions of the other points can also be derived from the average. The average is shown in Fig. 9.5A with a dashed line which shows that this is indeed what the network seems to learn.

Of course, the prediction of consecutive the y value can be made with the knowledge of the previous two points in a sequence. We can set this up in a similar way as earlier and test an MLP for the prediction.

Listing 9.4 sinSequence.ipynb (part 4)

```
#MLP2
inputs = layers.Input(shape=(2,))
h = layers.Dense(2, activation='relu')(inputs)
outputs= layers.Dense(1, activation='tanh')(h)
model = models.Model(inputs, outputs)

model.compile(loss='mean_squared_error', optimizer='adam')
print(model.summary())
model.fit(x_train, y_train, epochs=1000, batch_size=100, verbose=0)

# evaluate
y_pred = model.predict(x_test, batch_size=10, verbose=1)
plt.plot(y_test,'x')
plt.plot(y_pred,'o')
```

The results are much better and the predictions are quite good and can even be made better with more training. The main points that deviate from the correct results are the ones close to values $y = 1$ and $y = -1$. These values are a bit harder to reach, given that we used a sigmoidal tanh function where these values represent the extremes. Note that we only used two hidden neurons to keep the model even smaller than the previous one. While we used 10 hidden neurons for a total of 31 parameters in the previous experiment, here we are only using a model with 9 parameters.

Finally, we can implement this sequence prediction with a simple recurrent network. This is achieved with the Keras code in Listing 9.5.

Key to using the Keras RNN layer is that the input shape is expected to have the form

(batch_size, sequence_length, feature_dimension).

We thus included the reshaping at the beginning of this code. We are only using one node for the simple RNN node, and this model therefore has only five parameters (a weight and bias for the input connection, a weight and bias of the recurrent connection, and a weight for the output). Again, we can make the fit even better with more nodes or with more training, but the purpose here is to demonstrate the ability of the minimal networks. We could even remove the output node and use the output of the recurrent node as the prediction of the sequence with reasonable results. Such a model has only three parameters.

Listing 9.5 sinSequence.ipynb (part 5)

```
# RNN
x_train=np.reshape(x_train,(200,2,1))
x_test=np.reshape(x_test,(10,2,1))

inputs = layers.Input(batch_shape=(None,2,1))
x = layers.SimpleRNN(1, activation='tanh')(inputs)
outputs= layers.Dense(1, activation='tanh')(x)
model = models.Model(inputs, outputs)

model.compile(loss='mean_squared_error', optimizer='adam')
print(model.summary())

model.fit(x_train,y_train,epochs=1000,batch_size=100,verbose=0)
# evaluate
y_pred = model.predict(x_test, batch_size=10, verbose=1)
plt.plot(y_test,'x')
plt.plot(y_pred,'o')
```

9.3 Gated recurrent neural networks, natural language processing, and attention

As outlined earlier, the basic recurrent network has the form of a memory that takes earlier states into account. However, the influence of these states fades exponentially when the weight values are smaller than 1, which they have to be as otherwise the recurrent influence would exponentially overwhelm the input. The basic RNN is hence a form of short-term memory. Such a short-term memory is usually not sufficient for many applications. For example, in natural language processing it is necessary to take some context into account that might be remote relative to words at the current sequence position. Hence, some memories should only "kick in" at some appropriate time which itself might be triggered by another word. It is thus important to gate some of these memories until they are useful at a later state of processing.

9.3.1 Long short term memory (LSTM) and sentiment analysis

The first network which has taken longer-term memory into consideration is called **LSTM** which stands for "long short-term memory". This network is illustrated in Fig. 9.6.

This gated network introduces another cell state $c(t)$ which represents an intrinsic memory state. Its value is forwarded to the next time step and can be modified in each time step with two separate operations, a forgetting gate f_t and a input (write) gate i_t,

$$\mathbf{c}(t) = \mathbf{f}(t)\,\mathbf{c}(t-1) + \mathbf{i}(t)\,\tilde{\mathbf{c}}(t). \tag{9.9}$$

The new memory addition depends on the new input and is calculated as

$$\tilde{\mathbf{c}}(t) = \tanh(\mathbf{w}_c\{\mathbf{x}(t), \mathbf{h}(t-1)\} + \mathbf{b}_c) \tag{9.10}$$

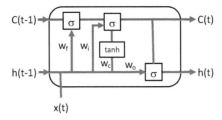

Fig. 9.6 Long Short Term Memory (LSTM; adapted from colah's blog) .

As a reminder, the curly brackets signify here a concatenation operation. This is like a usual hidden layer equation used in the basic RNN. The gating functions themselves are learned with corresponding weight values and a sigmoid gain function of the logistic variety to scale these terms to the range between 0 (total forgetting, no memory update) and 1 (keep memory state, add new input fully),

$$\mathbf{f}(t) = \sigma(\mathbf{w}_f\{\mathbf{x}(t), \mathbf{h}(t-1)\} + \mathbf{b}_f) \tag{9.11}$$
$$\mathbf{i}(t) = \sigma(\mathbf{w}_i\{\mathbf{x}(t), \mathbf{h}(t-1)\} + \mathbf{b}_i). \tag{9.12}$$

Finally, we produce an output for the recurrent node from this new memory state

$$\mathbf{h}(t) = o(t)\tanh(\mathbf{c}(t)) \tag{9.13}$$

which itself is gated by the learned influences of the inputs, namely

$$\mathbf{o}(t) = \sigma(\mathbf{w}_o\{\mathbf{x}(t), \mathbf{h}(t-1)\} + \mathbf{b}_o). \tag{9.14}$$

In order to demonstrate an LSTM in Keras we follow the common example of a sentiment analysis. Sentiment analysis is here just another example of classification in the context of giving documents some labels representing sentiments like good or bad. We use here the Large Movie Review Dataset (IMDB), which contains 50,000 movie reviews which are either positive or negative. The task is to use half the documents for training and test the other half if the sentiment of the test reviews can be predicted. Such a program is included in the Keras examples of which we provide here a simplified version.

This example gives us the opportunity to revisit text representations. In Chapter 8 we mentioned the bag of words representation. This representation consists of a large vector the size of the vocabulary with each component of this vector indicating the number of times this word occurs in the text. We now want to represent the text itself as a sequence of words, which is a much better way to approach natural language processing (NLP). With a one-hot representation of a vocabulary letter, we would then have a high-dimensional yet very sparse representation. A sequence would then be a sequence of such high-dimensional sparse vectors. Another way of word representations would be to give every word a unique integer. While this helps with the dimensionality of the representation, this representation does not capture relations between words. A common first step in NLP is therefore to learn an **embedding**. An embedding, more specifically a word embedding here, transforms an arbitrary representation to a dense vector space representation in which words that are commonly related within a task are close in embedding space. In Keras, we can realize this with an embedding layer. Keras datasets include the IMBD data set as a list of unique words as integers. The following code reads in the data, restricts the vocabulary size to 20,000 unique words, and then represents each document as a string of 8 unique words (maxlen = 8) to reduce the size of this example so we can execute it on a simple laptop. If the document has less than eight words, then the Keras function .pad_sequences() would using some 0 padding to make sure each document is of length maxlen here.

Listing 9.6 LSTM.ipynb (part 1)

```
from keras.preprocessing import sequence
from keras import models, layers, optimizers, datasets, utils, losses

vocabulary_size = 20000
maxlen = 8
batch_size = 32

(x_train, y_train), (x_test, y_test) = datasets.imdb.load_data(
    num_words=vocabulary_size)
x_train = sequence.pad_sequences(x_train, maxlen)
x_test = sequence.pad_sequences(x_test, maxlen)
```

We can then define the model, where the input is immediately funneled into the embedding layer so that this layer can be trained within the task. The embedding representation is then used in the LSTM layer, and finally we use a single sigmoid node for the classification of the sentiment. We also added dropout to the output of the recurrent layer for some regularization to prevent overfitting. Adding dropout to the recurrent layer is a bit trickier as small perturbations errors can stack up in the recurrent network dynamics and hence lead to problems of correct recall. An excellent treatment of this issue is given by Gal and Ghahramani in an NIPS paper called "A theoretical grounded application of dropout in recurrent neural networks." The recurrent layers in Keras therefore have parameters which include dropout in these layers that are strongly recommended. In this example, we used a high dropout rate.

Listing 9.7 LSTM.ipynb (part 2)

```
inputs = layers.Input(shape=(maxlen,))
e=layers.Embedding(max_features, 128)(inputs)
h=layers.LSTM(128, dropout=0.8, recurrent_dropout=0.8)(e)
h=layers.Dropout(0.7)(h)
outputs=layers.Dense(1, activation='sigmoid')(h)
model = models.Model(inputs, outputs)
```

This model is then compiled and trained on the binary cross-entropy as shown in Listing 9.8.

The evaluation accuracy is around 70 per cent after this short training. However, this is only a small example of a simple language processing task. In general, it is good to learn vector embeddings on better tasks such as a **language model** that aims to predict the next word in a sequence. Good word embeddings have been achieved with large data sets. Two popular ones are called **Word2Vec** and **GloVe**, and it is possible to download these to use for a pre-trained embedding. Using recurrent models with sophisticated word embeddings are among the best current language models.

Listing 9.8 LSTM.ipynb (part 3) with output

```
model.compile(loss='binary_crossentropy',
optimizer='adam',
metrics=['accuracy'])

model.fit(x_train, y_train,
batch_size=batch_size,
epochs=4,
validation_data=(x_test, y_test))
score, acc = model.evaluate(x_test, y_test,
batch_size=batch_size)
print('Test_accuracy:', acc)

Train on 25000 samples, validate on 25000 samples
Epoch 1/4
25000/25000 [==============================] - 69s 3ms/step -
loss: 0.6255 - acc: 0.6346 - val_loss: 0.5540 - val_acc: 0.7084
Epoch 2/4
25000/25000 [==============================] - 65s 3ms/step -
loss: 0.5342 - acc: 0.7339 - val_loss: 0.5421 - val_acc: 0.7140
Epoch 3/4
25000/25000 [==============================] - 66s 3ms/step -
loss: 0.4938 - acc: 0.7592 - val_loss: 0.5411 - val_acc: 0.7148
Epoch 4/4
25000/25000 [==============================] - 65s 3ms/step -
loss: 0.4633 - acc: 0.7801 - val_loss: 0.5611 - val_acc: 0.7159
25000/25000 [==============================] - 4s 160us/step
Test accuracy: 0.71588
```

9.3.2 Other gated architectures and attention

A popular slightly simplified variant of LSTM is the **gated recurrent unit (GRU)** shown in Fig. 9.7A. This model is defined by the following equations

$$\mathbf{z}(t) = \sigma(\mathbf{w}_f\{\mathbf{x}(t), \mathbf{h}(t-1)\}) \tag{9.15}$$

$$\mathbf{r}(t) = \sigma(\mathbf{w}_r\{\mathbf{x}(t), \mathbf{h}(t-1)\}) \tag{9.16}$$

$$\tilde{\mathbf{h}}(t) = \tanh(\mathbf{w}\{x(t), \mathbf{r}_t h(t-1)\}) \tag{9.17}$$

$$\mathbf{h}(t) = (1 - \mathbf{z}_t)\mathbf{h}(t-1) + \mathbf{z}_t\tilde{\mathbf{h}}_t. \tag{9.18}$$

This model has still a read gate r and a write gate z, but it uses the hidden state itself as the memory state. It is therefore a slightly more compact version of the LSTM with fewer parameters. Both the GRU and LSTM usually exhibit similar performance.

There are also a variety of other extensions of the basic gated recurrent units discussed above. A major additional step is to take the idea further in form of an external memory. The first version of such a model was called the neural Turing machine (NTM). The basic idea is to use a separate external memory with reading and writing gates. The memory itself is thereby a combination of an location-based memory and a content-addressable memory. It is also important that all such operations are differentiable in order to train such recurrent models with backpropagation through time. The advanced version of NTM is therefore called the **differentiable neural computer (DNC)**. Such an architecture is outlined in Fig. 9.7B.

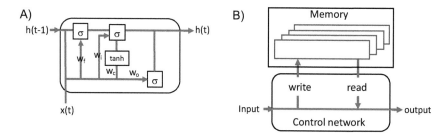

Fig. 9.7 (A) Gated recurrent unit (GRU; see Chris Olah's blog). (B) Differentiable neural computer (DNC; see <https://deepmind.com/blog/differentiable-neural-computers>.)

Instead of going into the details of variations of gated recurrent networks, it is useful to mention one more ingredient in recent models that seems to be crucial in boosting performance: **attention**. Attention has been considered an important part of human information processing since the release of William James' seminal book *The Principles of Psychology* in 1890. At its heart, attention captures the ability of humans to orient towards important information, or to weight certain information as greater than others and to inhibit others. Different forms of attention have been identified in the brain. One well-known fact is the ability of some networks in the early visual system to emphasize salient features such of having letter "A" in a sea of letters "C". This leads to the common effect that we perceive salient objects as "popping out," which greatly narrows down the search time for such objects.

This feature-based bottom-up attention is not the only effect. Indeed, our ability to direct attention, either to spatial locations or to objects, shows some form of top-down attention. Some consequences of attention on neuronal firings have been recorded. For example, Fig.9.8A shows experimental responses of neurons that are sensitive to objects moving in a certain direction in the visual scene. Response curves of neurons are called "tuning curves" in neuroscience. The squares show when the subject attends a "fixation point" and hence not attending the motion, while the circles show the effect of attending to motion. Interestingly, the modulation of the neuron activity is not additive but better described by multiplication. This is demonstrated in Fig. 9.8B with the program below. We draw a Gaussian which curves down slightly (blue curve). When adding a constant we get shifted dashed blue curve, whereas if we multiply the original curve with 1.5 we get the red curve that represents the experimental results in Fig. 9.8A.

Listing 9.9 attention.ipynb

```
import numpy as np
import matplotlib.pyplot as plt

f = lambda x: np.exp(-x**2)-0.2
x = np.linspace(-2,2,21)

plt.plot(x,f(x))
plt.plot(x,f(x)+.15,'b—')
plt.plot(x,f(x)*1.5,'r')
```

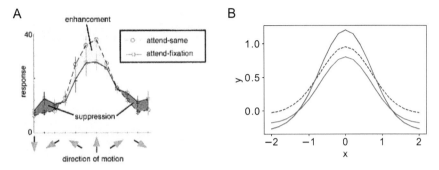

Fig. 9.8 Illustration of the effect of attention on the activation of neurons. (A) Example experimental results. Reprinted from Current Biology, 14 (9), Julio C Martinez-Trujillo and Stefan Treue, Feature-Based Attention Increases the Selectivity of Population Responses in Primate Visual Cortex, pp. 744-51, Figure 4a, doi.org/10.1016/j.cub.2004.04.028, Copyright ⓒ 2004 Cell Press. Published by Elsevier Ltd. All rights reserved). (B) Illustration of the additive and multiplicative effect on a tuning curve.

Including information processing principles of attention has been an important factor in machine learning. For example, attention has strongly influenced sequence-to-sequence processing such as in language translation. Gated memory networks already represent some form of attention since the the release of information that is triggered by some context can be seen as attention. In general, attention can be seen mathematically as some form of non-linear processing. The simplest form is thereby a multiplicative gating as shown earlier. For example, we can take the output of a regular layer $f(\mathbf{Wx})$ and multiply this with new parameters $\mathbf{V}$ as in

$$\mathbf{y} = \mathbf{V} * f(\mathbf{Wx}). \tag{9.19}$$

The attention parameters $\mathbf{V}$ can then be learned from supervised learning. It is now common to include such attention modules in modeling sequence-to-sequence processes. A good introductory tutorial of this subject is given by Jason Brownlee at <https://machinelearningmastery.com/encoder-decoder-attention-sequence-to-sequence-prediction-keras/>.

9.4   Models with symmetric lateral connections

9.4.1   Markov (conditional) random field

In the first part of this chapter we discussed a form of recurrent neural networks with re-entry connections. We now consider a special form of recurrent neural networks: those with symmetric connections

$$w_{ij} = w_{ji}. \tag{9.20}$$

Such networks have been an important part of the development of neural networks. Before going into more specific examples, let us first outline their relations to probabilistic graphical models.

In terms of probabilistic models, we can represent such bilateral neural networks as undirected Bayesian networks of random variables. The random variables are as usual illustrated as nodes in such networks. We illustrated non-directed networks earlier in Fig. 9.1. Here we want to show the usefulness of such models with a segmentation example. In Chapter 4, we discussed fully convolutional networks which we illustrate again in Fig. 9.9. The segmentation is based on the prediction of the class probability for every pixel of the image.

$$p(\mathbf{y}|\mathbf{x}) = \prod_i p(y_i|\mathbf{x}) \tag{9.21}$$

$$= \frac{1}{Z(\mathbf{x})} e^{\sum_i f(\mathbf{x};\mathbf{w})}, \tag{9.22}$$

where $\mathbf{x}$ are the input and $\mathbf{y}$ are the class labels. We used the output of the convolutional network $f(\mathbf{x};\mathbf{w})$ with a softmax function to convert this to probabilities, where $Z(\mathbf{x})$ is the normalization constant or partition function.

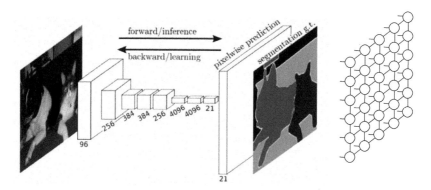

Fig. 9.9 Segmentation using a fully convolutional network with a Conditional Random Field layer as output layer.

We indicate here that we consider the class labels as independent from each other so that we could write the joined distribution as a product. However, there is a lot of information in the relations between the pixels, because we are looking for some objects in contiguous space. Therefore, there is a high probability that a pixel has the same label as a neighboring pixel. We could add such dependencies in our models with parameters v,

$$p(\mathbf{y}|\mathbf{x}) \frac{1}{Z(\mathbf{x})} e^{\sum_i f(\mathbf{x};\mathbf{w}) + \sum_i \sum_{nn} v_{i,i+nn}}, \tag{9.23}$$

where nn stands for the next neighbors. Of course, we could consider other interaction patterns beyond the nearest pixels. In the next section, we outline an example where all the output labels interact.

Training such networks, and Markov (conditional) random fields in general, requires algorithms like believe propagation to calculate the partition function efficiently. We will not discuss this area further but will instead discuss an interesting example that has historically attracted a lot of attention.

9.4.2 The Hopfield model

Steven Grossberg pioneered much of the field of recurrent neural networks and their relation to cognitive neuroscience in the early 1970s. We will discuss a specific example that has been popularized by John Hopfield. In the Hopfield model, each node receives an input and can communicate its activity to all other neurons. Hence, this is a special form of a conditional random field where all the output neurons interact. Such a network is illustrated on the left-side in Fig. 9.10. All the neurons in the network receive input and communicate the output. Thus, all the neurons in this network are visible nodes. In the next section we discuss the more general case with hidden nodes.

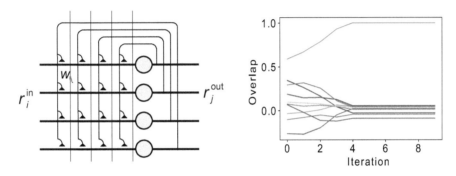

Fig. 9.10 A recurrent network with only visible nodes and symmetric lateral connections.

This type of networks has received a great deal of attention in neuroscience. It has been known for some time that an area of the archicortex called the hippocampus in humans is important for some form of memory, in particular episodic memory, the memory of specific events. This area has some interesting structures, including an area called CA3 which has a lot of collateral connections. In 1971, David Marr proposed an explanation for such networks, suggesting that they could facilitate associative memory, the type of memory recall that could be triggered by partial cues. The Hopfield model is a good abstraction of this kind of memory.

To demonstrate associative memory, we run a small experiment with binary neurons. We choose to represent these two states as -1 and 1. We can easily transform the network to other state representations, but it turns out that this representation helps with the compactness of the following program. We use hard threshold units in this example with the "update rule"

$$\mathbf{s}(t + 1) = \text{sign}(\mathbf{w}\mathbf{s}(t - 1)). \tag{9.24}$$

The sign function returns -1 if the argument is less than and otherwise 1. This is just another version of a threshold perceptron. We now want to store some patterns $\mathbf{x}^\mu$ in this network. The new part is now how we train this network. We use here the

Hebb rule: $\quad \mathbf{w} = \sum_\mu \mathbf{x}\mathbf{x}' \tag{9.25}$

This rule has a long history. It was verbally suggested by Donald O. Hebb in the 1940s and formalized by Eduardo R. Caianiello in 1961. This rule basically specifies that the connection between two neurons increases if both neurons are active (s=1) and decreases otherwise. A simulation of a network with 500 nodes that stores 10 random patterns is shown here.

Listing 9.10 hopfield.ipynb

```
import numpy as np
import matplotlib.pyplot as plt

pat=2*np.random.randint(2,size=(500,10))-1#Rand binary pattern
w=pat@pat.T                               #Hebbian learning
s = pat+10*np.random.randn(500,10)        #Initialize network
for t in range(10):
    s[:,t]=np.sign(w@s[:,t-1])            #Update network
plt.plot(s.T@pat/500)                     #plot overlaps
```

In the right-hand graph of Fig. 9.10 we show the results of this simulation by showing the overlap between the network states and the vectors representing the ten random patterns. The value of this overlap is 1 if the two vectors are the same, it is -1 if all the features are inverted, and 0 on average for random relations. After training, we start the network on a random version of one of the patterns. While the overlap between the network and the stored pattern is therefore not good initially, we can see that one patterns gets perfectly recalled (overlap = 1). It can be shown that the stored patterns are fix-points under the network dynamics. Interestingly, sometimes we can see that the overlap to one pattern goes to -1, so that the inverse of the pattern is also a fix-point under the network dynamics.

Before leaving the Hopfield model, it should be mentioned that there has been a theoretical results derived for this type of model, including its stochastic counterpart. We mentioned earlier that this network represents a dynamical system which has point attractors seen as the stationary states in the above simulations. This is a consequence of the symmetric weights as well as the monotonicity of the gain function used here. Braking such symmetries with associative learning rules or random asymmetries can brings us back to richer dynamics. The symmetric version of the stochastic model trained with Hebbian learning is related to spin models and, in particular, models called spin glasses. The phase structure of possible solutions in such states has been quite well characterized and can form the basis of a much deeper understanding of the possible behavior of such models.

9.4.3 The Boltzmann machine

A much more general form of such a network was introduced by Geoffrey Hinton and Terrance Sejnowski in the mid-1980s which they called the Boltzmann machine. These recurrent networks incorporate two more important aspects. One is that they considered hidden notes that are not connected to the outside world directly. As with perceptrons, hidden nodes allow an unlimited internal structure that allows in principle an unbounded complexity of internal computations. The second advancements over the basic Hopfield network is that the Boltzmann machine considers stochastic nodes and therefore represents a general probabilistic model.

Such a stochastic dynamic network, a recurrent system with hidden nodes, together with the adjustable connections, provide the system with enough degrees of freedom to approximate any dynamical system. While this has been recognized for a long time, finding practical training rules for such systems has been a major challenge for which there was only recently major progress. These machines use unsupervised learning to learn hierarchical representations based on the statistics of the world. Such representations are key to more advanced applications of machine learning and to human abilities.

The basic building block is a single-layer network with one visible layer and one hidden layer. An example of such a network is shown in Fig. 9.11. The nodes represent a

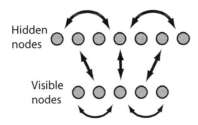

Hidden nodes

Visible nodes

Fig. 9.11 A Boltzmann machine with one visible and one hidden layer.

random variable similar to the Bayesian networks discussed earlier. We will specifically consider binary nodes that mimic neuronal states which are either firing or not. The connections between the weights w_{ij} specify how much they influence the on-state of connected nodes. Such systems can be described by an energy function. The energy between two nodes that are symmetrically connected with strength w_{ij} is

$$H^{nm} = -\frac{1}{2} \sum_{ij} w_{ij} s_i^n s_j^m.$$

(9.26)

The state variables, s, have superscripts n or m which can have values v or h to indicate visible and hidden nodes. We consider the probabilistic update rule,

$$p(s_i^n = +1) = \frac{1}{1 + \exp(-\beta \sum_j w_{ij} s_j^n)},$$

(9.27)

with inverse temperature, β, which is called the Glauber dynamics in physics, and describes the competitive interaction between minimizing the energy and the randomizing thermal force. The probability distribution for such a stochastic system is called the Boltzmann–Gibbs distribution. Following this distribution, the distribution of visible states, in thermal equilibrium, is given by

$$p(\mathbf{s}^v; \mathbf{w}) = \frac{1}{Z} \sum_{m \in h} \exp(-\beta H^{vm}),$$

(9.28)

where we summed over all hidden states. In other words, this function describes the distribution of visible states of a Boltzmann machine with specific parameters, $\mathbf{w}$, representing the weights of the recurrent network. The normalization term, $Z = \sum_{n,m} \exp(-\beta H^{nm})$, is again the partition function, which provides the correct normalization so that the sum of the probabilities of all states sums to 1.

Let us consider the case where we have chosen enough hidden nodes so that the system can, given the right weight values, implement a generative model of a given world. Thus, by choosing the right weight values, we want this dynamical system to approximate the probability function, $p(\mathbf{s}^v)$, of the sensory states (states of visible nodes) caused by the environment. To derive a learning rule, we need to define an objective function. In this case, we want to minimize the difference between two density functions. A common measure for the difference between two probabilistic distributions is the Kulbach–Leibler divergence,

$$\mathrm{KL}(p(\mathbf{s}^v), p(\mathbf{s}^v; \mathbf{w})) = \sum_{\mathbf{s}}^{v} p(\mathbf{s}^v) \log \frac{p(\mathbf{s}^v)}{p(\mathbf{s}^v; \mathbf{w})} \tag{9.29}$$

$$= \sum_{\mathbf{s}}^{v} p(\mathbf{s}^v) \log p(\mathbf{s}^v) - \sum_{\mathbf{s}}^{v} p(\mathbf{s}^v) \log p(\mathbf{s}^v; \mathbf{w}). \tag{9.30}$$

To minimize this divergence with a gradient method, we need to calculate the derivative of this "distance measure" with respect to the weights. The first term in the difference in Eqn 9.30 is the entropy of sensory states, which does not depend on the weights of the Boltzmann machine. Minimizing the Kulbach–Leibler divergence is therefore equivalent to maximizing the average log-likelihood function,

$$l(\mathbf{w}) = \sum_{\mathbf{s}}^{v} p(\mathbf{s}^v) \log p(\mathbf{s}^v; \mathbf{w}) = \langle \log p(\mathbf{s}^v; \mathbf{w}) \rangle. \tag{9.31}$$

Oc course, we have seen the argument for maximizing the log-likelihood function several times before, although we now put this into the context of a recurrent model. In other words, we treat the probability distribution produced by the Boltzmann machine used as a generative model as a function of the parameters, w_{ij}, and choose the parameters which maximize the likelihood of the training data (the actual world states). Therefore, the averages of the model are evaluated over actual visible states generated by the environment. The log-likelihood of the model increases the better the model approximates the world. A standard method of maximizing this function is gradient ascent, for which we need to calculate the derivative of $l(\mathbf{w})$ with respect to the weights. We omit the detailed derivation here, but we note that the resulting learning rule can be written in the form

$$\Delta w_{ij} = \eta \frac{\partial l}{\partial w_{ij}} = \eta \frac{\beta}{2} \left(\langle s_i s_j \rangle_{\mathrm{clamped}} - \langle s_i s_j \rangle_{\mathrm{free}} \right). \tag{9.32}$$

The meaning of the terms on the right-hand side is as follows. The term labelled "clamped" is the thermal average of the correlation between two nodes when the states of the visible nodes are fixed. The termed labelled "free" is the thermal average when the recurrent system is running freely. The Boltzmann machine can thus be trained, in principle, to represent any arbitrary density functions, given that the network has a sufficient number of hidden nodes.

This result is encouraging as it gives as an exact algorithm to train general recurrent networks to approximate arbitrary density functions. The learning rule looks interesting since the clamped phase could be associated with a sensory-driven agent during an

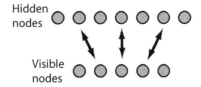

Fig. 9.12 Restricted Boltzmann machine in which recurrences within each layer are removed.

awake state, whereas the freely running state could be associated with a sleep phase. Unfortunately, it turns out that this learning rule is too demanding in practice. The reason for this is that the averages, indicated by the angular brackets in Eqn 9.32, have to be evaluated at thermal equilibrium. Thus, after applying each sensory state, the system has to run for a long time to minimize the initial transient response of the system. The same has to be done for the freely running phase. Even when the system reaches equilibrium, it has to be sampled for a long time to allow sufficient accuracy of the averages so that the difference of the two terms is meaningful. Further, the applicability of the gradient method can be questioned since such methods are even problematic in recurrent systems without hidden states since small changes of system parameters (weights) can trigger large changes in the dynamics of the dynamical systems. These problems prevented, until recently, more practical progress in this area. Hinton and colleagues developed more practical systems which are described next.

9.4.4 The restricted Boltzmann machine and contrastive Hebbian learning

Training of the Boltzmann machine with the above rule is challenging because the states of the nodes are always changing. Even with the visible states clamped, the states of the hidden nodes are continuously changing for two reasons. First, the update rule is probabilistic, which means that even with constant activity of the visible nodes, hidden nodes receive variable input. Second, the recurrent connections between hidden nodes can change the states of the hidden nodes rapidly and generate rich dynamics in the system. We certainly want to keep the probabilistic update rule since we need to generate different responses of the system in response to sensory data. However, we can simplify the system by eliminating recurrent connections within each layer, although connections between the layers are still bi-directional. While the simplification of omitting collateral connections is potentially severe, any of the abilities of general recurrent networks with hidden nodes can be recovered through the use of many layers, which bring back indirect recurrencies. A **restricted Boltzmann machine** (RBM) is shown in Fig. 9.12.

When applying the learning rule of Eqn 9.32 to one layer of an RBM, we can expect faster convergence of the rule due to the restricted dynamics in the hidden layer. We can also write the learning rule in a slightly different form by using the following procedure. A sensory input state is applied to the input layer, which triggers some probabilistic recognition in the hidden layer. The states of the visible and hidden nodes can then be used to update the expectation value of the correlation between these nodes, $\langle s_i^v s_j^h \rangle^0$, at the initial time step. The pattern in the hidden layer can then be used to reconstruct approximately the pattern of visible nodes. This **alternating Gibbs sampling** is illustrated in Fig. 9.13 for a connection between one visible node and one hidden node, although this learning can be done in parallel for all connections. The learning rule can then be written in the form,

$$\Delta w_{ij} \propto \langle s_i^v s_j^h \rangle^0 - \langle s_i^v s_j^h \rangle^\infty. \tag{9.33}$$

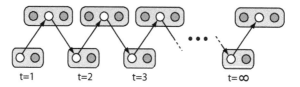

Fig. 9.13 Alternating Gibbs sampling.

Alternating Gibbs sampling becomes equivalent to the Boltzmann machine learning rule (Eqn 9.32) when repeating this procedure for an infinite number of time steps, at which point it produces pure fantasies. However, this procedure still requires averaging over long sequences of simulated network activities, and sufficient evaluations of thermal averages can still take a long time. Also, the learning rule of Eqn 9.33 does not seem to correspond to biological learning. While developmental learning also takes some time, it does not seems reasonable that the brain produces and evaluates long sequences of responses to individual sensory stimulations. Instead, it seems more reasonable to allow some finite number of alternations between hidden responses and the reconstruction of sensory states. While this does not formally correspond to the mathematically derived gradient leaning rule, it is an important step in solving the learning problem for practical problems, which is a form of **contrastive divergence** introduced by Geoffrey Hinton. It is heuristically clear that such a restricted training procedure can work. In each step we create only a rough approximation of ideal average fantasies, but the system learns the environment from many examples, so that it continuously improves its expectations. While it might be reasonable to use initially longer sequences, as infants might do, Hinton and colleagues showed that learning with only a few reconstructions is able to self-organize the system. The self-organization, which is based on input from the environment, is able to form internal representations that can be used to generate reasonable sensory expectations and which can also be used to recognize learned and novel sensory patterns.

The basic Bolzmann machine with a visible and hidden layer can easily be combined into hierarchical networks by using the activities of hidden nodes in one layer as inputs to the next layer. Hinton and colleagues have demonstrated the power of restricted Boltzmann machines for a number of examples. For example, they applied layered RBMs as auto-encoders where restricted alternating Gibbs sampling was used as pre-training to find appropriate initial internal representations that could be fine-tuned with backpropagation techniques to yield results surpassing support vector machines. This work was mentioned in Chapter 4 and shown in Fig. 4.7. A stacked RBM was thereby used as unsupervised Boltzmann

Example of basic RMB on MNIST data

While the principles behind RBMs are mathematically advanced, their implementation is straight forward. We can illustrate the principle with a simplified one layer model and training this on some examples from the MNIST data set. For this we load the MNIST dataset again from Keras, although we do not need Keras for the network in this program. The network consists of $784 = 28 \times 28$ nodes as this is the size of the input. We chose 100 hidden nodes. We then selected single examples for each number from the training set.

Listing 9.11 RBM.ipynb (part 1)

```
import numpy as np
import matplotlib.pyplot as plt
from keras.datasets import mnist

ndata=10; nhidden=100;  nvisible=28*28;  nepochs=200;  e=0.01;  noise
    =.05 ngibbs=5;   T=1./4
w= 0.1*np.random.randn(nvisible,nhidden)
vbias= np.zeros(nvisible);   hbias= np.zeros(nhidden)

(x_train, _), (_, _) = mnist.load_data()
x_train = x_train.reshape(60000,28*28)/255
x_train = np.array([x_train[34,:],x_train[8,:],x_train[5,:],x_train
    [7,:],x_train[9,:],x_train[0,:],x_train[32,:],x_train[15,:],
    x_train[17,:],x_train[22,:]])
```

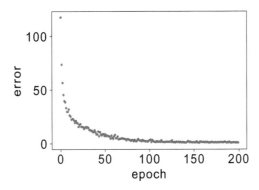

Fig. 9.14 Reconstruction error during training of MNIST examples.

We then train the network by applying a pattern, calculating the hidden activation that represents the probability, sampling the activation of the hidden state with this probability, using this activation to calculate the reconstruction activity for the input nodes, and then using the corresponding terms to modify the weight values.

Listing 9.12 RBM.ipynb (part 2)

```
sig = lambda x: 1 / (1 + np.exp(-x)) #sigmoid activation fcn

err = np.zeros(nepochs)
for epoch in range(nepochs): #train RBM
    for v in x_train:
        h = sig(v @ w + hbias)
        #sample hidden state
        hsample = h > np.random.rand(nhidden)
        vrecon = sig(w @ hsample + vbias)
        hrecon = sig(vrecon @ w + hbias)
        #update parameters
        w += e*(np.outer(v,h) - np.outer(vrecon,hrecon))
        hbias+= e*(h-hrecon);   vbias+= e*(v-vrecon)
    err[epoch] = ((v-vrecon)**2).sum()

plt.figure()
plt.plot(err,'.'); plt.xlabel('epoch'); plt.ylabel('error')
```

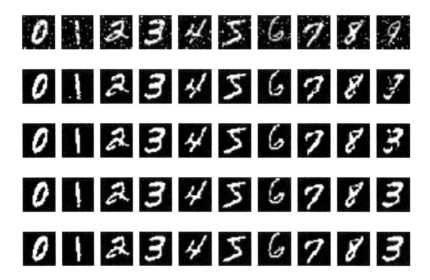

Fig. 9.15 Reconstruction of noisy version of the learned patterns. Each row is one iteration of Gibbs sampling.

For the reconstruction, we initialize the visible nodes with a noisy version of the image by flipping a certain percentage of pixels. The results shown in Fig. 9.14 show that most of the noise is easily removed in basically one iteration of recall through reconstruction. In the example shown, the only error was made in for the last digit. Of course, results will change with different noise examples.

Listing 9.13 RBM.ipynb (part 3)

```
r = np.random.rand(ndata,nvisible) < noise
flipped = (1-r)*x_train + r*(1.-x_train)   #flip random bits

for g in range(ngibbs):
    for i in range(10):
        plt.subplot(ngibbs,10,g*10+i+1);   plt.axis('off')
        plt.imshow(flipped[i].reshape(28,28),'gray')
        h = sig(1./T*(flipped[i] @ w+ hbias)) > np.random.rand(nhidden)
        flipped[i] = sig(1./T*(w @ h + vbias)) > np.random.rand(
            nvisible)
```

A simplified version of the RBM trained on some letters is included in folder
RBM example on the web resource page. The overage reconstruction error and some
examples of reconstructions after training are shown in Fig. 9.15.

10 Reinforcement learning

In supervised learning we assumed that a teacher supplies detailed information on the desired response of a learner. This was particularly suited to object recognition where we had a large number of labeled examples. A much more common learning condition is when an agent, such as a human or a robot, has to learn to make decisions in the environment. The agent in what follows is a machine learner that we implement in software, but it is useful to think about the agent as a system that can act in the world, like a robot or a human.

A good example of such a learning tasks for an agent is that of learning to play tennis. In this case the agent might try out moves and get rewarded by points the agent scores rather than a teacher who specifies every muscle movement we need to follow. Or, in the case of a robot, an engineer who designs every sequence of motor activations. One approach that resembles supervised learning is that of a trainer which demonstrates the correct moves. This type of supervised learning a called **imitation learning** in this context. Much of imitation learning follows the previous discussion so we will concentrate in this chapter on an important learning scenario where the agent only gets simple feedback after periods of actions in the form of reward or punishment without detailing which of the actions has contributed to the outcome. This type of learning scenario is called **reinforcement learning (RL)**.

We first formalize the learning problem in a Markov decision process and then discuss a variety of related algorithms for tabular functions. The second part of this chapter will use function approximators with neural networks which have made recent progress as deep RL.

10.1 Formalization of the problem setting

10.1.1 The reinforcement learning problem

Learning with reward signals has been studied by psychologists for many years under the term conditioning. This includes instrumental conditioning in which an action must be taken and hence a decision has to be made in order to find positive reward such as illustrated in Fig. 10.1.1A. In the illustrated experiment, a rodent is placed in a T-maze with food of different sizes at the different end of each horizontal arm of the T-maze. The rodent might wander around until it finds some reward. In the following trials it could then exploit this knowledge. In contrast, the classical conditioning illustrated in Fig. 10.1.1B are experimental setups in which the agent only observes the environment to learns reward associations.

It is useful to formalize such learning scenarios further with discrete states. We consider an agent that at time t is in a specific state s_t. A state describes thereby the environment such as a location at which the agent could be. Furthermore, we assume

Fundamentals of Machine Learning, Thomas P. Trappenberg, Oxford University Press (2020).
© Oxford University Press. DOI: 10.1093/oso/9780198828044.001.0001

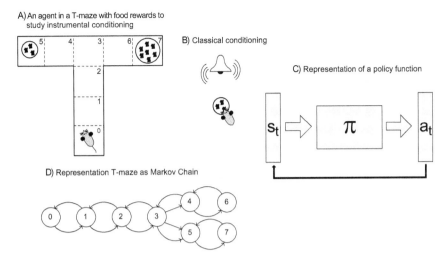

Fig. 10.1 (A) A rodent has to learn to transverse the maze and make a decision at the junction about which direction to go. Such a decision problem, which necessitates the action of an actor, is called instrumental conditioning in the animal learning literature. The corresponding Markov chain is shown in (D). (B) Experimental setting of classical conditioning. Such experiments do not require an action to be taken by the animal (agent). (C) The controller represents the implementation of a policy that provides the action to be taken given a specific state.

that the agent can take an action a_t from each state. In the context of a mobile agent, the action a_t is commonly provided by a motor command from a control program, but we can also think about these actions on a higher level such as turning right or left in the maze. The aim of reinforcement learning is to train a controller, the brain of the agent, to make the decision of which action to take from each state. This function is called the (control) policy in reinforcement learning

$$\textbf{Policy:} \quad \begin{matrix} a_t = \pi(s_t) & \text{deterministic} \\ \pi(a_t|s_t) & \text{stochastic.} \end{matrix} \quad (10.1)$$

We have thereby provided two formulations: a deterministic one with a regular function and a stochastic one by specifying a probability function. In general, it is useful to consider probabilistic settings. For example, even though the controller that executes the policy has the intention to move a vehicle forward, a malfunction in the program executes a tune routine. Hence, in this case, the policy specifies the probability that an action is taken, $\pi(a_t|s_s)$. We will outline most of the discussions in the deterministic setting for simplicity and to minimize notations. We use the probabilistic setting in later sections where appropriate and will continue outlining the formulations of the problem in both settings.

10.1.2 The environmental setting of a Markov decision process

There are two more functions we need to introduce that describe the environment in which the controller has to function. The first one is the

Transition function:
$$\begin{aligned} s_{t+1} &= \tau(s_t, a_t) \quad \text{deterministic} \\ \tau(s_{t+1}|s_t, a_t) &\quad \text{stochastic.} \end{aligned} \tag{10.2}$$

which simply specifies the resulting state when an agent takes action a_t from state s_t. Again, it is useful to consider a probabilistic setting since the actual state of an agent could be different than intended due to external factors which are not under the control of the agent. For example, even if the controller executes the forward function for a certain distance, a slope in the road might lead to an overshoot of the desired position. In such a probabilistic setting the transition function specifies a transition probability $\tau(s_{t+1}|s_t, a_t)$ of ending up in state s_{t+1}, when taking action a_t from state s_t.

We restrict the discussion here to the common assumption that the transition function depends only on the previous state and the intended action from the corresponding state. This is called the Markov condition. The series of states with transition probabilities is a Markov chain, and the one for the T-maze example is shown in Fig. 10.1.1D. A non-Markovian condition would be the case in which the next state depends on a series of previous states and actions, and our agent would then need a memory to make optimal decisions. The situation described by the Markov condition is quite natural as many decisions processes only depend on the current state. The Markov condition is therefore a good scenario and not a real limitation of the reinforcement learning methods we discuss later, but it will simplify some of the notations and discussions.

The second important environmental function encapsulates the assumption that the environment or a teacher provides reward according to the

Reward function:
$$\begin{aligned} r_{t+1} &= \rho(s_t, a_t) \quad \text{deterministic} \\ \rho(r_{t+1}|s_t, a_t) &\quad \text{stochastic.} \end{aligned} \tag{10.3}$$

This reward functions returns the value of reward when the agent is entering state s_{t+1} by taking action a_t from state s_t. In most cases, the reward only depends on the state it enters, but therefore it depends on the previous state and the action taken from this state. In the probabilistic setting the reward $\rho(s_{t+1}|s_t, a_t)$ is a probability of receiving reward in the state s_{t+1} when taking action a_t from state s_t.

The environmental functions τ and ρ, together with the specifications of the set of states S and actions A, define the environment in which we want to make decisions. Since we restricted our discussion to Markov chains, the corresponding decision process is called a **Markov decision process (MDP)**. Note that we assume in our notation that the agent knows in which state it is in. While we will see that this is easy in simulations as shown later, this is a major problem in practice when the state needs to be derived from observations. For example, this is a common occurrence in robotics where we have sensors such as cameras or gyroscopes from which we want to estimate the pose of a robot. Moreover, we have to infer the states usually from limited observations. This general setting is commonly referred to as the partially observable Markov decision process (POMDP). We discuss the basic ideas first in the MDP setting, then later discuss DeepRL that can be applied directly to a POMDP setting.

RL faces several challenges. One is called the credit assignment problem. This includes which action (spatial credit assignment) and at which time (temporal credit assignment) of the system should be given credit for the achievement of reward. Another important aspect that is new in contrast to supervised learning is that the agent must search for solutions by trying different actions. The agent must therefore generally play an active role in exploring options. Even if the agent finds a solution that give it some reward, the question might remain if this is a good solution or if the agent should search for a better solution or stick to the known rewards. This problem is commonly stated as **"exploration versus exploitation trade-off**." Let us assume that the rodent (agent) found the smaller food reward at the end of the left arm of the T-maze. It is then likely that the rodent will turn left in subsequent trials to receive food reward. Thus the agent learned that the action of taking a left turn and going to the end of the arm is associated with food reward. Of course, in this case the rodent could also receive larger reward when exploring the right arm of the maze, which illustrates again the exploration–exploitation trade-off in such learning settings.

Many of the applications of reinforcement learning now apply deep networks as a learner. However, we will start formalizing the discussion of RL with the more traditional tabular representation of functions which will give us the opportunity of discussing exact examples without function approximation. We will later return to the use of function approximators.

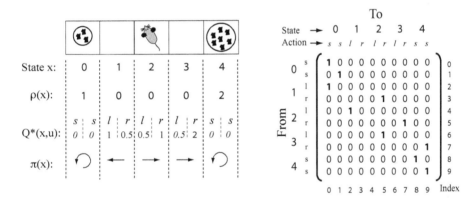

Fig. 10.2 Example experiment with the simplified T-maze where we concentrate on the more interesting horizontal portion of the maze (linear maze). The right hand side shows the corresponding transition matrix for the optimal policy.

To illustrate the different reinforcement learning schemes discussed in this chapter, we will apply these algorithms to a simplified version of the T-maze example mentioned above. To keep the programs minimal and clean, we concentrate on the upper linear part for the maze as illustrated in Fig. 10.2. States s of the maze are labeled 0 to 4. A reward of value 1 is provided in state 0 and a reward of 2 is provided in state 4. The discrete Q-function has 10 values corresponding to each possible action in each state. In states 1, 2, and 3 these are the actions move *left* or move *right*. The states with the reward, states 0 and 4, are terminal states and the agent would stay in these states if unprompted to move. We coded this with action labeled as 0 in the figure.

In order to start coding these examples, we will define some simple functions as shown below. The first two functions are the environmental functions of the transition function $\tau(s, a)$ and the reward function $\rho(s)$. Note that these functions are usually not known by the agent, but we will come back to this point. In addition, we provide several helper functions, one which calculates the policy from a value function as discussed shortly, and a function $\mathrm{idx}(a)$ to transforms the action representation $a \in \{-1, 1\}$ to the corresponding indices $\mathrm{idx} \in \{0, 1\}$, which we need for the specific implementation of the actions in this example.

Listing 10.1 RL.ipynb (Part 1)

```
## Reinforcement learning in 1d maze
import numpy as np
import matplotlib.pyplot as plt

def tau(s,a):
    if s==0 or s==4:  return(s)
    else:        return(s+a)
def rho(s,a):
    return (s==1 and a==-1)+2*(s==3 and a == 1)
def calc_policy(Q):
    policy=np.zeros(5)
    for s in range(0,5):
        action_idx=np.argmax(Q[s,:])
        policy[s]=2*action_idx -1
        policy[0]=policy[4]=0
    return policy.astype(int)
def idx(a):
    return(int((a+1)/2))
```

10.1.3 Return and value functions

The goal of the agent is to maximize the total expected reward in the future from every initial state. This quantity is called return in economics. Of course, if we assume that this goes on forever, then this return should be infinite, and we have henceforth to be a bit more careful. One common choice is to define the return as the average reward in a finite time interval, also called the finite horizon case. Another common form to keep the return finite is to use a discounted return in which an agent values immediate reward more than a reward to be obtained far in the future. To capture this we define a discount factor $0 < \gamma < 1$. In the example program we will use a value of $\gamma = 0.5$,

Listing 10.2 RL.ipynb (Part 2)

```
## discount factor
gamma=0.5;
```

although values much closer to 1 such as $\gamma = 0.99$, are common. For this case we now define a **state-action value function**. This function gives us a numerical value of the return (all future discounted reward) when the agent is in state s and takes action a and then follows the policy for the following actions,

Value function (state-action): $Q^\pi(s, a) = \rho(s, a) + \sum_{t=1}^{\infty} \gamma^t \rho(s_t, \pi(s_t)).$ (10.4)

In other words, this functions tells us how good action a is in state s, and the knowledge of this value function should thus guide the actions of an agent. The aim of value-based reinforcement learning is to estimate this function. Here, we consider first the deterministic case and return to another formulation in the stochastic case for finite horizon cases later.

Sometimes we are only interested in the value function even when we follow the policy for the first step in the action sequence from state s. Then, this value function does then not depend explicitly on the action, only indirectly of course on the policy, and is defined as the total discounted return from state $s = s_0$ following policy π,

$$\textbf{Value function (state):} \quad V^\pi(s) = Q^\pi(s, \pi(s)). \tag{10.5}$$

The goal of RL is to find the policy which maximized the return. If the agents knows the

$$\textbf{Optimal value function:} \quad V^*(s) = \max_a Q^*(s, a), \tag{10.6}$$

then the optimal policy is simply given by taking the action that leads to the biggest expected return, namely

$$\textbf{Optimal policy:} \quad \pi^*(s) = \arg\max_a Q^*(s, a). \tag{10.7}$$

This function is implemented here with the python code for `calc_policy`.

The optimal value function and the optimal policy are closely related. We will discuss in the following several methods to calculate or estimate the value function from which the policy can be derived. These methods can be put under the heading of **value-search**. Corresponding agents, or part of the corresponding RL algorithms, are commonly called **critic**. There are also methods to learn the policy directly. Such methods are called **policy-search** and the corresponding agents are called an **actor**. At the end we will argue that combining these approaches in **actor–critic scheme** has attractive features, and such schemes are increasingly used in practical applications with the help of neural networks as function approximators. We will work our way towards this exciting area.

10.2 Model-based reinforcement learning

In this section we assume that the agent has a model of the environment, which includes both, the knowledge of reward states $\rho(s, a)$ and the transfer functions $\tau(s, a)$. The knowledge of these functions, or a model thereof, is required for model-based RL. The basic challenge in practical applications is to learn these functions from examples of the agent acting in the environment. Here we are more concerned with showing how to calculate optimal policies if we know these functions.

10.2.1 The basic Bellman equation

The key to learning the value functions is the realization that the right-hand side of Eqn 10.4 can be written in terms of the Q-function itself, namely

$$Q^\pi(s, a) = \rho(s, a) + \gamma \sum_{t=1}^{\infty} \gamma^{t-1} \rho(s_t, \pi(s_t))$$

$$= \rho(s,a) + \gamma \left[\rho(\tau(s,a), \pi(\tau(s,a))) + \gamma \sum_{t=2}^{\infty} \gamma^{t-2} \rho(s_t, \pi(s_t)) \right].$$

The term in the square bracket is equal to the value function of the state that is reached after the transition $\tau(s,a)$

$$Q^\pi(\tau(s,a), \pi(\tau(s,a))) = V^\pi(\tau(s,a)). \tag{10.8}$$

The Q-function and the V-function are here equivalent since we are following the policy in these steps. Using this fact in the equation above, we get the

π **Bellman equation:** $\quad Q^\pi(s,a) = \rho(s,a) + \gamma Q^\pi(\tau(s,a), \pi(\tau(s,a))). \quad$ (10.9)

If we combine this with known dynamic equations in the continuous time domain, then this becomes the Hamilton–Jacobi–Bellman equation. often encountered in engineering.

As stated earlier, we here assume that the reward function $\rho(s,a)$ and the transition functions $\tau(s,a)$ are known. At this point the agent follows a specified policy $\pi(s)$. Let us further assume that we have n_s states and n_a possible actions in each state. We have thus $n_s \times n_a$ unknown quantities $Q^\pi(s,a)$ which are governed by the Bellman equation. More precisely, the Bellman Eqn 10.9 are $n_s \times n_a$ coupled linear equations of the unknowns $Q^\pi(s,a)$. It is then convenient to write this equation system with vectors

$$\mathbf{Q}^\pi = \mathbf{R} + \gamma \mathbf{T}^\pi \mathbf{Q}^\pi \tag{10.10}$$

where T^π is an appropriate transition matrix which depends on the policy. This equation can also be written as

$$\mathbf{R} = (\mathbb{1} - \gamma \mathbf{T}^\pi) \mathbf{Q}^\pi, \tag{10.11}$$

where $\mathbb{1}$ is the identity matrix. This equation has the solution

$$\mathbf{Q}^\pi = (\mathbb{1} - \gamma \mathbf{T}^\pi)^{-1} \mathbf{R} \tag{10.12}$$

if the inverse exists. In other words, as long as the agent knows the reward function and the transition function, it can calculate the value function for a specific policy without taking even a single step. This is an example of a deliberative system where the agent can use the models of reward and the environment to calculate optimal decisions, hence the designation as model-based RL.

To demonstrate how to solve the Bellman equation with linear algebra tools, we need to define the corresponding vectors and matrices as used in Eqn 10.12. We therefore order quantities such as ρ and Q with 10 indices. The first corresponds to $(s = 0, u = -1)$, the second to $(s = 0, u = 1)$, the third to $(s = 1, u = -1)$, etc. The reward vector can thus be coded as:

Listing 10.3 RL.ipynb (Part 3)

```
print('—>␣Analytic␣solution␣for␣optimal␣policy')

# Defining reward vector R
i=0; R=np.zeros(10)
for s in range(0,5):
    for a in range(-1,2,2):
        R[i]=rho(s,a)
        i += 1
```

The transition matrix depends on the policy, so we need to choose one. We chose the one specified on the left in Fig. 10.2 where the agent would move to the left in state $s = 1$ and to the right in states $s = 2$ and $s = 3$. This happens to be the optimal solution, as we will show later, so that this will also give us a solution for the optimal value function. We use this policy to construct the transition matrix by hand as shown on the right in Fig. 10.2. For example, if we are in state $s = 4$ and move to the left, $a = -1$, corresponding to the from-index = 7, then we end up in state $s = 3$, from which the policy says go right, $a = 1$. This correspond to the to-index=9. Thus, the transition matrix should have an entry $T(7, 9) = 1$. Going through all the cases results in

Listing 10.4 RL.ipynb (Part 4)

```
# Defining transition matrix
T=np.zeros([10,10]);
T[0,0]=1; T[1,1]=1; T[2,0]=1; T[3,5]=1; T[4,2]=1
T[5,7]=1; T[6,5]=1; T[7,9]=1; T[8,8]=1; T[9,9]=1
```

With this we can solve this linear matrix equations with the `inv()` function in the linear algebra package of NumPy,

Listing 10.5 RL.ipynb (Part 5)

```
# Calculate Q-function
Q=np.linalg.inv(np.eye(10)-gamma*T) @ np.transpose(R)
Q=np.reshape(Q,[5,2])
```

We reshaped the resulting Q-function so that the first row shows the values for left movements in each state and the second row shows the values for a right movement in each state. From this we can calculate which movement to take in each state, namely just the action corresponding to the maximum value in each column,

Listing 10.6 RL.ipynb (Part 6)

```
policy=calc_policy(Q)
```

Finally we print the results with

Listing 10.7 RL.ipynb (Part 7)

```
print('Q_values:_\n',np.transpose(Q))
print('policy:_\n',np.transpose(policy))
```

which gives

Listing 10.8 RL.ipynb (Part 8)

```
—> Analytic solution for optimal policy
Q values:
[[0.   1.   0.5 0.5 1. ]
 [0.   0.5 1.   2.   0. ]]
policy:
[ 0 -1  1  1  0]
```

The agent is moving left in state 1 as this would lead to an immediate reward of 1 and moving right in the other states as this would result in a larger reward, even when taking the discounting for more steps into account. Of course, at this point our argument is circular as we started with the assumption that we use the optimal policy as specified in the transition matrix at the start. We will soon see how to start with an arbitrary policy an improve this to find the optimal strategy. Also note that the transition matrix was perfect in the sense that the intended move always leads to the intended end state. A probabilistic extension of this transition matrix is quite useful in describing more realistic situations.

In the code we save the optimal Q-values for the optimal policy

Listing 10.9 RL.ipynb (Part 9)

```
Qana=Q
```

so that we can later plot the differences to the other solution methods.

The Bellman equations are a set of n coupled linear equations for n unknown Q-values, and we have solved these here with linear algebra function to find an inverse of a matrix. Finding the inverse of a function can be implemented with different algorithms such as Gauss elimination. However, it is much more common to use an iterative procedure to solve the Bellman equation. For this iterative algorithm we starts with an estimation of the Q-function, let's call this Q_i^π, and improve it by calculating the right-hand side of the Bellman equation,

Dynamic programming: $\quad Q_{i+1}^\pi(s,a) \leftarrow \rho(s,a) + \gamma Q_i^\pi(\tau(s,a), \pi(\tau(s,a)))$.
$$(10.13)$$

The fixed-point of this equation, that is, the values that does not change with these iterations, are the desired values of Q^π. Another way of thinking about this algorithm is that the Bellman equality is only true for the correct Q^π values. For our guess, the difference between the left- and right-hand side is not 0, but we are minimizing this with the iterative procedure above. The corresponding code is

Listing 10.10 RL.ipynb (Part 10)

```
print('—>_Dynamic_Programing')

Q=np.zeros([5,2])
for iter in range(3):
    for s in range(0,5):
        for a in range(-1,2,2):
            act = np.int(policy[tau(s,a)])
            Q[s,idx(a)]=rho(s,a)+gamma*Q[tau(s,a),idx(act)]

print('Q_values:_\n',np.transpose(Q))
print('policy:_\n',np.transpose(policy))

—> Dynamic Programming:
Q values:
[[0.   1.   0.5 0.5 0. ]
 [0.   0.5 1.   2.   0. ]]
policy:
[ 0 -1  1  1  0]
```

which is, of course, the same correct solution as found with the explicit matrix inversion. This iterative method is a much more common implementation and it does not require the explicit coding of the transition matrix. Iterative approaches will be used in all further methods discussed later. Note that we have only used three iterations to converge on the correct solution. While here we set the number of iterations by hand, in practice we iterate until the changes in the values are sufficiently small.

10.2.2 Policy iteration

The goal of RL is of course to find the policy which maximizes the return. So far we have only discussed a method to calculate the value for a given policy. However, we can start with an arbitrary policy and can use the corresponding value function to improve the policy by defining a new policy which is given by taken the actions from each state that gives us the best next return value,

$$\textbf{Policy iteration:} \pi(s) \leftarrow \arg\max_a Q^\pi(s, a). \tag{10.14}$$

For the new policy, we can then calculate the corresponding Q-function and then use this Q-function to improve the policy again. Iterating over the policy gives us the

$$\textbf{Optimal policy:} \quad \pi^*(s). \tag{10.15}$$

The corresponding value function is Q^*. In the maze example we can see that the maximum in each column of the Q-matrix is the policy we started with. This is the optimal policy, as we stated earlier.

The corresponding code for our maze example is

Listing 10.11 RL.ipynb (Part 11)

```
print('——>_Policy_iteration')

Q=np.zeros([5,2])
policy=calc_policy(Q)
for iter in range(3):
    for s in range(0,5):
        for a in range(-1,2,2):
            act = np.int(policy[tau(s,a)])
            Q[s,idx(a)]=rho(s,a)+gamma*Q[tau(s,a),idx(act)]
    policy=calc_policy(Q)

print('Q_values:_\n',np.transpose(Q))
print('policy:_\n',np.transpose(policy))

——> Policy iteration
Q values:
[[0.   1.   0.5 0.5 0. ]
 [0.   0.5 1.   2.   0. ]]
policy:
[ 0 -1  1  1  0]
```

again leading to the correct result. Note that in this example we again iterated only three times over the policies. In principle, we could and should iterate several times for each policy in order to converge to a stable estimate for this Q^π. However, the improvements will lead very quickly to a stable state, at least in this simple example.

10.2.3 Bellman function for optimal policy and value (Q) iteration

Since we are primarily interested in the optimal policy, we could try to solve the Bellman equation immediately for this policy,

$$Q^*(s,a) = \rho(s,a) + \gamma Q^*(\tau(s,a), \pi^*(\tau(s,a))). \quad (10.16)$$

The problem is that this equation now depends on the unknown π^*. However, we can check in each state all the actions and take the one which gives us the best return. This should be equivalent to the equation above in the optimal case. Hence we propose the

Optimal Bellman equation: $Q^*(s,a) = \rho(s,a) + \gamma \max_{a'} Q^*(\tau(s,a), a'). \quad (10.17)$

We can solve this equation again with the iterative method when the transfer function and the reward functions are known,

Q-iteration: $Q^*_{i+1}(s,a) \leftarrow \rho(s,a) + \gamma \max_{a'} Q^*(\tau(s,a), a'). \quad (10.18)$

The corresponding code for our maze example is

Listing 10.12 RL.ipynb (Part 12)

```
print('--->_Q-iteration')

Q_new=np.zeros([5,2])
Q=np.zeros([5,2])
policy = np.zeros(5)
for iter in range(3):
    for s in range(0,5):
        for a in range(-1,2,2):
            maxValue = np.maximum(Q[tau(s,a),0],Q[tau(s,a),1])
            Q_new[s,idx(a)]=rho(s,a)+gamma*maxValue
    Q=np.copy(Q_new)

policy=calc_policy(Q)
print('Q_values:_\n',np.transpose(Q))
print('policy:_\n',np.transpose(policy))

---> Q-iteration
Q values:
[[0.  1.  0.5 0.5 0. ]
 [0.  0.5 1.  2.  0. ]]
policy:
[ 0 -1  1  1  0]
```

In this example we again used only three iterations which are sufficient to reach the correct values. In practice, we can terminate the program if the changes are sufficiently small, which we did not implement here to keep the code short.

There is an interesting difference between this value iteration method and the previous policy iteration method. In the policy iteration method we followed the policy to calculate the updated value function. We call such a method **on-policy**. In contrast, in the value (Q) iteration, we check out all possible actions from this state for the update of the value function. Such a procedure is called **off-policy**.

10.3 Model-free reinforcement learning

10.3.1 Temporal difference method for value iteration

Above we assumed a model of the environment by an explicit knowledge of the functions $\tau(s, a)$ and $\rho(s, a)$. While the Bellman equations have been known since the 1950s, their usefulness has been limited due to the fact that finding the environmental functions can be difficult. This is one of the reasons that such RL techniques have not gained more applications at that point. We could use modeling techniques and some sampling strategies to learn these functions with machine learning techniques and then use model-based RL as described above to find the optimal policy. For example, we can use demonstrations of actions by a teacher as a form of supervised learning for the models. As mentioned earlier, such supervised learning is commonly called imitation learning in the context of robotics and RL. We are not following this line of thought here but will instead combine here the sampling directly with reinforcement learning by exploring the environment. This approach has helped to apply RL to many more applications. Since we do not need to know the environmental functions, this approach is called **model-free**.

We will start again with a version for a specific policy by choosing a policy and estimate the Q-function for this policy. As in the iterative methods earlier, we want to minimize the difference between the left- and right-hand sides of the Bellman equation. But we can not calculate the right-hand side since we do not know the transition function and the reward function. However, we can just take a step according to our policy $u = \pi(s)$ and observe a reward r_{i+1} and the next state s_{i+1}. Now, since this is only one sample, we should use this as update of the value function only with a small learning rate α. The corresponding algorithm is

SARSA: $Q_{i+1}(s_i, a_i) = Q_i(s_i, a_i) + \alpha\left[(r_{i+1} + \gamma Q_i(s_{i+1}, a_{i+1}) - Q_i(s_i, u_i)\right].$ (10.19)

The name comes from the fact that we are in a state from which we take an action and observe an reward and then go to the next state and take action:

$$s \to a \to r \to s \to a.$$

The term in the square brackets on the right-hand side of Eqn 10.19 is called the **temporal difference** since it is the difference between the expected value earlier at some point and the new estimate from the actual reward and the following estimate at the next temporal evaluation point. Note that we are following the policy, and the methods is therefore again an on-policy method.

The next step is to use the estimate of the Q-function to improve policy. However, since we are mainly interested in the optimal policy, we should improve the policy by taking the steps that maximizes the reward. However, one problem in this scheme is that we have to estimate the Q-values by sampling so that we have to make sure we trade off exploitation with exploration. A common way to choose the policy in this scheme is the

ϵ-greedy policy: $p\left(\arg\max_a Q(s, a)\right) = 1 - \epsilon.$ (10.20)

So, we are really evaluating the optimal policy that requires us to make the exploration 0 at the end, $\epsilon \to 0$.

The corresponding code for the SARSA is:

Listing 10.13 RL.ipynb (Part 13)

```
print('—>_SARSA')

Q=np.zeros([5,2])
error = []
alpha=1;
for trial in range(200):
    policy=calc_policy(Q)
    s=2
    for t in range(0,5):
        a=policy[s]
        if np.random.rand()<0.1: a=-a #epsilon greedy
        a2=idx(policy[tau(s,a)])
        TD=rho(s,a)+gamma*Q[tau(s,a),a2]-Q[s,idx(a)]
        Q[s,idx(a)]=Q[s,idx(a)]+alpha*TD
        s=tau(s,a)
error.append(np.sum(np.sum(np.abs(np.subtract(Q,Qana)))))

print('Q_values:_\n',np.transpose(Q))
print('policy:_\n',np.transpose(policy))
plt.figure(); plt.plot(error)
plt.xlabel('iteration'); plt.ylabel('error')

—> SARSA
Q values:
[[0.   1.   0.5 0.5 0. ]
 [0.   0.5 1.   2.   0. ]]
policy:
[ 0 -1  1  1  0]
```

Fig. 10.3 shows that the difference between the Q-value of this algorithm and the Q-value of the analytic solution goes to 0 and hence converges to the correct solution. Sometimes this can take more iterations because exploring off-policy states is not frequent. Of course, this also depends on the exploration strategy.

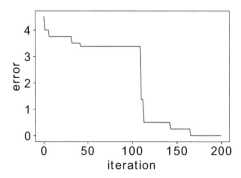

Fig. 10.3 Example learning curve of the SARSA algorithm. The error is the absolute difference between the Q-value of this algorithm and the Q-value calculated analytically above.

Note that we have set the learning rate $\alpha = 1$ for this example, which makes the update rule look similar to the iterative method of the model-based case

$$Q_{i+1}(s_i, a_i) = (r_{i+1} + \gamma Q_i(s_{i+1}, a_{i+1}). \tag{10.21}$$

However, there is a major difference. Previously we iterated over all possible states with the knowledge of the transition function and the reward function; thus an agent does not really have to explore the environment and can just "sit there" and calculate what the optimal action is. This is the benefit of model-based reinforcement learning. In contrast, here we discuss the case where we do not know the transition function and the reward function and hence have to explore the environment by acting in it. As this is usually associated with a physical movement, this takes times and hence limits the exploration we can do. Thus, it is common that an agent can not explore all possible states in large environments. Also, a learning rate of $\alpha = 1$ is not always advisable since a more common setting is that reward itself is probabilistic. A smaller value of α then represents a form of taking a sliding average and hence estimating the expected value of the reward.

Episode 1   Episode 2   Episode 3   0   Episode 4

Fig. 10.4 Example of the "back-propagation" of the reward (not to be confused with the back-propagation algorithm in supervised learning). In this example, an episode always starts in the left-most state and the policy is to always to go right. A reward is received in the right-most state.

It is useful to go through some iterations of the SARSA algorithm by hand for a linear-maze example. In the example shown in Fig. 10.4, we changed the situation to a linear maze in which the state always starts at the left-most state and a reward of $r = 1$ is received in the right-most state. The policy is to always go right, which is also the optimal policy in this situation. At the first time step of the first episode we are in the left-most state and evaluate the value of going right. In the corresponding state to the right there is no reward given, and the value function is also 0. So the value function of this state-action is 0. The same is true for every step until we are in the state before the reward state. At this point the value is updated to the reward of the next state. In the second episode the value of the first and second state remains 0, but the third state is updated to $\gamma * 1$ since the value of the next state following the policy is given by 1, and we discount this by γ. Going through more episodes it can be seen that the value "back-propagates" by one step in each episode. Note that this back-propagation of the value is not to be confused with the backpropagation algorithm in supervised learning. Also, notice that the values for the Q-function for going left are not updated as we only followed optimal policy deterministically. Some exploration steps will eventually update these values, although it might take a long time until these values propagate through the system.

There is one important additional basic algorithm that we need to mention in this section on temporal difference learning. This final algorithm is to use an alternative way to estimate the value function using an off-policy approach for the estimation step from each visited state. That is, we check all possible actions from the state that we evaluate state and update the value function with the maximal expected return,

$$Q\text{-learning: } Q_{i+1}(s_i, a_i) = Q_i(s_i, a_i) + \alpha \left[(r_{i+1} + \gamma \max_{a'} Q_i(s_{i+1}, a') - Q_i(s_i, a_i) \right]$$
(10.22)

We still have to explore the environment which usually follows the optimal estimated policy, with some allowance for exploration such as ϵ-greedy or a softmax exploration strategy. The corresponding code for the Q-learning is

Listing 10.14 RL.ipynb (Part 14)

```
print('--->_Q-Learning:')

Q=np.zeros([5,2])
alpha=1
error = []
for trial in range(200):
    policy=calc_policy(Q)
    s=2
    for t in range(0,5):
        a=policy[s]
        if np.random.rand()<0.1: a=-a #epsilon greedy
        TD=rho(s,a)+gamma*np.maximum(Q[tau(s,a),0],Q[tau(s,a),1])-Q[s,
            idx(a)]
        Q[s,idx(a)]=Q[s,idx(a)]+alpha*TD
        Q[0]=0;Q[4]=0;
        s=tau(s,a)
    error.append(np.sum(np.sum(np.abs(np.subtract(Q,Qana)))))

print('Q_values:_\n',np.transpose(Q))
print('policy:_\n',np.transpose(policy))
plt.plot(error,'r');
plt.xlabel('iteration'); plt.ylabel('error')

---> Q-Learning:
Q values:
[[0.   1.   0.5 0.5 0. ]
 [0.   0.5 1.   2.   0. ]]
policy:
[ 0 -1  1  1  0]
```

10.3.2 TD(λ)

The example of the linear maze in the previous section has shown that the expectation of reward propagates backwards in each episode which thus requires multiple repetitions of the episodes in order to evaluate the value function. The reason for this is that we only give credit for making a step to a valuable state to the previous step and hence only update the corresponding value function. A different approach is to keep track of which states have led to the reward and assign the credit to each step that was visited. However, because we discount the reward proportional to the time it takes to get to the rewarded state, we need to also take this into account.

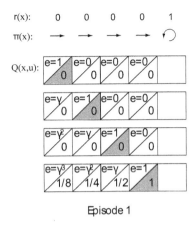

Episode 1

Fig. 10.5 Example of the "back-propagation" of the reward in the TD(1) algorithm. Compared to the slow back-propagation in the TD(0) algorithm, as shown in Fig. 10.4, the added memory allows for the credit assignment in the whole episode.

To realize this we introduce an eligibility trace that we call $e(s, a)$. At the beginning, this eligibility trace is set to 0 for all the states. For each visited state we set the eligibility state to 1 for this current state, and we discount the eligibility for all the other states by γ. This is demonstrated in Fig. 10.5. In the figure we indicate the eligibility trace at every time step. Note how the eligibility trace is building up during one episode until reaching the rewarded state, at which time the values of all the states are updated in the right proportion. This algorithm does therefore only need one optimal episode to find the correct value function, at least in this case with a learning rate of $\alpha = 1$. Thus to change a TD algorithm to a TD(1), we change the build up the eligibility trace in each step

$$e(s, a) \leftarrow e(s, a)\gamma \quad \text{for all } s, a \tag{10.23}$$

and update all Q-values proportional to the TD error of this step multiplied by the eligibility trace,

$$Q(s, a) \leftarrow Q(s, a) + \alpha TD * e(s, a). \tag{10.24}$$

While this algorithms requires some memory, we see that we only need to store an eligibility trace which indirectly specifies the sequence the agent took. It is also easy to extend this algorithm to a more general form called TD(λ) where we can interpolate between the original TD algorithm with no eligibility trace, called TD(0), with the perfect memory trace of TD(1). An exponential decay of an eligibility trace can be implemented simply by including a factor λ in Eqn 10.23,

$$e(s, a) \leftarrow e(s, a)\gamma\lambda \quad \text{for all } s, a. \tag{10.25}$$

This algorithm is implemented for the Q-learning version of temporal difference learning in the code shown in Listing 10.15.

Listing 10.15 RL.ipynb (Part 15)

```
print('—>_TD(lambda)_for_Q−learning:')

Q=np.zeros([5,2])
alpha=1
error = []
eligibility=np.zeros([5,2])
lam=0.7

for trial in range(200):
    policy=calc_policy(Q)
    s=2
        for t in range(0,5):
        a=policy[s]
        if np.random.rand()<0.1: a=−a #epsilon greedy
        TD=rho(s,a)+gamma*np.maximum(Q[tau(s,a),0],Q[tau(s,a),1])−Q[s,
            idx(a)]
        eligibility *=gamma*lam
        eligibility[s,idx(a)]=1
        for si in range(1,4):
            for ai in range(2):
                Q[si,ai]=Q[si,ai]+alpha*TD*eligibility[si,ai]
        Q[0]=0;Q[4]=0;
        s=tau(s,a)
        error.append(np.sum(np.sum(np.abs(np.subtract(Q,Qana)))))

print('Q_values:_\n',np.transpose(Q))
print('policy:_\n',np.transpose(policy))
plt.plot(error,'r');
plt.xlabel('iteration'); plt.ylabel('error')

—> TD(lambda) for Q−learning
Q values:
[[0.          0.99999999 0.49999994 0.49998045 0.          ]
 [0.          0.25       1.         2.         0.          ]]
policy:
[ 0 −1  1  1  0]
```

TD(λ) made famous by Gerald Tesauro in the early 1990s for achieving human level performance in playing backgammon. In addition, Tesauro's solution used neural networks as a function approximator which is important for capturing the high-dimensional state-action space. This will be discussed in the next section.

10.4 Deep reinforcement learning

10.4.1 Value-function approximation with ANN

Up to this point we have outlined the basic ideas behind reinforcement learning algorithms. We will now move on to an important topic to scale these ideas to real-world applications. The previous method we used tabulated the values for the functions. For example, the value function in the above programs were look-up tables or arrays in programming terms that specified the value function for each discrete state and action. Correspondingly, this lead to tables for the policy. Such algorithms are now commonly referred to as tabular RL algorithms. The problem with this approach is that these tables can be very big for large state and action dimensionality. Indeed, the increased computational demand of calculating these quantities in many real-world applications is often prohibitive, in particular in a stochastic setting where we have to sample in the state-action space.

To illustrate this point with a popular example, let us think how tabular RL would look if we implement learning to play a computer game. Let us discuss the example of Atari 2600 games that have been implemented in an arcade learning environment by Michael Bowling and colleagues at the University of Alberta. This environment simulates video input of 210×160 RGB video at 60Hz. An example of these video screens is shown in Fig. 10.6. The state space of these games is equivalent to a state input vector of length 100,800 every 1/60 of a second. Even if each pixel is only allowed to have, say, 8 bit representations, equivalent to $2^8 = 256$ possible values, and all the pixel values are independent, there would be 256^{100800} possible states. Clearly this is impossible to implement with the tabular methods cited earlier. Bellman noticed this practical limitations and coined the phrase "curse of dimensionality." The principle idea for overcoming the curse of dimensionality is to use function approximators to represent the functions, and it comes at no surprise that we will specifically use deep neural networks for these function approximations.

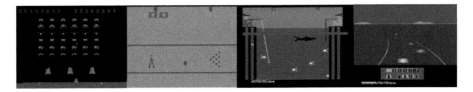

Fig. 10.6 Examples of video screens of the Atari 2600 game simulator.

Several types of function approximators have been used in the past. Linear function approximation (linear regression) is often discussed in engineering books as this provides some good baseline and is somewhat tractable analytically. However, many real world applications are highly non-linear, and it is the reason we have discussed neural networks. Neural networks have been applied to RL for some time. A nice example of the success of TD(λ) was mentioned above for playing backgammon. We will now show how to implement such basic networks for reinforcement learning.

To illustrate the basic idea of using neural networks with RL, we return to our maze example. The basic form of the implementation of the Q-function with a neural network is to make a neural network that receives as input a state and an action, and which then outputs the Q-values as shown in Fig. 10.7 with network A. In order to train this network with supervised learning we would need examples of the value function, which we of course don't have. However, we discussed how we can estimate such values with temporal differences while exploring the trajectories in the environment. For example, we can start with an arbitrary Q-function, use SARSA to estimate an improved version of Q, and then use this as a desired state in a mean square loss function. That is, we can define the following error term (loss function)

$$E(s_t, a_t) = (r_{t+1} + \gamma Q(s_{t+1}, u_{t+1}; w) - Q(s_t, a_t; w))^2 \qquad (10.26)$$

and use back propagation to train the weights of the network that represent the Q-function.

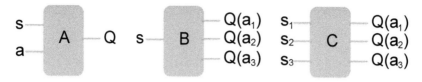

Fig. 10.7 Different ways to implement a function approximator for the value function.

While the neural network approach to SARSA can be applied immediately to a continuous state and action space, many applications have a finite and relatively small set of possible actions, and it is more common to use a Q-leaning (off-policy) strategy in this case. Here we have to compare the Q-values of all the possible actions from a specific state. While we could just iterate over the previous network, we can also learn a network that provides the Q-values for all the possible actions. This approach has been taken by Riedmiller in 2005 with the neurally fitted Q-iteration (NFQ) algorithm. The basic idea is shown in Fig. 10.7 with network B. In this case we can train the network with the following loss-function

$$E(s_t, a_t) = (r_{t+1} + \gamma \max_a Q(s_{t+1}, a; w) - Q(s_t, a_t; w))^2 \qquad (10.27)$$

which corresponds to training the connections to the winning node as well as all the connections feeding into it through backpropagation. To apply this strategy to the maze example, we will here represent the state vector as a 1-hot vector. For example, if the agent is in state 2 then we can write the 1-hot input vector to the network as `s=np.array([0,0,1,0,0])`. Such a network is illustrated in Fig. 10.7C. We then have to modify our helper functions slightly to calculate the next state, and we also need a small function to identify if the state is a final state.

Listing 10.16 RLmlp.ipynb (Part 1)

```python
import numpy as np
import matplotlib.pyplot as plt
from keras import models, layers, optimizers

def tau(s,a):
    if (s[0] and s[4]) == 0 : s=np.roll(s,a)
    return s

def rho(s):
    return ((s[0]==1)+2*(s[4]==1))

def terminal_state(s):
    return (s[0]==1 or s[4]==1)

gamma=0.5
invT = 1
```

The variable `invT` represents the inverse temperature for the exploration. It is set very high at the beginning, but we will later decay this value. So there is a lot of exploration at the beginning but much less later.

We then define a small dense network with five inputs for the state vector, ten hidden nodes, and two output nodes, each representing the Q-value for each possible action, that of going left or right.

Listing 10.17 RLmlp.ipynb (Part 2)

```
# the network
inputs = layers.Input(shape=(5,))
h = layers.Dense(10, activation='relu')(inputs)
outputs = layers.Dense(2, activation='linear')(h)

model = models.Model(inputs=inputs, outputs=outputs)
RMSprop = optimizers.RMSprop(lr=0.01)
model.compile(loss='mse', optimizer=RMSprop)
```

To train the network we repeat several trials where we start the agent in state 2 and proceed for maximal 5 time steps. We include in this example a decay of the exploration rate (`invT`) as already mentioned so that the final estimates are closer to the analytical values. From the current state we use the network to predict the corresponding Q-value and then move one step ahead to calculate the target for the gradient learning as $r + Q(next\_s)$. The network is then updated right away.

Listing 10.18 RLmlp.ipynb (Part 3)

```
for trial in range(400):
    s= np.array([0, 0, 1, 0, 0])
    for t in range(0,5):
        if terminal_state(s): break
        if trial > 30 and invT > 0.1: invT -= 0.001
        prediction=model.predict(s.reshape(1,5), steps=1, verbose=0)
        aidx=np.argmax(prediction)
        if np.random.rand() < invT : aidx=1-aidx
        a=2*aidx-1
        next_s = tau(s,a)
        if terminal_state(next_s):
            y = rho(next_s)
        else:
            y = gamma*np.max(model.predict(next_s.reshape(1,5), steps=1,
                verbose=0))
        prediction[0,aidx]=y
        model.fit(s.reshape(1,5), prediction, epochs=1, verbose=0)
        s = np.copy(next_s)
```

After the exploration we can evaluate the final policy and value functions.

Listing 10.19 RLmlp.ipynb (Part 4)

```
policy = np.zeros(5)
Q=[]
s = np.array([1,0,0,0,0])
for i in range(0,5):
    Qs=model.predict(s.reshape(1,5), steps=1)
    Q.append(Qs)
    aidx=np.argmax(Qs)
    policy[i]=2*aidx-1
    s = np.roll(s,1)
print(np.transpose(Q))
print('policy:',np.transpose(policy))
```

The resulting values should reflect the right solution. While this program seems to be overkill in this simple case, RL with function approximation opens up a whole new world of possibilities. In particular, it gets us away from tabular methods which somewhat alleviate the curse of dimensionality as we can now deal with a finite set of parameters even in an infinite (continuous) state space. Also, while we use a simple model here, we can now combine this with the advancements in deep learning.

10.4.2 Deep Q-learning

At the time of TD-Gammon, the MLP with one hidden layer has been the state of the art, more elaborate models with more hidden layers have been difficult to train. However, deep learning has now made major progress based on several factors, including faster computers with specialized processors such as GPUs, larger databases with lots of training example, the rediscovery of convolutional networks, and better regularization techniques. The combination of deep learning with reinforcement learning has recently made mayor breakthroughs in AI. These breakthroughs have been demonstrated nicely by learning to play Atari games and and winning the Chinese board game Go against a grandmaster by the deep RL learning system called AlphaGo by Google DeepMind. The Atari games are a great example of learning directly from sensory data in an environment that is much more complex than typical low-dimensional environments to which RL systems have been applied before. Mastering the game Go is relevant as it has been considered one of the most challenging examples for AI and was thought to require deep intuition by the players. Before AlphaGo, computer versions of Go players have only been able to play on an advanced novice level.

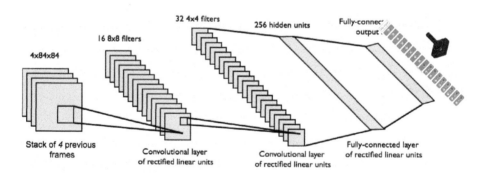

Fig. 10.8 Outline of the DQN network used to learn playing Atari games. Adapted from Nature, 518 (7540), Volodymyr Mnih, Koray Kavukcuoglu, David Silver, Andrei A. Rusu, Joel Veness, Marc G. Bellemare, Alex Graves, Martin Riedmiller, Andreas K. Fidjeland, Georg Ostrovski, Stig Petersen, Charles Beattie, Amir Sadik, Ioannis Antonoglou, Helen King, Dharshan Kumaran, Daan Wierstra, Shane Legg, and Demis Hassabis, Human-level control through deep reinforcement learning, pp. 529{533, Figure 1, doi.org/10.1038/nature14236, Copyright © 2015, Springer Nature.

DQN (deep Q-learning network) is the basic network that has been used by Mnih (2014/15) to learn to play Atari games from the Arcade Games Console benchmark environment. The network is basically a convolutional network as shown in Fig. 10.8 which takes video frames as input and outputs Q-values for the possible joystick actions. While we have already outlined the basic strategy of using the TD error with back propagation to train such networks in such an RL task, which basically represents the NFQ approach, Mnih et al. have made several important additions that achieve these results. In particular, an important factor in the original DQN network was the use of **experience replay**. Experience replay is now a common technique for the following reason. It is common that the learning rate has to be fairly small during learning to prevent single instances from dominating. This means that specific episodes only have a very small contribution and one would need a large amount of episodes. In replay, we memorize a chosen action and use mini-batches of random samples for training.

Another common problem regarding why we would need small learning rates is that we need some time to propagate Q-values and values can fluctuate a lot. A second important factor in the practical use of such networks is the use of a **target Q-network**. In this technique, we freeze the parameters of the Q-network for the estimation of the future reward. Let us call these weights w'. We then calculate the temporal difference as

$$E = (r + \gamma maxQ(s', a', w') - Q(s, a, w))^2 \tag{10.28}$$

$$\rightarrow \frac{\partial E}{\partial w} = (r + \gamma maxQ(s', a', w') - Q(s, a, w))\frac{\partial Q}{\partial w}. \tag{10.29}$$

The weights of this target network are updated only periodically.

There are a variety of other techniques that are used in conjunction with the basic models. For example, **clipping rewards** or some form of **normalizing the network** can help to prevent an extreme buildup of Q-values. There are other techniques to keep the network somewhat stable since small changes in rewards can cause large fluctuations in policies. Another important aspects of even larger applications is to find a good starting position to generate valuable responses. That is, if one starts playing the games with random weights it is unlikely to get to a point were sensible learning can take place. Indeed, AlphaGo used supervised learning on expert data to train the system initially, while the RL procedures could then continue and advance the system to the point where it could outperform human players. A combination of RL with supervised learning in form of imitation learning is therefore a common techniques, in particular in robotics applications. However, instead of looking further into these techniques here, there are two more major techniques that are important and discussed next.

10.5 Actors and actor-critics

10.5.1 Policy search

So far we have focused on finding a value function and we derived from this the greedy policy as the action that leads to the state with the largest return. The value function can be seen as a **critic** to adapt the policy. Another approach, especially when using function approximators, is to consider a parameterized policy directly and to search for good parameters of the policy. Such an approach is called an **actor**. We need to find parameters that maximize the payoff. We illustrated such a setting in Fig. 10.1.1C. It is now time to think about the implementation of this actor as deep neural network which takes observations such as pictures from a camera and produces outputs such as motor commands for a mobile robot.

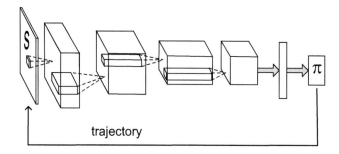

Fig. 10.9 Illustration of an actor that is implemented with a deep neural network.

We will discuss this approach in a stochastic setting with finite horizon episodes that is commonly used for the policy search discussed in the following. In a stochastic setting, the reward is stochastic so that we need to sample over trajectories. A trajectory in the list of all state and action taken in an episode,

$$x = \{s_0, a_0, s_1, a_1, ..., s_T, a_T\}. \tag{10.30}$$

Since the policy and the transitions are also probabilistic, we can write the probability if a trajectory $p(x) = p(s_0, a_0, s_1, a_1, ..., s_T, a_T)$ as

$$p(x|; \mathbf{w}) = p(s_0) \prod_{t=0}^{T} \tau(s_{t+1}|s_t, a_t)\pi(a_t|s_t; \mathbf{w}). \tag{10.31}$$

We indicated here which of the probabilities depend on the parameters of the model as it is these we want to learn. In the stochastic case, the reward is stochastic and we need to sample over trajectories. Since we use here the finite horizon case we do not need discounting, and the objective function can simply be written as the average value of the reward over repeated episodes.

Actor value function: $$J(\mathbf{w}) = E[\sum_{t=0}^{T} \rho(s_t, \pi(a_t|s_t; \mathbf{w}))]_{x \sim p(x|\mathbf{w})}. \tag{10.32}$$

This is an expected value so that we need to sample to find an approximation of this value

$$J(\mathbf{w}) \approx \frac{1}{N_x} \sum_{x=1}^{} N_x \sum_{t=0}^{T} \rho(s_t, \pi(a_t|s_t; \mathbf{w})), \tag{10.33}$$

where N_x are the number of trials in the sample. To find the parameters that maximize this objective function we follow a gradient, as usual. Thus, we have to find the gradient of the expectation value over trajectories,

$$\nabla_w J = \int_x \nabla_w p(x|\mathbf{w})\rho(x)dx. \tag{10.34}$$

Since $p(x|\mathbf{w})$ is the product of several terms, it is useful to take consider the logarithm of this term

$$\nabla_w \log p(x|\mathbf{w}) = \frac{1}{p(x|\mathbf{w})} \nabla_w p(x|\mathbf{w}), \tag{10.35}$$

so that we can replace the gradient term in Eqn 10.37,

$$\nabla_w J = \int_x p(x|\mathbf{w}) \nabla_w \log p(x|\mathbf{w}) \rho(x) dx. \tag{10.36}$$

If we now expand the log-probability of a trajectory

$$\nabla_w \log p(x|\mathbf{w}) = \nabla_w \log(s_0) + \nabla_w \log \pi(a|s; \mathbf{w}) + \nabla_w \log \tau(s'|s, a) \tag{10.37}$$

and the probability of the first state and the transition probability do not depend the model parameters, $\nabla_w \log(s_0) = 0$ and $\nabla_w \log \tau(s'|s, a) = 0$, we see that we do not need a model to evaluate the gradient. Also, we can now write the gradient of loss function again as an expected value,

$$\nabla_w J = E[\nabla_w \log \pi(a|s; \mathbf{w}) \rho(x)]_{x \sim \pi(a|s; \mathbf{w})} \tag{10.38}$$

This nice result for model-free learning of the actor is called the policy gradient theorem. With this theorem we see that we can estimate the gradient by sampling the log-probabilities of the policies and multiplying this with the sample rewards of the trajectories,

$$\nabla_w J \approx \frac{1}{N_x} \sum_{x=1}^{T} N_x \sum_{t=0}^{T} \log \pi(a_t|s_t; \mathbf{w}) [\sum_{t=0}^{T} \rho(s_t, \pi(a_t|s_t; \mathbf{w}))]. \tag{10.39}$$

This concludes the principle idea of training an actor model. This algorithm is called

$$\textbf{REINFORCE:} \quad w_{t+1} \leftarrow w_t - \alpha \langle \nabla_w log(\pi) R \rangle, \tag{10.40}$$

where R stands for the accumulated reward of a trajectory. Unfortunately, in practice it turns out that the samples for the gradient of the log-policies usually have very high variance so that the sampling becomes prohibitive. One trick to make this variance smaller is to only take the change of R with each sample from the average of some batch or samples $\bar{R}$ into account. This **baseline** version is given by

$$\textbf{REINFORCE with baseline:} \quad w_{t+1} \leftarrow w_t - \alpha \langle \nabla_w log(\pi)(R - \bar{R}) \rangle, \tag{10.41}$$

and there have been a variety of other tricks introduced in the literature. However, an important other method is introduced in the next section.

10.5.2 Actor-critic schemes

It is now easy to introduce an important architecture for reinforcement learning, that of the **actor-critic** architecture. The principle idea is to replace the estimate of the accumulated reward of a trajectory with a better estimate of the values of the visited states. We have discussed the estimation of the Q-function at length in the previous sections and we can now combine the two approaches. We simply replace R with Q in the REINFORCE algorithm

$$\textbf{Actor-critic:} \quad w_{t+1} \leftarrow w_t - \alpha \langle \nabla_w log(\pi)Q \rangle. \tag{10.42}$$

The Q-function itself can be learned with a temporal difference method,

$$w_{t+1} \leftarrow w_t - \alpha(r_t - V(s_{t+1}) - V(s_t))\nabla_w log(\pi). \tag{10.43}$$

Such actor-critic architectures are now the common implementations of reinforcement learning with function approximation. Implementations of many recent deep Rl algorithms is provided by Matthias Plappert at <https://github.com/keras-rl/keras-rl>.

As already suggested, training a neural network while exploiting it to suggest actions is dangerous and usually leads to oscillations and instabilities. One reason is that when Q-values are close to each other, then small changes in the Q-values can lead to drastic changes in response actions that can cause problems and inconsistencies in learning. In this respect, actor-based reinforcement learning seems to have some advantages, but building a appropriate parameterization of actions has it's own challenges. However, combining actors and critics has been shown to build much more robust systems. The basic scheme is illustrated in Fig.10.10 on the left, and in the context of using neural networks on the right. Another implementation is DDAC (deterministic deep actor-critic) as shown in Fig. 10.12.

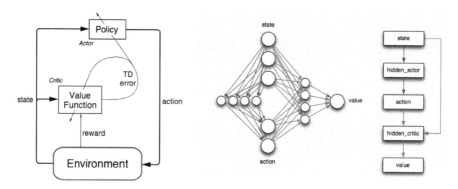

Fig. 10.10 Outline of the actor-critic approach (Sutton-Barto; 1998) on the left and the neurally fitted Q-learning actor-critic (NFQAC) network (Rückstiess, 2010) on the right.

10.6   Reinforcement learning in the brain

Throughout this book we briefly mentioned some relations of some aspects of machine learning and the brain. This included the basic filters of Gabor-like functions in the visual system, some ability of human of leveraging Bayesian decision-making in taking priors into account, the layered structure of neural networks, and the implementation of associative memory with recurrent networks. While these are important components to consider in neuroscience, one of the most amazing stories of the interaction between

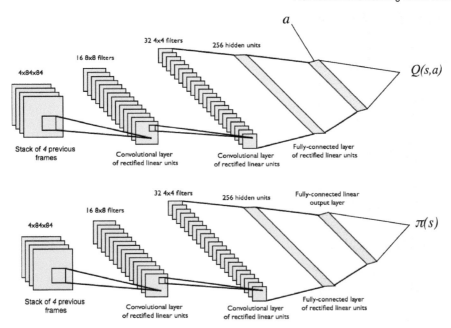

Fig. 10.11 Deep Deterministic Actor-Critic (DDAC) network (from Lillicrap, 2015).

learning theory, behavioural cognitive science, and system neuroscience is related to reinforcement learning. This brief section presents a brief outlook into this fascinating area.

We started this chapter by alluding to classical animal learning experiments of conditioning. One of the most famous of these is the experiment by Ivan Pavlov at the turn of the 20th century showing a conditioned flex of salvation in dogs following predictive tones. Such conditioning behaviour was then modeled by Robert A. Rescorla and Allan R. Wagner in 1972. The basic form of the Rescorla–Wagner model has a form of

$$\Delta V = \alpha\beta(\lambda - V), \tag{10.44}$$

where what is described here is the associative strength between a stimulus and a reward prediction: α describes the salience of a stimulus, β is some learning rate. The most interesting part is the expression in brackets that represents the difference between the real reward and the expectation of reward. This model is hence a form of temporal difference model. Relating reinforcement learning to models of behavioral conditioning is already an interesting step. However, an even bigger step was made when Wolfram Schulz, Peter Dayan, and Read Montague related the neural signals found by Wolfram Schulz in dopaminergic neurons in some specific areas of the midbrain.

The upper panel in Fig. 10.12 shows that these neurons become active if an unexpected reward is given. The lower example shows the activation of the same neurons when a predictor of a reward is given later in the trial. The experiment demonstrates the backpropagation of the reward prediction, and the experiments have been decribed successfully with TD learning. The midbrain collection of nuclei called

No prediction
Reward occurs

(No CS)   R

Reward predicted
Reward occurs

CS   R

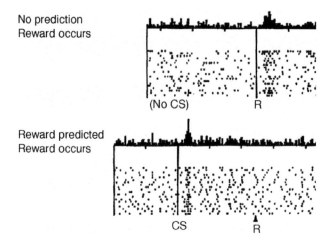

Fig. 10.12 Recordings of the activity of Dopamineric neurons in the basal ganglia. (from Schulz, Dayan, Montegeu, 1997).

the basal ganglia has since been implicated in habitual decision-making that is akin to the model-free reinforcement learning decribed by the TD mechanisms.

However, human have not only a habitual decision system but we are also commonly able to initiate deliberative goal directed behavior. Such model-based decision-making must hence also be present in the brain.

11   Artificial intelligence, the brain, and our society

Machine learning is now basically equated with artificial intelligence (AI), and AI is aving an increasing impact on our society. This brief final chapter outlines the relation between machine learning and AI, the brain, and our society. We want to clarify some possible misconceptions, and to highlight some legitimate concerns as well as opportunities and unavoidable shifts in our society.

I hope that this book has given a sense of the amazing achievements in the machine learning community that will facilitate a new chapter in automation. Machine learning has already gained a considerable foothold in several industries, and it seems we have only just scratched the surface. Current applications are based primarily on the ability to learn to detect complex patterns in high-dimensional data. While this can help with many applications, such as computer vision and speech recognition, it also runs the risk of compromising privacy or misinterpreting data in data mining. In addition, automation on a large scale will have considerable influence on our economy and how wealth is created. It is therefore important to evaluate the impact of new technologies for our society.

The popular notion of equating machine learning with AI is clearly based on the progress with applications that have been difficult to tackle with traditional computer systems in te past and which seems to mimic more human abilities. A typical example is a computer vision system based on deep learning that can outperform humans, or machine assistants based on recurrent networks that respond to natural language. While it is good that these technologies have come to a wider attention in our society, the labeling itself might include the risk of mistinterpretation of what this technology can or cannot do.

In this context, it is interesting and appropriate to study the relations of machine learning with human abilities. We can even start to compare machine learning methods directly with possible analogies in brain processing. We will start this brief exploration by outlining the relation of machine learning and the brain before discussing the relations of machine learning and AI in more general terms. We will then close with some thoughts on the impact of machine learning onto our society.

11.1   Different levels of modeling and the brain

What stands out from the studies of machine learning is a new way of approaching modeling. In the introductory chapter, we outlined that the meaning of modeling is to describe a system in a simplified way which allows us to make predictions and thus encapsulates in some sense the essence of our knowledge. In this sense,

Fundamentals of Machine Learning, Thomas P. Trappenberg, Oxford University Press (2020).
© Oxford University Press. DOI: 10.1093/oso/9780198828044.001.0001

machine learning goes beyond simply providing convenient algorithms to solve some automation problems. Learning to represent or extract meaningful entities might not be equivalent to meaning itself, but it is certainly related.

To illuminate further what we mean here, let us discuss different types of describing a system by looking at an example of modeling a natural phenomenon, that of a falling leaf from a tree. In order to understand and describe such a situation we might think back to our physics lessons and digest the situation with a description embedded in physical laws. If we begin with an apple for convenience, we can start with gravity and understand that the apple falls straight down. Treating the apple as a point mass, we can even quantitatively predict the timing of the trajectory with high precision. Going back to the leaf, it gets a bit more complicated. We now need to take the airflow into account, which turns out to be a much more complex endeavor, requiring the study of flow dynamics. Analytically solving this problem is extremely complicated and maybe impossible in some practical applications. However, going back to the first principles of physics is still an excellent way to go about describing the situation of a falling leaf when using approximations to make numerical predictions with a computer.

Let us now bring a human perspective into the picture. A human is observing the scene and wants to catch the falling leaf. What must the human do to do achieve this? In essence, we need to decode sensory information, mostly from the eyes in this situation, to get information about the dimensions of the object and combine this with prior knowledge about typical falling patterns of leaves. Also, it might be important to take other information into account such as the amount of wind from tactile sensors in the face. In other words, we have a situation as discussed in this book where we want to make predictions from high-dimensional sensory data based on previous observations from which we learn. Thus, the point here is that there is a role for different type of modeling, either from physical principles, modeling with considering stochastic factor as in Bayesian networks, or building predictive models with deep neural networks. Physical modeling will provide us with the best accuracy of predictions if we get everything right, although the solution is highly specific to this particular situation. Humans are able to catch a leaf even though we are not using physical modeling every time we do so. There is some evidence that humans are able to provide some optimal reasoning in the Bayesian sense by taking appropriate factors into account such as priors of the probabilities of common outcomes. However, the fact that Bayesian models have been successful in describing some human behavior in cognitive science does not necessarily mean that Bayesian mathematics is implemented in our brains verbatim. Given that neural networks are general function approximators and have the ability to approximate a lot of theoretical models, it is interesting to ask how such Bayesian functions can be approximated and implemented in neural tissues.

What does seem clear is that the brain is set up perfectly for the type of modeling that is captured by deep learning. The brain is a deep neural network in the sense that it is a structure of processing elements with several stages of processing that form a layered hierarchical structure. In addition, the brain has the ability to change network parameters such as synaptic efficacies. Also, it has been shown recently that representational learning seems to capture some of the representational organization found in the brain. A good example was mentioned in Chapter 2, that of the existence of receptive fields that can be approximated by Gabor functions in the early visual system. It has by now been shown many times that such filters emerge in early layers of neural networks when trained on natural images, at least when taking some additional constrains into account such as encouraging a sparse representation. There is now even more evidence that deep CNNs can capture a lot of the statistics in functional brain imaging data deeper in the visual system. Even without direct experimental evidence, it is clear that there is the need, in human information processing, to transform high-dimensional sensory spaces into higher-level descriptors and possibly a semantic latent space that can be used for advanced reasoning. The ability to implement such capabilities with networks of simple elements and the ability of the brain to learn such parameters alone offers sound evidence that studying machine learning in neuroscience is a good idea.

In addition, neural networks in the brain are not only feed-forward. It is well established that there are many recurrencies in the brain. This starts in the peripheral nervous system such as the retina in our eyes. The retina itself not only comprises of sensory cells such as rods and cones but it also has several neural processing layers that include collateral connections. Most sensory signals then pass through a midbrain structure called the thalamus that includes some regions with inhibitory collateral connections. It is also known that information goes back and forth between the thalamus and the neocortex. There are many other examples of system wide recurrencies in the brain. We outlined in Chapter 9 how recurrent neural networks can be used for advanced temporal processing. Thus, there is plenty of evidence that the brain exhibits factors of deep learning.

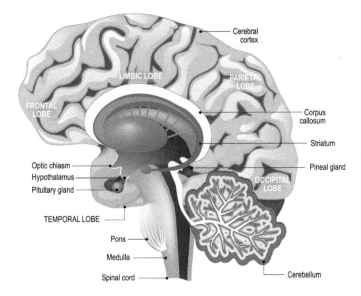

Fig. 11.1 Outline of the human brain that shows some of the structures. The neocortex that is often identified as the brain wraps around many nuclei in the center of the brain and the upper brain stem.

However, it is also useful to recognize that there are many elements and structures in the brain that go beyond the descriptions of neural networks as machine learning algorithms. To start with, the brain has advanced structures that seems to go beyond the architectures typically discussed in machine learning. Let us just point to some of the structure in the brain as illustrated in Fig. 11.1. A prominent part of the brain is the neocortex which is the wrinkly layer of tissue that covers most of the brain. Even in this fairly homogeneous-looking tissue there is a lot of structure. There are anatomical differences such as the ratio of different neuron types or the thickness of layers in different parts of the neocortex. The neocortex itself is made up of layers and sublayers, and the thickness of these layers varies in different parts of the neocortex.

There are also a number of parts of the brain. For example, the cerebellum is a very different structure compared to the neocortex and contains actually the largest number of neurons in the brain. The midbrain is surrounded by the neocortex. This brain area has many distinguishable clusters called nuclei, a collection of which form the basal ganglia. We mentioned this structures in conjunction with evidence of temporal difference learning in Chapter 10. Clearly, there seems to be some functional organization in the brain that have not thus far been paralleled by deep networks.

Moreover, it is unclear if the mode of electrical activation of neurons is the only information-processing machinery. There are many other aspects of potential information-processing abilities in the brain that have been identified. For example, neurons are not the only cells in the brain. There are others such as glia, that can form networks in which information can be processed. Also, there are extensive chemical networks within neurons. Some of these networks can be identified via their role in forming memories, but there are potential other consequences. Research about the role of information transmission in the dendrites is evolving beyond the traditional view of them acting only as passive conductors. There are indications of how more intricate subthreshold computations, backpropagating action potentials, and calcium waves could have important roles in human information processing. The point here is simply that there is a large source of complexity in the brain that we do not see at this point replicated in machine learning systems.

In summary, deep learning helps us to understand the potential of information processing in neuronal networks. However, we can not claim that we understand all the building blocks of minds; "real intelligence" can, at this point, not simply be reduced to deep learning.

11.2 Machine learning and artificial intelligence

AI is now discussed frequently in the media. Many of these reports seem to focus largely on concerns about and potential dangers of this technology, or the imagined technologies. It is important for any scientific discipline to discuss the relationship new technologies and sciences may have with our society. New technologies have always forced us to reflect on this, and it is not limited to AI. Inventions such as explosives, genetic interventions, and computers, have profound consequences for our society and environment. Discussion of the impact of technology should cover as broad a social span as possible.

It might be timely now to point out that this new discussion of AI seems mainly to be fueled by the advancements in machine learning. It is this aspect of AI that I want to discuss here. While AI is certainly the more recognized term in the broader public, it

Fig. 11.2 The thinker robot. Human shape and pose can be deceiving.

might lead to some overestimation of what we achieved with machine learning. There are now many concerns that AI might lead to the development of machines that evolve to harm human deliberately. I would like to argue that there is already a substantial danger in machines and technologies used by humans now, but the concerns are largely overstates when it comes to machine learning.

AI is a diverse field of study. Most of it is about strategies and technologies to enable applications that require advanced control. AI is sometimes divided into two principle approaches, that of symbolic AI and that of sub-symbolic AI. Symbolic approaches are concerned with reasoning systems based on pre-defined knowledge representations that are encapsulated in symbols, hence symbolic AI. Such symbolic systems can use some form of an explicit logic method for inference to derive some conclusions. This type of AI has dominated much of the AI field at least since the 1970s, and is now often called "Good Old-Fashioned AI," or GOFAI for short.

In contrast to GOFAI, machine learning is a main area of sub-symbolic AI that underlies most of the recent advancements that have brought AI to public attention. More specifically, machine learning focuses on methods to use data to built models that can then classify or forecast data that have not been seen before. This is a form of anticipation. These forecasts are based on the generalizations which the models learned form the training data and some form of regularization, including the assumptions build into the structure of the model. We have argued that building models in this way has advanced considerably to the point where it is thought that we can even learn meaning or semantic knowledge from data that would help to build the symbolic knowledge that underlies symbolic AI. Hence, there is the possibility that the traditional distinct area of AI will become linked to each other through machine learning, although this part of AI is still in its infancy.

An important implication of intelligence is that there is some form of reasoning involved. There might be some form of looking at processed data that can be viewed as some form of reasoning, but for the most part, the machinery used in today's machine learning lacks reasoning capabilities. There is often an attempt to make sense of the learned representation of a specific instance of machine learning or to extract some rules that summarize the functions in human-readable forms. Such descriptions might sound like human reasoning, though one needs to be careful in distinguishing here human post-hoc analysis from the abilities of machines to use reasoning capabilities to form new solutions. Reasoning is until now practically absent from machine learning, at least in the large areas of applications that are commonly discussed in machine learning. There are now examples of machines that produce visual art and music, an area that is now termed creative machine learning. Recurrent networks and stochastic sampling from latent spaces are behind much of these achievements. Exploring the consequences of machine learning in such creative ways is very inspiring and could lead to new developments. However, such creations should not be mistaken for representing logical reasoning systems. At least, this is not part of the mainstream machine learning.

An important discussion when it comes to defining advanced human abilities is the question of consciousness. Consciousness is certainly an important factor that underlines many of our deepest questions. It has been discussed at length in some philosophical and scientific circles. From these discussions, it is clear that a difficult question is about the "hard problem," that of understanding how consciousness feels to others. However, on the more mechanistic side it seems that some form of self-awareness is an integral part, or even a prerequisite of consciousness. It has been argued that some form of recurrency or "re-entry" can facilitate self-awareness, so that we might already have some machinery for this within recurrent neural networks. However, at this point it seems that most deep learners are reflective systems that basically learn to represent density functions of world states but have little machinery for reasoning based on their own reflection.

In summary, while a discussion of AI and the potential of learning machines is important, there seems to be some misconception of the abilities of machine learning when it comes to using reasoning for their own advancement. We do not know at this point how such systems could work, and while this alone can raise some concern, the more outlandish depictions of the thread posed to society by AI are clearly unfounded.

11.3 The impact of machine learning technology on society

While these thoughts delve deep into philosophical questions about the machineries of the mind, it might be good to end this chapter with a brief discussion about the more direct impact that machine learning currently has on our society and what it could have in the near future.

There can be no doubt that there is already a strong influence of machine learning on our society which is reflected by a wave of new start-ups. Speech recognition and natural language processing has advanced to a level where we now have electronic personal assistants. While such electronic personal assistants might merely be fancy toys or minor conveniences for some people, they can dramatically improve the quality of life for others. Of course, there are many potential problems included in this technology, such as the potential for providing unintentional access to personal information via sending speech thought the Internet and processing it remotely. Thus, while the machine learning components are important enablers of such technology, it is difficult to reconcile the fact that some of the worries attributed to AI are instead related to web technology. Indeed, machine learning might be part of the solution here, as the speech recognition and natural language processing aspect could be run locally instead of using a backend that requires that information is send into the cloud.

Even the discussion regarding which part of technology is to blame seems to be missing the point. What is needed is a more frank discussions and evaluation of what role technologies play within our society. To this end, we need to recognize that technology in general already enacts a strong influence on our society. Modern humans would barely be able to survive without the aid of technology for staying warm and getting food. Furthermore, certain technologies now have a much deeper impact on our society and our personal interactions through technologies such as social media. There is an increasing realization that our innate sensitivities in communications can be negatively affected by communications through social media. Also, while technology is often developed to help with mundane tasks, this automation has not led to a decrease of working hours as was originally thought. Instead, it has largely shifted the balance in the workforce; safer working environments fall on the positive side of this shift, falling employment in many parts of the workforce on the negative. New technologies can have drastic and immediate consequences. There is an increase in fatal car accidents caused by texting while driving, and even the risk of being exposed to new man-made pollutants can in part be attributed to new technologies. Thus, there is a real need to consider the impacts of technologies on our society.

With regards to machine learning specifically, there are new capabilities that can be used to solve problems as well as potential applications that create new concerns. A real problem is that machine learning methods can be used to aggregate information in a way that can be compromising for individuals. Traditionally, data are anonymized by simply removing personal identifiers such as names or social insurance numbers. However, machine learning has the capability to link data that are in isolation not informative enough to be linked to individuals. For example, data collected from what seems to be simple daily tasks such as shopping can now be used to target individuals via advertising. While such individualization of services can be helpful for some, it generally brings the danger of reinforcing prejudice in categorizations of common targets.

Another area of concern is that machine learning methods often have problems with reproducibility and a clear understanding of their generalization abilities to previously unexplored areas of their state space. These difficulties are a direct consequence of building high-dimensional non-linear models. It is now well recognized that reproducing results of machine learners can be difficult. While such systems are robust in many ways, it seems difficult to develop a full understanding of the impact of all hyperparameters in a model and all the consequences of a specific training set. Furthermore, it is difficult at this time to understand what the networks have learned and how to evaluate their performance, say, in different domains that have not been covered by the training data. Understanding the robustness of machine learners is now an emergent research topic in machine learning.

While there are certainly many areas of concern, we should not forget that machine learning can help to solve many problems. Progress in autonomous systems can help operations of robots in danger zones like deep oceans or disaster zones. Or, while surveillance cameras can be useful in reducing crime, there is a legitimate concern about privacy when human operators watch the footage. Machine learning models can be trained to recognize behaviours with safety implications, often even more reliable than human operators. Such systems remove the need of human operators in such safety systems, and this alone may be enough to alleviate would remove some privacy concerns.

Another interesting discussion is with regard to self-driving cars. A lot of the progress in autonomous systems and robotics has been made due to the advancements in machine learning, with the increased abilities in computer vision and localization techniques. Cars can be built with many cameras covering all directions and additional sensors that outperform human sensors. Machine learning gives us the capabilities to integrate such sensor information for advance recognition systems that will ultimately increase the safety on our streets. Of course, the evaluation of the robustness of these systems and how their operation fits in with the current legal system regarding culpability if things go wrong are important factors that will need more deliberation. Thus, the problem does not lie in the technology per se but rather how we as a society decide to use it. For example, we could build redundant systems that surpass human abilities in pedestrian recognition, though the added cost of building them might prevent its implementation. The popularity of AI and machine learning in recent years has now opened this discussion, an important one to have.

While we focused here on safety concerns, it is important to consider the impact that new technology will bring to our economy and therefore our society as a whole. Automation has been an essential part in the development of our economy and hence society at least since the Industrial Revolution, although we could argue that technologies such as farming equipment had significant impacts much further back into the past. Automation has contributed to globalization though the economy of scales; large factories with cheap labor could produce goods that would otherwise be cost-prohibitive. Unfortunately, such globalization and scales of production also lead to a huge impact on our environment. Building sustainable and resilient communities is now increasingly viewed as important for the future of humankind. This is where the automation and individualization capabilities enabled though machine learning and other technological advancements bring new opportunities of a more refined economy that caters to local needs with local productions.

For example, 3-dimensional printers are able to produce some parts locally that were once produced using only specialized machines and often be shipped half way around the world. This availability of specific, local solutions to local economies, such as sustainable farming in different climates, is to be greatly welcomed. Technological advancements in farming have always led the way in advancements in technology. While the trend has been to use larger machines and flooding of chemicals to foster high yields from small areas, precision agriculture now seeks to optimize operations. For example, recognizing weeds and enabling spot spraying reduces the amount of herbicides use. Ideally, with physical weeding, we could eliminate the need for chemical solutions. Moreover, such forms of automation allow the farming of areas that have been too costly to farm in the past; enabling low-density farming or mixed crop

Fig. 11.3 Some author with a prototype of a weeding robot developed by Nexus Robotics.

operations.

Machine learning is advancing rapidly. There are areas that use learned models to extrapolate to predict domains that have not been covered by the training examples. Such uses of machine learning can be viewed as providing "artificial creativity". The results of such applications of machine learning can inspire, as demonstrated by some interesting applications of machine learning to art.

Preventing misguided use of machine learning and AI, as with any other technology, is a strong responsibility placed on our society. It is clear and widely accepted that we must devote more time as a society to reflect on the path we wish to take. In order to do so, we need education in this area, and possibly legislation and technology that can prevent some misuse. However, I believe that the greatest challenge comes from the changes in our economies and society brought forward by increased automation. Labor that has dominated wealth creation in the pre-industrial and industrial age will be replaced by automation where labor is replaced by energy. The challenge we face as a society is how to distribute created wealth within the society. Such shifts in our society are unavoidable, and it is up to us and our chosen societal structure as to how to use technology for the common good. These are issues that go far beyond machine learning in itself.

Index

representational learning 2, 73–6
Rescorla–Wagner model 231
ResNet 83
restricted Boltzmann machine 201–5
retina 235
return 210
reverse model algorithm 119–20
reward function 208
ridge regression 102–3
risk 6
risk function 62–4
ROC curve 43

saddle points 100
SARSA 217
scatter plots 29–30
segmentation 85–6
self-driving cars 240
self-supervised generative models 170–4
semantic hashing 76
sensitivity 42
sentiment analysis 191
sequence processing 184–90
sequential minimal optimization algorithm
    58
Shannon entropy 53
sigmoid function 148
sigmoidal perceptron 107–12
signal decomposition 73–4
skip connections 83
sklearn 38–65
slag variables 58
SMOTE 47
society 238–41
soft margin classifier 58
softmax function 160
sparse representation 74–5
Spyder 17–18
square-error loss function 146
standard deviation 125
state-action value function 210
statistical inference 136
statistical learning theory 61–4
statistical machine learning 3
stochastic gradient descent 99, 111
stochastic neural networks 161
stride 78
structural learning 156
sub-symbolic artifical intelligence 237
summary statistics 29
supervised generative models 163–7
supervised learning 2, 5, 7, 9, 62
support vector classifier 39–40
support vector machines 55–65
support vector regression 64–5
support vectors 58
symbolic artifical intelligence 237

t-distributed stochastic neighbor embedding
    51
tabular RL algorithms 222
tanh 11, 175, 186
target Q-network 227
TD(λ) 220–2
temporal difference 217–20
tensor 5, 20, 35
test set 49
text processing 167–70, 191–2
thalamus 235
threshold gain function 67
threshold logical unit 66–8
threshold perceptron 67–8
Tikhonov regularization 102
timing programs 25
transfer function 67
transfer learning 87
transition function 208
true data distribution 158
true positive/negative 41
true positive rate 42–3
true underlying world 5

UCI machine learning repository 30
under-sampling 47
uniform distribution 128
universal function approximator 113
unsupervised learning 2, 49
up-sampling 86

validation set 48
value function 210–11
    approximation 222–6
value iteration 216, 217–20
value-search 211
variance 10, 125, 126
variational autoencoder 13, 175–8
VC dimensions 64
vector 5, 20
vectorized code 26–8
VGG16 81–2, 86
video games 3, 223, 226–7
visible neurons 183
visual cortex 13, 37
vocabulary 168

wavelet (transform) 74
weight decay 88, 102
weight parameter 67
"what-and-where" networks 85–6
white box methods 14
Wolpert's "No free lunch" theorem 13
word embedding 191–2
Word2Vec 92

YOLO 85